The New Aesthetics of Deculturation

Also available from Bloomsbury

The Aesthetic Marx, ed. Samir Gandesha, Johan F. Hartle
Transitional Aesthetics: Contemporary Art at the Edge of Europe, Uros Cvoro
Aesthetics of Ugliness: A Critical Edition, Karl Rosenkranz

The New Aesthetics of Deculturation

Neoliberalism, Fundamentalism, and Kitsch

Thorsten Botz-Bornstein

BLOOMSBURY ACADEMIC

LONDON • NEW YORK • OXFORD • NEW DELHI • SYDNEY

BLOOMSBURY ACADEMIC
Bloomsbury Publishing Plc
50 Bedford Square, London, WC1B 3DP, UK
1385 Broadway, New York, NY 10018, USA
29 Earlsfort Terrace, Dublin 2, Ireland

BLOOMSBURY, BLOOMSBURY ACADEMIC and the Diana logo
are trademarks of Bloomsbury Publishing Plc

First published in Great Britain 2019
Paperback edition first published 2021

Copyright © Thorsten Botz-Bornstein, 2019

Cover design by Maria Rajka
Cover image © Alexandre Cappellari / Alamy Stock Photo

A catalogue record for this book is available from the British Library.

A catalog record for this book is available from the Library of Congress.

ISBN: HB: 978-1-3500-8634-0
PB: 978-1-3502-4369-9
ePDF: 978-1-3500-8635-7
eBook: 978-1-3500-8636-4

Typeset by Deanta Global Publishing Services, Chennai, India

To find out more about our authors and books visit
www.bloomsbury.com and sign up for our newsletters.

...sia creando, nel caso peggiore, al posto del vecchio clerico-fascismo un nuovo tecno-fascismo (che potrebbe comunque realizzarsi solo a patto di chiamarsi anti-fascismo); sia, com'è ormai più probabile, creando come un contesto alla propria ideologia edonistica, un contesto di falsa tolleranza e di falso laicismo: di falsa realizzazione, cioè, dei diritti civili.

Pier-Paolo Pasolini, Lettera luterane

Contents

Foreword

Globalization is a fact. Of course, there have been other instances of globalization throughout history, but the phenomenon today is a total and global one. But what actually characterizes this phenomenon? It is the disappearance of the very notion of culture—defined as a horizon implicitly imbued with meaning, a communications system (language), and the shared values of a given society. Of course, every culture has its history and its conflicts, and every representational system is also a form of symbolic domination; except for the anthropological monads of those societies often believed to be primitive (both primitive and isolated), every culture is subjected to expansion, acculturation, and mutations. But from colonial and postcolonial history to the class conflict and the feminist protest against a patriarchy that is so universally rooted in cultures that it almost appears as though it springs from nature itself, we have learned not to essentialize the concept of culture. Similarly, art is not simply the product of culture either: it is autonomous and travels, as the Mona Lisa and Bach have, to find an audience far from its original home. Revealed religions, too, butt heads with the cultures from which they emerge, but they subsequently enter into a permanent dialectic of universalization and enculturation/inculturation, of fusion with local cultures.

In the old dialectic between universality and cultural specificity, culture always persisted. The opening of the world between the sixteenth and the nineteenth centuries ensured that there are no more "monad cultures," or even civilizational areas, as conceptualized by Braudel, but the connections fostered by globalization, far from destroying cultures, have instead, sustained them and infused them with openness and mutation. The triumph of the free market, which implies the standardization of systems of production, measurement, and circulation, initially only affected merchandises or commodities.

But the paradigm has changed. Contemporary globalization is the extension of this standardization to all fields of human activity, and consequentially the destruction of indigenous cultures because they form an obstacle to this standardization. It is much more than the commercialization of all human activities that was already denounced by Marx. Instead, it is very much the de-realization of human activity that was so well described by Jean Baudrillard.

And the reality that is disappearing is the culture that provided an anchor and depth to the object that moves.

And yet, this destruction happens without any violence, other than the symbolic kind, because cultural globalization, unlike the institution of free trade areas, does not need to destroy "enclosures," corporations, and local particularisms: there is no need to send in an American fleet as was done to open the Japanese ports. Deculturation imposes itself because it is wanted, because it appears good, and because it presents itself as the way to go par excellence. The return to protectionism and national sovereignty (as the Brexiters hope for) will obviously not put an end to globalization: it no longer needs a free market of goods and migrants to spread because it is no longer driven by products and the workforce, but by meaning.

Globalization ignores cultures: it defines itself precisely through the uniformization of modes of consumption, of the circulation of ideas as well as objects, of communication. It goes well beyond the free market in the purely economic sense of the term because what is traded is not merely goods, but all kinds of things detached from their original cultures. Globalization decultures and decontextualizes, detaches things, isolates them, and throws them into the global marketspace where they float and reassemble, often in a random way, and connect with other elements in the most unlikely fashion. Surrealism had anticipated this: the Mona Lisa bore a mustache and a urinal became a work of art. This kind of association is understood as kitsch in aesthetics: kitsch is its own reference.

But what Botz-Bornstein shows is that everything is kitsch—from art to ethics and knowledge; everything is but a hazardous recomposition of signifiers that refers only back to itself and the spectator's gaze, and the spectator only looks for that which he or she has already found: narcissistic evidence.

In his book, Botz-Bornstein endeavors to show how the different fields of human activity are reshaped by globalization: art, of course, but also truth, rationality, and measurements. This is what establishes the originality of this book.

Deculturation is both the condition and the consequence of globalization. Everything begins with this initial phenomenon. Of course, individual cultures do not necessarily cease to exist, but they become subcultures, more tribal than anything else, and are in turn themselves retroactively reworked by globalization. In this sense, populism is the expression of kitsch in politics: far from returning to a foundation, far from opposing globalization with authenticity, it transforms national or regional culture into a heterogeneous cobbling of symbols without content (flags, the crucifix, recipes, landscapes from postal cards, etc.), whose goal is merely to fight the other (the migrant) who is so fluid and nomadic that nothing can "hold" him or her, whether it be borders or discriminating signs. What remains of national culture is transformed into folklore by populists, and the folklore, once traditional rural society has disappeared, is kitsch. One may thus add politics to the list of domains seized by the kitsch which Botz-Bornstein studies: what could be more kitsch than the ruling figures of today, from Trump or Putin to Erdogan and Kim Jong Un? What could be more kitsch than the populist aesthetic and rhetoric that plays on the same wavelength of self-referential narcissism? Like kitsch, the identity that populists defend ("our identity is who we are") is tautological.

Deculturation results in the replacement of culture by a double system of codification and normativity. This code is a system of communication in which each symbol is explicit and univocal. Of course, there are codes in every culture: whether it be traffic laws, penal codes, or etiquette, in which every action or word is permitted to have only a single meaning that can be immediately understood by the other party. But with globalization, everything becomes a code because there is no longer any shared implicit understanding and there can thus no longer exist any creative ambiguity.

Of the first to be affected by this process is obviously language: when a language is globalized, as is the case with English, it must detach itself from its original culture, eliminate words that are overly polysemic or ambiguous, as well as terms that can only be understood in relation to literature, history, or a terroir. The language can only rely on itself. "Globish" is kitsch by definition. Google's automatic translation, although otherwise efficient, functions in a horizontal manner: it compares existing texts and cannot rely on anything but what is already present on Google. Thus we have here the first characteristic of a code: it is self-referential, because circulating in the global space is only possible if one is detached from all context.

The second characteristic is that it cannot be ambiguous. Emoticons and smileys are there to provide univocal meaning to what is being said: "this is a joke," such is the feeling I experience after selecting from the list of possible and clearly identifiable feelings, a list created by the managers of social media that is intended to function from Japan to Montmartre to California. The explicit codification of sexuality likewise seeks to eliminate the ambiguities of seduction, which can be experienced differently by men and women. That such explicitness is necessary demonstrates that there is, in fact, a common implied understanding (culture) that is lacking, but also that in this system *the implicit no longer can or should be*. The result, however, is that the explicit meaning must be learned, and ergo be taught, because it is not built on any preexisting structure, because it is its own repository.

Globalization is by definition the expansion of systems of normativity, and therefore it is also the expansion of systems of learning (since nothing is a given), with sanctions for those who did not understand or learn. This goes beyond tribunals to the exclusion from social media (Twitter or Facebook). There are no misuses or misunderstandings, because not being capable of making oneself well understood is in of itself a mistake: the guilty one did not respect the law of the explicit.

Religions too have fallen into this trap of deculturation, and they make their return as normative systems rather than as spiritual ones (such is the case with the obsessive prohibition of abortion and the myth of sharia). Since nothing is any longer inscribed in an implicit cultural understanding, knowledge is no longer the domain of *Bildung*: an education existing within a cultural context where the content of lessons makes only sense when viewed as a guide to life and in relation to other people. Instead, knowledge is understood as the mastery of an explicit norm, which, once again, relies only on itself. And it is here, after demonstrating that the essence of representation in a globalized word is "kitsch," that Botz-Bornstein introduces his pertinent critique of excellence. How can we measure that which has no content?

Globalization is thus defined as the expansion of a system of codified norms, which rely only on themselves. This explains the emergence of the Shanghai system of university rankings. By definition, since it wishes to be universal, this system ignores the concept of culture altogether (and not only national cultures). Globalization is not a new culture; it is the absence of culture. The first consequence of this is the disappearance of the humanities, which is a paradox, given that universities were built upon the very concept of the humanities. But the humanities are not replaced by "hard" sciences, because the latter has its own domain and is evaluated by its own results (biology, physics, etc.). Instead, the humanities are replaced by an imitation of science, which uses the same terms, algorithms, and acts as though it were science much in the way kitsch acts as though it were beautiful. And like kitsch, this scientism does not operate based on the truth, but on its own auto-referential standards (it speaks only of itself) and on the satisfaction of the user, wherein lies its narcissism.

Paradoxically, this kitsch in the human sciences was not imposed by any government. Rather, the Shanghai criteria are enthusiastically embraced by our colleagues, who wish to appear on the board of excellence, as though we were in primary school. It is then enough to jargonize and chant the magic terms ("benchmark": the new overseer of excellence) and to practice a binary game of dependent variables and independent variables (this dualist couple is always an essential aspect of puritanism, both in sex and in science and art).

Yet this binary coding system destroys the context. This system tries to explicitly isolate the variables from their context to make them into objective data without seeing that, in the social sciences, by definition, it is the context that creates the meaning.

One cannot then be surprised at the silence of the social sciences regarding the great problems of society. This silence cannot necessarily be blamed on individual "scholars," who do give their opinions at every turn in the media (the famous op-ed in important newspapers). But they cannot hold their weight against public intellectuals who are much better trained in the rhetoric of public debates, or against the "people" of the internet: these millions of little monads, who before the invention of the internet, resembled those barflies that monologued from the end of the counter at indifferent bartenders as they cleaned glasses, but have today found an extraordinary echo chamber on the internet where all opinions are equalized—or rather, all statements are transformed into opinions. It is amusing to see so many stars and personalities solemnly announce that they are shutting down their Twitter or Facebook accounts because they are harassed by "bullshit" (another concept well discussed by Botz-Bornstein): they have failed to understand that the narcissism that spreads on social media is no longer "their" narcissism, the narcissism of (the) stars and the elites, but instead the narcissism of everyone. There are no longer stars and fans, only ego-equals.

The obvious question that poses itself is: how can truth be (re?)grounded outside of a system that relies only on itself? But what is then meant by truth: transcendence (the sacred), consensus (culture), or demonstration (science)? Religions no longer fulfill this role. The great epic stories have not disappeared: but they have returned in the shape of what we call radicalism. Consensus is no longer a social contract; instead, it has become an identity. And what is exported under the pretense of "scientific rigor" from the hard sciences is nothing but a caricature, a cosmetic system of norms which produces nothing but a repetition of the same.

One must nonetheless avoid the trap of nostalgia. The humanities did not prevent fascism, or even Nazism (Heidegger, Evola, Pound), and the education in Soviet schools adored the "great authors" of classic literature (Hugo, Zola).

One must not be nostalgic for a "safe" world, which never existed, but to notice the disappearance of the question of truth: it is today but a simulacrum/travesty/illusion. The great difference between this and the philosophy of the death of God (Kierkegaard, Nietzsche) is that the latter recognized the consequences of its act: anguish. Anguish, because it leaves a gap, a hole, a lacking, a doubt that may perhaps be staved off by art, writing, or engagement. Kitsch does not assume any responsibility, which is why it is the new opium of the people. Moreover, it's cheap.

Olivier Roy

Acknowledgments

Two articles roughly corresponding to Chapters 2 and 3 in this book have been published previously, and I thank the following journals for having granted the permissions to reprint revised and extended versions of their articles: *Philosophy and Literature*, which published "Kitsch and Bullshit" in its issue 39:2 in 2015; and *Aesthetics and Literature*, which published "The Aesthetic Experiences of Kitsch and Bullshit" in its issue 26 in 2016. Some of the material found in Chapter 1 has been used in "A Hermeneutic Answer to the Crisis of the Universities: Reflections on Bureaucracy, Business Culture and the Global University," published in 2016 in *Eastward Bound: The Politics, Economics and Pedagogy of Western Higher Education in Asia and the Middle East* (editors K. Gray, S. Keck and H. Bachir); and "Science, Culture, and the University," published in *The Crisis of the Human Sciences: False Objectivity and the Decline of Creativity* (ed. T. Botz-Bornstein).

Introduction

What is the predominant aesthetics of the twenty-first century? According to British sociologists Ruth Holliday and Tracey Potts, "We are on the point of drowning in kitsch. A casual survey of the British metropolitan high street offers ample evidence of the kitschification of everyday life" (Holliday and Potts: 1). Kitsch has been defined as a tasteless copy of an existing style or as the systematic display of bad taste or artistic deficiency. Garden gnomes are kitsch, just like cheap paintings for tourists, which are technically correct but express their "truths" too directly and too straightforwardly, often in the form of clichés. Some people play with kitsch by using irony, which can lead to interesting results. However, most of the time, kitsch has negative connotations. Most dictators have attempted to reinforce their authority with the help of kitsch propaganda. The former Libyan leader Muammar Gaddafi has been called "the kitsch-dictator" (Marshall 2011), and Saddam Hussein, who designed his own monuments in a Stalinist spirit (Makiya 2011), is one of the few turn-of-the-century leaders able to debate Gaddafi's title. Saddam's "Victory Arch" monument consists of two sets of giant forearms and swords draped with a net containing a gruesome collection of enemy helmets. For the arms, the sculptor had to use casts of Saddam's own arms.

Kitsch used to be the taste of uneducated masses propelled into consumer culture by an emergent capitalism. Jean Baudrillard describes kitsch as the "culture of the parvenus requiring their panoply" (1970: 166). In the twenty-first century, kitsch is present in a much larger variety of places. Neoliberal culture has created its own kitsch world of which Dubai is a good example. In terms of capitalist hubris and exuberance, Dubai is outdoing everybody else. The city's multilevel fantasy collage of gaudiness sparks a kitsch vertigo arguably more supreme than the one achieved in Las Vegas and Macao. Modernist megalomania and retro kitsch aspirations like the neoclassical-motif syndrome and the village-in-the-city syndrome are here concentrated on a few square kilometers.

Another new kitsch hub is terrorism. Most of the over 300 jihadi propaganda images analyzed by the US Military Academy at West Point (the majority is from Al-Qaeda) show romantic, literal, and naive images of a mythical world presenting sunrises, superimpositions, softened contours, and fading colors.[1] Rüdiger Lohlker writes that Al-Qaeda writer Dhu I-Bijadayn, famous for the launching of the jihadi technical magazine *Al-Qaeda Airlines*, displays "a fascination with some gothic elements (skulls and bones) and kitsch" (Lohlker 2014b: 9). The graphic ISIS images and videos of a later generation of terrorists offer even more explicit kitsch expressions as they cultivate the art of violence for its shock value. Explosions and bodies flying through the air are repeated from different angles and in slow motion. The aesthetics of ISIS is an aesthetics of the "too much."

Deculturation

Why is there so much kitsch? One reason is that we are living at the age of hyperbole. There is simply too much of everything: extreme sports, doping, eating contests, hyper-skinny models, mass shootings, addictions, etc. However, kitsch is determined by a deeper pattern, which is the pattern of deculturation. Humans need truths to believe in, but in the past, those truths tended to be transmitted through cultures. In the neoliberal world, truth is increasingly produced instantaneously without cultural mediation. Kitsch employs this mechanism in the realm of aesthetics, and the sudden explosion of kitsch must be seen as a symptom of a large-scale civilizational development.

The term "deculturation" emerged in sociology in debates about the effects of colonialism and subsequent loss of culture—for example, in Bourdieu's early *Sociologie de l'Algérie* (1958). We speak of deculturation when a particular group is deprived of one or more aspects of its culture. The entire process of modernization has been seen as such a process of deculturation. John Tomlinson writes that modernity is "technologically and economically powerful but culturally weak" (Tomlinson 1991: 174). Today, the deculturation process is accelerated through globalization.

The largest part of this book examines neoliberal deculturation and narcissistic kitsch politics in the fields of education, culture, politics, and business. If we see kitsch not merely as an aesthetic expression but, in a more metaphorical fashion, as a "cultural category" (cf. Baudrillard 1970: 166), we can make interesting statements about "political kitsch," "administrative kitsch," "communicative kitsch," etc.

A major place where the consequences of deculturation are flagrant is religion. The global rise of religious fundamentalism is linked to the separation of religious practice from indigenous cultures in which it used to be embedded and which could prevent it from becoming kitsch. In a globalized world, religion is deterritorialized and can conceive of itself as independent from local political and cultural constraints. In the last two decades, we have witnessed a significant shift of traditional forms of religious practice like Catholicism, Hanafi Islam, or classical Protestant denominations toward so-called charismatic forms of religiosity like Evangelicalism, Salafism, or Chabad-Lubavitch. Those fundamentalist religions are puritan, radical cults functional in any cultural context because their teachings represent pure truths unmediated and unfiltered by cultural components. Theological reflection is no longer stimulated by the "other" (by culture, philosophy, or literature), but religion has become a self-sufficient takeaway cult.

Islam scholar Olivier Roy has shown that religious radicalization occurs when religions attempt to define themselves as culturally neutral and "pure." Being disconnected from concrete cultural values, religious truths tend to become absolute. Fundamentalist religions see themselves not as cultural phenomena but as positive quasi-sciences. In his book *Holy Ignorance: When Religion and Culture Part Ways* (2013), Roy reiterates his older thesis that the separation of religion from culture has had negative consequences for religion. Instead of secularizing religion, it merely isolates religion from culture and enables its pursuit in terms of an anti-cultural purification:

> What we are witnessing today is the militant reformulation of religion in a secularized space that has given religion its autonomy and therefore the conditions for its expansion. Secularization and globalization have forced religions to break away from culture, to think of themselves as autonomous and to reconstruct themselves in a space that is no longer territorial and is therefore no longer subject to politics. (Roy 2013: 2)

Though the arguments sound counterintuitive they are plausible: secular societies help produce religious fundamentalism through deculturation.

Decultured education

Another area where the production of such "absolute" truths can be observed is contemporary education. It is fascinating to compare Roy's analysis with

Bill Readings's findings on the separation of learning and culture in neoliberal, corporate universities. In his book *The University in Ruins* (1996), Readings shows how in globalized, neoliberal universities, any appeal to virtues and values anchored in local cultures has become impossible. In a neoliberal environment, the idea of culture is no longer available as a referent because any qualitative content of learning is not supposed to refer to culturally specific things or ideas. Instead, universities function in terms of "excellence." Excellence is a vague term not because it refers to too many things but, on the contrary, because it is pure and content-less. There is an amazing parallelism in Roy's critique of religions and Reading's critique of education: Roy calls deculturation what Readings calls "dereferentialization." The equivalent of fundamentalism's pure truth is excellence in the neoliberal university.

In the last thirty years, learning has been separated from culture by insisting on standardization and quantified learning outcomes. In 2015 the *Guardian* wrote:

> The corridors of our universities are stalked by soft-footed technocrats who draw down six-figure salaries in exchange for implementing "right-sizing" exercises and "internationalization programs," while harried academics are forced to deal with a wall of bureaucracy that is being constructed, form-by-form, between them and their students. Research is centrally mandated and programmatic; time— once the academic's greatest resource—must be accounted for in meticulous detail; and everywhere, and at all times, the onus is on academics to "monetize" their activities, to establish financial values for their "outputs," and to justify their existence according to the remorseless and nightmarish logic of the markets. (Preston 2015)

A year earlier, in 2014, the *Guardian* had printed an article in which an anonymous academic criticized the fact that "universities focus too much on measuring activity [and not on] quality." The author regrets that the "meaningless pursuit of 'quality' is transforming academics into part-time administrators." In the past, "quality" could be spelled out in terms of culture; today it has been replaced with "value-neutral" measuring activities (*The Guardian* 2014). Scholars working in the human sciences find this particularly disturbing. Originally, the humanities were about culture as their primary task was to define the human being as a cultural being. Philosophers and humanists have developed various theories about how the cultural capacities of human beings can be enhanced. Being human means "being culture" writes Keyan Tomaselli: "Being human cannot be encapsulated in the relative crudity offered by numbers. Being human requires a soul" (2010: 2). In a globalized environment, the idea of culture is no longer available as an educational referent because the content of learning is not supposed to refer to culturally specific objects or ideas. As a result, the only remaining accepted reference is the culturally neutral term "excellence." The overabundance of excellence rhetoric in neoliberal environments is suspicious. On university websites, "excellence initiatives" and "Centers for Excellence" address excellence along with words such as "beyond-par" and "world-class." Excellence has become an absolute value similar to the "truth" of religious fundamentalists. Being measurable and packaged with the help of quantifying methods, excellence-based knowledge is suitable for immediate "takeaway" consumption in globalized environments. However, "excellence" is just as empty as the idea of "being yourself," which is, according to Renato Busarello, the implicit imperative of all neoliberalism (Busarello: 84).

In the end, self-declared excellence strategies could even take hold of religion itself. Roy notes the "market-driven formatting" and standardization in religious fundamentalism resulting in the "insistence on the norm rather than on love and compassion" (Roy: 8).

Liberalism

Who is responsible for all this? Capitalism and neoliberalism produced deculturation by shifting their focus to economically exploitable and technical knowledge. However, neoliberalism is not the only culprit. A paradoxical interlinking of conservative neoliberalism and progressive, leftist liberalism has contributed to the separation of culture from domains like education. Christopher Lasch traces in his book on narcissism decultured education to a liberal aversion of "genteel culture, overemphasis on academic subjects, 'gentleman's education', and the 'cultured'" (Lasch 1979: 135). He describes not the conservative but the leftist agenda. In the 1960s, cultural refinement became suspect because "higher education and 'culture' should not in any case be 'desired by the mob'" (135). Leftist thought remolded those convictions into progressive liberal ideologies holding that anything cultural is elitist and must be refused. Progressive liberalism saw "the full flowering of the school as a major agency of industrial recruitment, selection, and certification" (135). Soon cultural elitism became a common charge and education was supposed to avoid culture. Progressive liberals and capitalist neoliberals joined hands as they agreed on one point: learning should no longer be associated with the assimilation of culture.

On the one hand, progressive liberalism has had a truly liberating effect on education and other social domains because it broke with parochial traditions. On the other hand, since it did so mainly by creating new universal norms, the "liberation" required large administrative machines able to implement those norms. Progressive education offers less freedom but abstract constraints. It became determined by an "unimaginative educational bureaucracy" (Lasch: 147), and liberty is mainly understood as a sphere determined by consumption enabled by free trade. Those who can still remember earlier periods of the university experience this liberalism as a restriction of freedom.

Political correctness

Both brands of liberalism, the left-wing and the right-wing ones, propagate the cold mechanics of abstract, decultured ideas of excellence most suitable for shapeless humans without cultural qualities. Political correctness was born on these premises. Liberalism's supposed value neutrality is due to the fanatical adherence to culture neutrality. The African American sociologist Orlando Patterson writes:

> It is now wholly incorrect politically even to utter the word *culture* as an explanation in any other context than counterattacks against hereditarians. Indeed, so far has this politically correct position gone that it is not uncommon for people who even tentatively point to social and cultural problems to be labelled and condemned as racists. (Patterson: 144–45)

PC becomes symptomatic for the confused state of the battlefield of liberalism. Coming originally from conservative centers of power who wanted to hide the neoliberal tactics behind the facade of neutrality, PC would soon be used to denounce certain left-wing behaviors and attitudes. Later it could be seen as a "postmodern" assault on truth driven by leftist relativism. However, once again, both left and right liberals agree on one thing: "that the purpose of education is to induce correct opinion rather than to search for wisdom and liberate the mind" (Lea: 29). This means that both the left-wing liberal and the right-wing liberal foster deculturation. Both are working on a new orthodoxy of correctness. In (neo)liberal education students will still be asked to acquire knowledge, but this knowledge should not imply the transmission of concrete cultural heritages. Students will still be asked to acquire thinking skills, but this should happen through training and by taking newly invented critical thinking classes. Or students can submit themselves to the decultured forms of philosophy offered by the analytic tradition. In spite of the progressive potential that leftist liberals were trying to import into the realm of education, schools and academia are confined to a

> new kind of paternalism, which has risen from the ruins of the old paternalism of kings, priests, authoritarian fathers, slavemasters, and landed overlords. Capitalism has severed the ties of personal dependence only to revive dependence under cover of bureaucratic rationality. Having overthrown feudalism and slavery and then outgrown its own personal and familial form, capitalism has evolved a new political ideology, welfare liberalism, which absolves individuals of moral responsibility and treats them as victims of social circumstance. It has evolved new modes of social control, which deal with the deviant as a patient and substitute medical rehabilitation for punishment. (Lasch: 218)

Excellence rhetoric

Lasch's analysis of the crisis of Western education in terms of deculturation sees narcissism as the compulsive desire to obtain a very abstract form of success, which becomes most obvious in the desire to become famous simply for being famous. This is nothing other than the desire to be excellent. Lasch explains that the good or the virtue desired by the narcissist "has no reference to anything outside the self. The new ideal of success has no content," which means that "the only important attribute of celebrity is that it is celebrated; no one can say why" (Lasch: 47). The neoliberal obsession with excellence is rooted in this kind of narcissism. Management specialist Eugene Emerson Jennings, who has described managers as narcissists, coined the formula "performance means to arrive." Lasch concludes that "the manager's view of the world . . . is that of the narcissist, who sees the world as a mirror of himself and has no interest in external events except as they throw back a reflection of his own image" (47). Without calling it such, Lasch describes the excellence-syndrome produced by deculturation. Work itself has become abstract through the process of industrialization. Marx's term "*Entfremdung*" implies a first act of deculturation. After Marx, the working environment became even more abstract and impersonal through bureaucratization as it was divorced from performance: "When work loses its tangible, palpable quality, it loses the character of the transformation of matter by human ingenuity" (Lasch: 102). The deculturation of working life is a process stretching over hundred years at the end of which we find the narcissistic work ethics of excellence.

Kitsch

The reflections on narcissism lead us to kitsch. On the aesthetic level, deculturation is embodied by kitsch. So far, the term "kitsch" has been used mainly metaphorically. We have kitsch religion (fundamentalism) and kitsch education. A similar "fundamentalism via deculturation" pattern is at work in nationalism.[2] Ulrich Steinvorth finds that "the spread of kitsch goes along with the spread of nationalism and other forms of identification with communities, such as religious fanaticism" (Steinvorth: 212). Excellence rhetoric in education and management is another example of kitsch. However, in aesthetics, kitsch is decultured art.

Like the deculturation of working life, kitsch emerged at the age of industrialization. Kitsch is aesthetic excellence, and it occurs when art is not achieved through lengthy processes of cultural mediation, but when the value of an aesthetic expression (its beauty) is produced and enjoyed instantaneously. Similar to the absolute truths of fundamentalist religions and neoliberalism, kitsch happens when aesthetic values are separated from cultural contexts. Kitsch wants aesthetic enjoyment quickly and without bothering about culture. Kitsch is aesthetic fundamentalism as it strives for excellence in the form of a culturally empty type of beauty.

When condemning kitsch, I do not intend to deprive art of all emotionality. On the contrary, most of the time art *should* be emotional. However, the emotions should be reflected against a cultural background. The latter is the case in the poems of Sir Walter Scott (which would otherwise be kitsch), but it is not the case in the paintings of Thomas Kincade. It is therefore better to say that kitsch is not emotional enough. Steinvorth finds that "kitsch not only blinds us to facts by presenting them as more pleasant than they are, but also numbs us, crippling the cognition that emotions provide" (Steinvorth: 213).

Kitsch is not only a product of deculturation but also—and in perfect accordance with Roy's hypothesis—a product of secularization. There is a strong link between the kitsch and the secular world, which Roger Scruton observed like nobody else. For Scruton "the loss of religious certainty facilitated the birth of kitsch. Faith exalts the human heart, removing it from the marketplace, making it sacred and unexchangeable. Under the jurisdiction of religion, our deeper feelings are sacralized" (Scruton 1999).

People always had, and many still have, religious feelings. Modernity and secularization did not make those feelings disappear but shifted them toward areas where they look out of place. The most inappropriate "new home" for those feelings is the economy. Instead of remaining restricted to art and religion, sentimentality has entered the world of the market and the result is kitsch. According to Elisha McIntyre, kitsch is "imitating other attempts to represent the divine and this second degree results in a replica of emotion rather than holiness" (McIntyre: 91).

In retrospect, this had an effect on religion itself. Theologian Johan Cilliers believes that religion "no longer mediates salvation but sentiment" (Cilliers: 3) but that religious sentimentalities have become kitsch. Those explanations echo Karsten Harries's idea that "religious kitsch elicits religious devotion without an encounter with God" (Harries: 80). While Roy holds that secularization created fundamentalism, those authors hold that secularization created kitsch.

Modern or postmodern culture is affected by the same pattern. The fact that European city centers have become so similar to Disneyland is due to the kind of secularization described by Scruton. Those urban spaces were more authentic in the past because they had "something sacred" about them. In other words, those spaces were cultural while now, after their transformation into commercial zones, they are decultured and desacralized. Despite the immense efforts made to preserve the cultural heritage of cities, they have become kitsch.

Excellence civilization

The infernal machine of quantification set in motion by the neoliberal world resembles that of religious fundamentalism and kitsch. Fundamentalism produces an autonomous reality based on what it believes to be excellent. By constantly referring to its own truths to establish "The Truth," it negates the social and historical reality that religion was originally supposed to serve. Quantifying methods serve the same purpose, which is particularly obvious in those methods supposed to lead to "excellence." That's why the anonymous academic in the *Guardian* complained about the explosion of "value-neutral" measuring activities. Most often those methods are dependent on a category of efficiency whose value-status has been narcissistically established by the method itself. Those approaches toward reality lack the sphere of the (cultural) other, which is similar to what happens in fundamentalism. Fundamentalism is "otherless" because religion occupies the entire life sphere and religion cannot be reflected against a cultural truth (philosophy, literature, etc.). In bureaucratic reason, the capacity to reflect truths against a broader spectrum of culture is lost, too.

The phenomenon of deculturation and culture's exodus toward excellence is not a passing fad but one of the biggest challenges of modern civilization. Already in the 1940s, Lionel Trilling described modernity as determined by the "disenchantment of our culture with culture itself" (Trilling 1943: 3). At that time, deculturing modernism could still be contradicted by developing anti-modern critiques. This became impossible once classical modernism had morphed into modernism's phase 2, that is, into "postmodernism." Together with modernist convictions, postmodernism began to dissolve the remnants of Western culture into a soup of aesthetic and ethical relativism. Disillusioned by the collapse of the Soviet bloc in the late 1980s, modernists of the second phase (postmodernists) deconstructed values because they saw them as paternalistic and imperialistic. The soup had been prepared a long time beforehand. In 1962, Claude Lévi-Strauss declared in *La Pensée sauvage* that "the last aim of the human sciences is not to constitute man but to dissolve man" (1962: 326). Lipovetsky and Charles call the postmodern phase, which takes over modernity through relativism, "hypermodernity" (2004: 49). Kitsch remains one of the most emblematic features of this cultural development. As modernism exhausts itself aesthetically, it can no longer transmit emotions appropriately. "Tonal music, figurative painting, rhyming and regular verse—all seemed, at the time of the modernist experiments, to have exhausted their capacity for sincere emotional expression," writes Scruton (1999). As a result, one part of civilization goes for intellectualized expressions of the atonal, the nonfigurative, and the experimental; the other part goes for kitsch. The latter shift does not concern aesthetics alone. Exaggerations, the explosion of images and information as well as fake news characterize a hypermodernity whose main "truth" category has become kitsch.

Still the new modernists do not get tired repeating that cultural values are linked to old authoritarian structures and need to be abandoned. Ethical scruples derived from concrete cultures are declared arbitrary because they are "merely" historically determined. True ethics must be decultured. This is how the "postmodern" deconstruction of values gives way to a naive kitsch philosophy associating borders, authorities, and males with violence. Sooner or later, this curious mixture of pacifism and anarchism will see value neutrality as the only viable option for running a society. On the one hand, those new modernists deconstruct culture via a simplistic form of anti-foundational thinking; on the other hand, they rely on a cultural analysis led by "objective" methods such as quantification, psychoanalytically informed clinical criteria, and identity politics. The result is a nonculture of excellence. Worse, the deconstruction pacifists are rarely aware that the new decultured individuals can so easily be swallowed by the simultaneously emerging neoliberal economy. They are not aware how much leftist and rightist thinking are beginning to overlap and to fuse.

An immense catalyzer of this fusion of left and right is the internet. One of the deepest concerns of both libertarians and liberals is the existence of borders. To be free means to be without borders and the internet has overcome borders. However, through this freedom, the nomadic individual of the postmodern age will also become the prime victim of "the market," especially since the market discovered that those individuals, who have lost all cultural references, are narcissists and therefore an easy prey.

Image culture

This book establishes conceptual links between religious fundamentalism, neoliberal culture/economics, and kitsch. All three thrive in a postindustrial environment of globalization and information culture. Globalization and deterritorialization foster the production of such cultureless truths and in the twenty-first century, they appear in the form of Salafist religious values, quantified cultures of excellence, and kitsch. All three create alternative worlds with alternative truths. It is thus not surprising that kitsch thrives so well in environments determined by the dynamics of the information society. Social media are narcissistic because they enable individuals to recycle their own "selves" without being confronted with the culture of the "other." The rise of self-centered "alternative truths" and conspiracy theories is linked to the above fundamentalism-neoliberalism-kitsch pattern of deculturation. The internet fosters narcissist instincts and therefore also kitsch. In the image culture of the internet narcissism is on the rise. A "Narcissism and Social Networking" study by the University of Würzburg in Germany found that social media networks give narcissists "easy access to a large audience and allows them to selectively post information for the purpose of self-promotion [and to] meticulously cultivate their image" (Würzburg University 2017). The authors conclude that "the link between narcissism and the behavior in social media follows the pattern of a self-reinforcing spiral."

In a decultured world, the self becomes the only remaining ontological and axiological anchor because truths will no longer be extracted from concrete cultural contexts. The distribution of information on the internet avoids confrontations with "other" ideas or simply with "the other." Nicholas Negroponte, the founder of the MIT Media Lab, wrote in the 1970s that the ideal newspaper of the future will be called *Daily Me* (Harper 1997). The internet fosters perpetual narcissist acts of self-discovery and the fascination with selfies is the most literal manifestation of this phenomenon.

On the internet, words have become unnecessary because now "we have the instantaneity of the moment fixed on some million pixels." That's the opinion of Elsa Godart (Godart: 46). However, the word (logos) is essential for any critical discourse. Ancient Greek philosophy was based on rational discourse operating with words whereas image culture is dominated by the effect of the sensible on the intelligible. As a result, we have the image but lost the imaginary because the imaginary requires discursive thinking. Godart concludes that "without logos there is no imaginary. Imagination is no longer a living source able to apprehend the world. There are no reveries or inspirations in the artistic sense" (121).

If the word still appears, it has become an image, too. The word tends to be taken for granted as a sign. Texts serve to inform and to document and interpretations via the logos have become increasingly difficult. This means that the process of reading is no longer seen as a cultural activity. It is only a small step from this kind of image culture to a culture of narcissism. Godart believes that the selfie inaugurates the erasure of the logos as the rational structure around which society is organized. In 1990, when the high-speed internet was introduced, one could already have predicted the emergence of selfies. Already Lasch had singled out the proliferation of images as a catalyzer of narcissism. Today the image flood has turned society into a spectacle in which the individual attempts to participate narcissistically via selfies.

Kitsch is an "alternative aesthetic truth," which will become clear in this book when comparing Harry Frankfurt's popular analysis of alternative truths (the famous "bullshit theory") with the rules of kitsch in aesthetics. Kitsch abounds when narcissistic self-enjoyment becomes the major aesthetic reference. Alternative truths are not due to misinformation but to the kitschification of truth. Similar to religious truth current in fundamentalism, they are mounted on circular self-affirmations. Quantified truths based on a culturally empty idea of excellence follow the same pattern. What all those "truths" have in common is that they are not dialectically derived from confrontations with concrete cultural realities but establish themselves autonomously by affirming their own truth.

Liberalism and deculturation

This book criticizes not only the "conservative" side of liberalism (which tends to be called neoliberalism) but also the deculturing policies of progressive or leftist liberalism. I described above the educational strategies current in both progressive and conservative liberalism. When I criticize in this book liberalism, I address a compound including leftist liberalism and conservative neoliberalism as both attempt to organize society scientifically and produce a limited and naive vision of a *homo aequalis* supposed to have no moral or cultural ambitions, but who is led by the rudimentary imperatives of political correctness. The *homo aequalis* is a hard-working consumer who respects the law and the market. She is not embedded in a culture.

The quantified reality created by algorithms is not only the work of hyper-capitalist neoliberalism, but also the work of progressive liberalism. Neoliberalism embraces the other in terms of efficiency as an object functioning inside a market. Progressive liberalism embraces the other as an abstraction via ethical imperatives of tolerance, the law, and political correctness. In both cases, there is no concrete other that can be evaluated, accepted, or refused. Neither the nonculture of kitsch nor the nonculture of excellence (both of which Dubai has combined within one and the same place) are the products of harsh, globalized capitalism and conservative neoliberalism alone. They are also the results of "progressive" thinking common among leftist liberals. Both neoliberals and progressive liberals put forward a cultureless notion of excellence, and both do so in the name of freedom. As liberals preach freedom for everybody, the logical consequence is that the liberal self must be "liberated" from all cultural contingencies. In a liberal world, the liberal is freest when she has accepted her own cultural disembodiment and embraced an existence that is not more cultural than kitsch. Kitsch becomes the last utopia, which Milan Kundera sensed when writing that the "brotherhood of men on earth will be possible only on the base of kitsch" (1984: 251).

To understand the parallels between conservative neoliberalism and progressive liberalism it is necessary to identify the root of liberal thought more precisely. Jean-Claude Michéa (2007) has shown that the modern phenomenon of liberalism arose from the necessity of pacification. After centuries of wars, violence, and Hobbesian insights into the fundamentally evil nature of the human being, the most urgent task of politics at the time of Enlightenment became ideological pacification. When we respect the choices of each other in the realm of ethics, religion, and aesthetics, society will be pacified. Those intentions, which prepared the ground for a modern culture of tolerance, are certainly laudable. However, their continuous application in modern states has led to the mechanical and rigid use of liberal convictions in terms of ideologies, assumptions about the universality of values, standardizations, and the requirement of transparency of even the most insignificant opinions.

All those problems can be traced to deculturation. Since all beliefs and cultural determinations had to be excluded from the public sphere and be relegated to the private sphere, abstract notions of "rights" and the "free market" became the only acceptable moral standards. Deculturation became the modern liberals' obsession. The initial intention had been to create a free environment in which laws establish a balance between powers to avoid conflicts. However, those abstract imperatives of tolerance and freedom became totalitarian in their own right as they banned concrete values and culture. The good could no longer be established with reference to cultures but only quantitatively, that is, culturally neutrally. This good was supposed to represent an absolute truth, which brings liberalism close to religious fundamentalism where the category of "good life" is derived—equally circularly and narcissistically—from noncultural religious prescriptions.

Though rightist ("free market") and the leftist ("human rights") liberal approaches differ from each other in many respects, both are based on a similar ideology of deculturation. Culture prevents the liberal machine from running smoothly. In liberal societies, individuals are best served when seeing themselves not as cultural subjects but as abstract, quantified entities. They can still pursue cultural interests privately, but public expressions should be cleansed of moral-cultural connotations. Conservative and progressive liberals agree on this. Neoliberals refuse culture because culture-based arguments disturb the freedom of the market. They refuse ethical arguments that are not derived from the justice of the market. Progressive liberals have different motives, but the results are the same.

The anti-cultural tyranny is not always easy to recognize because most typically, leftist liberals will superpose their idea of culture with a fuzzy concept of "class." Once this rhetoric has been adopted, even language will be dismissed as class-based: in an ideal society, language is not supposed to determine life, but a new, simple, noncultural language must be invented. This language should be easy to learn for everybody, after which it will become the standard for everybody. In both cases, culture is seen as an element that can only disturb the development of free and modern societies.

The decultured world of progressive liberals is not different from the world of multinationals who build soulless cities like Dubai. Both agree that knowledge needs to be transformed into culturally neutral information. The further resemblance of both liberalisms with fundamentalism is even more mindboggling. Liberal ideologies correspond with Roy's description of fundamentalism for which culture becomes an obstacle "in a space where information has replaced knowledge" (Roy 2013: 6).

Dubai

Dubai is a perfect example of a "kitsch through deculturation" syndrome driven by neoliberal policies as well as by globalization. Dubai is a globalized city marked by consumerism and internal fragmentation, with an artificial economy dependent on borrowed capital. Dubai is a financial mirage or, according to Sean O'Grady (2009), a "sub-prime in the desert." This alone makes it unreal. However, Dubai also appears as unreal because of its lack of urban history or local identity. Dubai lacks *cultural* reality. According to Qatar-based architect Ali Alraouf, Dubai is the result of the pursuit of planning whims unwilling to offer a sense of contextual authenticity (Alarouf 2005). The city is filled with architectural icons "designed from the top down by starting from a desired image and moving to its physical manifestation" (Elsheshtawy: 187). The result is an unreal city founded on narcissistic structures. This means that Dubai impresses not merely through its kitsch aesthetics, but also through its kitsch *structure*. Dubai has a narcissistically self-enclosed penchant as its existence is auto-fed by its own virtual productions. The real estate crash in 2008 spelled an end to plans that most people believed to be too fancy from the onset, but an endless series of rollover of debts and access to emergency financing postponed any "game over." A real ground of the economy could never be established. Because Dubai has no place in the "real world" it creates its own world. However, it does so not by imitating—like Disneyland—romantic parts of *other* real cultures but rather by insisting on its aesthetic self-sufficiency. Malls provide the simulation not of culture but of the natural world represented by lakes, meadows, and ski resorts. Dubai develops toward the narcissistic world that Umberto Eco described as the mall in Los Angeles reproducing neighborhoods of Los Angeles (Eco 1998: 53). Much more than Disneyland, Dubai is the perfect example of narcissistic kitsch through deculturation as it creates a world emptied of *any* culture. The creation of islands in the sea—a peculiar undertaking in a country that has plenty of empty desert space—denotes the same pattern of narcissistic self-sufficiency. The artificial island that lodges the Burj Al Arab Hotel is located about three hundred meters away from the beach and is conceived in the form of a private city-state following its own laws. In Dubai, social and professional functions are not planned in the form of cities or compounds, but of archipelagos: Internet City, Media City, the Financial Center, as well as the Gold and Jewelry Park. Each island represents a certain part of the world and the entire project will lead—metaphorically speaking—to the creation of a new world. Dubai's islandization strategy represents the most aggressive neoliberal attempt at creating legal relativism within a globalized world that has lost its (cultural) standards. While earlier Hong Kong underwent a complex process of deculturation to develop a "tendency towards placelessness and timelessness" that was later reverted (Abbas 1996: 215), for Dubai the placeless and timeless option was part of its concept from the beginning. Dubai's *basis* is deculturation. The city never attempted to be more than a computer-generated image and *immediately* engaged in self-abstraction, which is the most radical act of deculturation.

Liberal utopias

All decultured civilizations—no matter if progressive or neoliberal—share two characteristics: they rely on excellence and they produce kitsch. When culture is abolished, the only recognized realities are an abstract idea of social justice or human rights (for leftist) and economic growth (for rightist). Next, those ideas of human rights and economic growth will be exalted, most probably by using variations of the term "excellence." Growth will be mystified via positivist methods (algorithms and statistics) based on relatively obscure standards. For example, neoliberals like to define the gross GDP (Gross Domestic Product) by taking into account pollution and future accidents, which are produced by the neoliberal economy, but which can be dissimulated through "rational" calculations. Those pseudo-scientific fictions depicting growth in terms of excellence have much in common with kitsch. They are inappropriate though at the same time they work—like kitsch—along the lines of utmost neatness and precision.

Conservative liberals (neoliberals) replace culture with the market because markets function better when the environment is decultured. Progressive liberals work toward a similar aim. The "value" that matters for both is an abstract form of justice. For both liberals, much of this justice will be established through economic reasoning and in the market. Both are striving for a liberal utopia determined by excellence. This is paradoxical because initially, liberalism was against utopias as utopias contain values enabling the fanatic adherence to utopian visions. The utopia is rather a matter of socialist philosophies. According to Michéa, liberalism was based on realism, empiricism, and moderation (2007: 192). Even in the church, "liberalization" meant moderation in the sense of secularization. Roy points out that secularization, which went hand in hand with the advance of liberal movements, "was experienced as more of a positive thing (except of course in the Churches of the Awakening), [as] it was moving in the direction of what would become liberal Protestantism, far removed from religious excess" (Roy: 60).

The liberal utopia is a peculiar utopia based on human rights and the market. It has been established realistically and empirically, preferably with the help of algorithms; and it will be defended with the same utopian fanaticism that liberalism initially intended to contradict. The system of liberalism is supposed to be based not on ideology but simply on truth. It is this belief in the validity of truths disconnected from reflections on culture that makes many liberal statements sound religious.

In the postwar economy, as it created a utopia of its own, liberalism began looking more and more like an ideology. More precisely, it created the utopia of a value-free anti-utopia. Both liberalisms are based on a decultured form of rationality. Both believe in the existence of a pacific and harmonious society regulated not by culture but by rights and the market. In a liberal world, wars will still occur, but they will be fought on a smaller scale because individualization and the absence of cultural identities make the occurrence of large-scale wars more and more unlikely. That said, liberalism fosters the war of everybody against everybody. But those "small wars" will not be fought with weapons but rather in the form of legal wars or commercial wars because nobody will be ready to fight for anything other than for justice and for the market.

Education remains the black sheep of both liberalisms. Both see it more as a problem than as a solution because education is traditionally linked to cultures. For the neoliberal, education is a waste of time except if it teaches (in the form of training) technology and knowledge about justice or about the market economy. For the progressive liberal, educating children is an act of symbolic violence and should be limited to the teaching of human rights. In both cases, liberty is understood abstractly not as the liberty to choose values, but as the liberty to switch from one market to the other. For the liberal, it is politically correct to change the country for fiscal reasons as long as one does not move to a non-liberal country. Cultural convictions or adherences of any kind are taboo. This innocent and naive vision of human life in terms of justice and the market is kitsch the more so as it is—like kitsch—inoffensive, cute, and morally empty.

The narcissistic culture of quantification

Many truths based on quantification are "kitsch truths." In kitsch, aesthetic truths are derived from immediate experiences of enjoyment that lack cultural depth. The person who enjoys art in a kitsch way will usually not have those cultural references. The result is the creation of alternative truths or—if the mechanism persists—of alternative realities. In this sense, algorithms, which have begun to determine many parts of our existences, have invented a separate reality. Algorithms tell us which books we like, based on previous choices. In algorithms, signs are quantified and classified along the guidelines of abstract forms of excellence. The narcissist structure of this model is obvious. Interactive robots whose personality is constructed around our personal algorithms will soon serve us as "accompanying mobile robots." Algorithms create a culture of narcissism. The company Lyrebird developed robots that perfectly imitate our voice.

Liberals will hold that following algorithms makes us free *just because* we are merely following ourselves. True, we are free because we are not linked to any form of cultures established by other elements than those based on ourselves. The internet user who follows her own algorithms does not follow others. The world governed by algorithms can thus be propagated as a world of maximal freedom, especially since it goes across national borders. However, in reality we are not free because algorithms lock us into the bubble of our own preferences or into their synthetically created narcissistic, quantified, alternative reality. Neoliberal technocrats will explain those limitations as a maximized freedom. We are not essentialized through our culture (race, gender, ethnicity, etc.) but we have to accept our own essentialization through quantification. We are supposed to construe this essentialization as an act of freedom because what has been quantified are *our own* choices. However, this is not freedom because our choices have not been guided by free decisions. It is rather a "kitsch-life" guided by narcissism. Real freedom has been stifled by the calculators' ambition to construct the image of statistical regularity (an alternative reality) that users are supposed to accept as the result of their free choice.

The parallel with religious fundamentalism is not exaggerated. First, both algorithms and fundamentalists work toward deculturation. Second, they replace culture with abstract notions of universal truths based on cultureless notions of excellence. Once truths are disconnected from cultural realities, the next step will be the production of alternative truths and alternative realities. This is the specialty of both fundamentalism and algorithm culture.

Neoconservative and progressive liberalism share the above paradoxical starting point, and it is not surprising that both end up with similar solutions. Both propose a pseudo-rational and contradictory concept of freedom that finds its most contemporary expression in algorithm culture. The liberty of algorithms is based on deculturation. The freedom of liberalism (no matter which kind) is a freedom based on narcissism. I see kitsch not only in neoliberalism with its bombastic aesthetics, exaggerated belief in the individual, or the exaltation of social Darwinism. I also see it in progressive liberalism with its humanitarian appeals to pity or what French writer Philippe Muray has called a hypocrite culture of "bons sentiments."

Liberalism and kitsch

Neoliberal attitudes toward kitsch are straightforward: everybody is free to like whatever she wants, and even kitsch producers should be allowed to benefit from the sale of ugliness as long as they do not force other people into buying it. Questions of taste are irrelevant because taste cannot be quantified. The *progressive* liberal kitsch defender's position is more complicated. Robert Solomon has described how progressive liberals attribute the disdain for kitsch to "economic class distinctions and manufacturing values rather than aesthetic evaluation as such. Much of the literature attacking kitsch is political rather than aesthetic" (Solomon: 238). This argument needs to be disentangled. The leftist faces a conundrum. Though, from a leftist point of view, the capitalist origin of mass-produced kitsch needs to be criticized, the *consumers* of kitsch should not be discriminated but defended: "Though ironically much of [the critique] comes from Marxists and their kin who despise the mass-marketing origins of kitsch, at the same time . . . they would defend the people who are most likely to purchase such objects" (Solomon: 238). The leftist liberal recognizes kitsch as an undesirable by-product of capitalism. But at the same time, kitsch cannot be criticized because that would denote class snobbism. Solomon describes the paradox of the liberal kitsch man, which is based on a paradox of liberalism that will be elucidated below. The progressive liberal is against kitsch but will simultaneously defend kitsch on the grounds of tolerance. As a result, Holliday and Potts have noted that liberals now have "lesser difficulties accepting the industrially influenced (mass-) cultural trash which had posed a big problem for the previous generations" (Holliday and Potts: 21).

The paradox of freedom

Liberalism suffers from the paradox of freedom. The problem is rooted in the paradoxical combination of individualism and universalism, a combination present in liberalism ever since its conception. In liberalism, individuals are not supposed to define themselves as free because they are different. The liberal is merely free because she is following the universal rule of freedom. At the same time, progressive liberalism preaches a politics ready to tolerate differences. But how can differences be reconciled with the other principle of liberalism, which is universalism? The principles of liberalism are universal laws not supposed to be corrupted by contingencies such as cultural affinities. Liberalism (and that goes for the progressive and the conservative branch) is universalist because its basis is rationalism. This book will show that rationality without culture is pseudo-rationalism. By following the rationalism of deculturation the liberal ends up as a deracinated, neutral human being. Why should this be called rational?

Both liberals and neoliberals rarely recognize this paradox. In the eyes of the liberal, the freest individual is culturally neutral and only determined by an abstract form of rationality. The liberated individual should find absolute happiness by following the algorithms of her own preferences. The politics of liberalism (no matter which kind) has created a sphere of excellence that corresponds to the "shallow" liberalism already criticized by Nietzsche.

Instead of abandoning liberalism altogether, this book tries to design a better, self-critical image of liberalism by criticizing the circular reasoning of self-confirmation to which liberalism has been submitted. Both neoliberalism and progressive liberalism are caricatures of what "liberal" was once supposed to be. Liberalism has degenerated into a fundamentalist philosophy of quantification producing a kitsch reality. The politics of fundamentalism, neoliberal economics, and kitsch, all three of which thrive in postindustrial environment in which cultural landmarks are dwindling, are difficult to contain. But the awareness that those three phenomena, which are otherwise very dissimilar, have a common root will make it easier to spot them.

Which culture?

This book, which points to the deculturation in several domains, is not simply nostalgic. True, I criticize relatively recent developments: scientification, overrationalization, technologization, and the corporate culture of quantification take place in the present. But criticizing the present does not necessarily mean that one wants to go back to a pre-global past. The past was not always better than the present: kitsch and fundamentalism exist since centuries and are only differently materialized in neoliberal and global times. Chapter 6 on Nietzsche, Burckhardt, Evola, and Meinecke provides historical dimensions to the problem of deculturation showing that the crisis of liberalism begins in the nineteenth century.

How do I define culture? I use the term "culture" in a very broad sense of a force regulating human relations. This definition is broad enough to include the national and the social and even class. Culture is concrete and dynamic, which distinguishes it from the abstract and static codes of, for example, political correctness. Culture contains emotions, choices, values, desires, perceptions, attitudes, interests, expectations, and sensibilities; it is the reality of human life, and the book's claim is that this reality is getting lost in the neoliberal world. Indirectly, this concept of culture is opposed to that of civilization, which has (at least in some languages) always alluded to the utilitarian, outer aspect of human existence in the sense of material, technical, and economic. In this sense, this book aims to continue a value-oriented and idea-oriented tradition along the lines of a neohumanist agenda of *Bildung*, of historicism, and of historical criticism based on the work of Giambattista Vico and Johann Gottfried Herder. In these philosophies, culture is perceived as the "real" essence of humans, society, and their achievements. Reculturation must be defined in this sense, considering all reservations that are necessary in certain cases. Far-right thinkers regretting the deconstruction of societies' cultural foundations present their reculturation project as the reinvigoration of language, heritage, feeling, spirituality, communities, and sometimes religion. Each of those notions needs to be critically evaluated to avoid "nostalgicism."

Describing deculturation is an ambiguous project as noted already Oswald Spengler when construing the end of the occident. Spengler's thoughts appear nostalgic as they portray the erasure of culture through a civilization that was, at Spengler's time, represented by Cecil Rhodes (36–37). At the same time, Spengler sees this process as inevitable because much culture had become decadent. It had to be taken down by "civilization" (32). Today we are not confronted with Cecil Rhodes but with the civilization of Silicon Valley. Interpreting the decline of culture remains a project as ambiguous as ever.

Notes

1   On the aesthetics of ISIS see Botz-Bornstein 2019.
2   Steinvorth finds that "the spread of kitsch goes along with the spread of nationalism and other forms of identification with communities, such as religious fanaticism" (Steinvorth: 212).

A Religion of Excellence

We are living in times of deculturation. The appeal to values anchored in local cultures has become more and more difficult, which is nowhere more obvious than in universities. In the eighteenth century, universities could still be used for the purpose of national cultural revival. "The early European universities combined an evolving sense of self-identity—partly grounded on the site and partly derived from the surrounding cities," writes Simon Marginson (2011). In today's universities, knowledge is globalized. Bill Readings has shown that the deculturation of the university began with the growth of American universities. American society is a contractual community and the establishment of "American culture" could not be seen as an end of education. As a result, the only "value" permitted became a neoliberal notion of excellence. To be excellent means to be "efficient," but it is left open what concrete values this efficiency is supposed to establish. In America, writes Readings, "the idea of the nation is always already an abstraction [and] excellence can thus most easily gain ground" (33). Christopher Lasch has described the liberal break with parochial ethnic traditions as "Americanization" (Lasch: 135), explaining that the excellence culture of corporate capitalism "has replaced character building with permissiveness, the cure of souls with the cure of the psyche, blind justice with therapeutic justice, philosophy with social science, personal authority with an equally irrational authority of professional experts" (221). The phenomenon is not limited to America but, according to Bryan Turner, "the tension between universalism and nationalism [was] always present at the university. [It] made the university a creator of national language and culture [but] has been vitiated by the globalization of knowledge and the university" (Turner: 73–75).

Allan Bloom traced the decline of culture to other sources. There is a crisis of cultural transmission in which the "decay of the family's traditional role as the transmitter of tradition" plays an important role: "Nobody believes that the old books do, or even could, contain the truth. So books have become, at best, 'culture' i.e., boring" (Bloom: 58). Bloom does not criticize conservative-neoliberal policies but rather a leftist cultural attitude of openness and tolerance, which brought about deculturation. Lasch does something similar when pointing to the loss of history. The collapse of historical culture coming with the disappearance of patriotism and political optimism leads to a public consciousness that finds the past irrelevant (Lasch: xiv). This stream of critique has been developed in the 1990s by Sowell (1993), Bernstein (1994), and Sykes (1995).

During the twenty years that have passed since the publication of Readings's *The University in Ruins*, the neoliberal education model has expanded. Excellence became a rule and could be defined as a global standard. A frantic culture of evaluations, quantitative measuring, control, and standardization is ubiquitous. Even in Europe, learning contents are no longer determined by a corresponding culture but by Programme for International Student Assessment (PISA). On the world's university websites, we find almost identical mission statements containing multiple references to excellence no matter in which part of the world the university is located. Knowledge and education have been impersonalized. Everybody is supposed to fill in the same charts of goal achievement and everybody must live up to the same abstract notion of excellence. Knowledge has become information and schools have become training centers in which teachers coach students how to acquire this information.

The Gulf countries and excellence culture

The most extreme cases of this culture are not found in the United States but in the region of the Arabian/Persian Gulf, and it is worthwhile examining this culture as a paramount example of deculturation. Historically, in the Gulf region, the idea of culture-free excellence was accepted very quickly. By transplanting institutions and by importing American educational models into a region that has no strong cultural pull, neoliberal educational strategies could be implemented without meeting much resistance. In the late 1990s, when American branch campuses were opened in the Gulf States because "governments and citizens in the Gulf states were expressing dissatisfaction with the quality education at domestic universities" (Tétreault 2012: 56), the neoliberal notion of excellence facilitated the transfer of knowledge from one sphere to the other. The Gulf welcomed excellence more warmly than anybody else. Some Gulf States were just about to attempt the shift from an oil-based economy to an information-based economy, and the launching of corporate university initiatives was seen as a way of achieving this aim. Many Gulf universities invested in neoliberal business models to cooperate with American universities, often fully paying the setup and operation costs. The most outstanding example is the Qatar Foundation, which is directly dependent on and funded by the Qatari government. Another example is the Dubai Knowledge Village (DKV), which is equally heavily funded by the local government. Doha's Education city includes Cornell, Georgetown, Virginia Commonwealth, Northwestern, and Texas A&M while DKV includes twenty-two international universities, among which are the universities of Michigan State, Middlesex, New Brunswick, Wollongong, and Bradford. Abu Dhabi hosts New York University and the Sorbonne. Most of those universities receive enough money to channel it back into their home institutions (see Vora 2013: 161).

Universities in the Gulf Cooperation Council (GCC) have embraced excellence as a mantra for success and as a brand name for a new type of educational corporatism. Most universities have a Center for Excellence, which can also be called "Center for Excellence in Teaching and Learning," "Center for Excellence and Distinction" or "Center for Achievement and Excellence." The *International Indian* writes that "Education and Excellence go hand in hand in UAE," and the Dubai Healthcare City claims to work "in a culture that champions excellence." Universities advertise "Outstanding Academic Excellence Scholarship," "Business Excellence specialization," "Smart Learning Excellence," and an "Emirates ID's Track Record in Excellence" quantifies excellence in all Emirates. There is also a "Dubai Government Excellence Program" for education and the Canadian University of Dubai's "Centre of Excellence for Innovation and Creativity" (CEIC) develops collaborative strategies to support the advancement of the green economy in Dubai. Above that, "excellence initiatives" all over the territory offer seminars like the "Dubai Achieving Excellence in Higher Education Seminar" or the "Annual Forum on e-Learning Excellence in the Middle East" (Zayed University).

In the UAE universities, "excellence" is, together with "global," the most used term in marketing texts. On websites, the very first statement typically addresses excellence. The American University of the Emirates (Dubai) "remains convinced that since its opening, it has made great strides towards developing a culture of excellence" (website). In a country whose prime minister, Sheik Mohammed bin Rashid Al-Maktoum, has named his own book *My Vision: Challenges in the Race for Excellence*, universities need to follow the call. Dubai University's Centre of Excellence "aims to support the vision of the ruler of Dubai." Maktoum's vision of Dubai as a Smart City (typically understood as a "sensing city" making use of algorithms to regulate traffic and services) is linked to the rhetoric of excellence.[1] The connection between excellence and new technologies seems to be intrinsic. The software producer National Instruments Arabia (NI) claims to cater directly to Centers of Excellence (CoE) and with the "Smart City," excellence has moved to the realm of urban planning, making the future of Dubai as mythical and vague as neoliberal excellence itself. The virtual character of an urbanization able to "transcend time and space" (Junemo: 183) and even to create an "illusive history" (Elsheshtawy 2010: 72) is closely linked to the autonomous and narcissistic reality trying to ground itself on a culturally empty idea of "excellence."

In spite of this overwhelming rhetoric, the neoliberal idea of the "knowledge society" or "knowledge economy" remains very vague in the Gulf. The excellence language does not correlate to the actual tertiary levels of education. Though "since 2007 almost every government economic or planning document issued by the State of Qatar has made explicit reference to the knowledge economy" (Weber: 62), Wiseman et al. detect "a potential contradiction between the expectations of Arabian Gulf countries and their perceived capacity to reach those goals (e.g., seemingly low quality and low impact education system)" (3). According to Davidson, there is "a question mark over the enforcement of minimum standards [as] ministries have been slow to develop quality control bodies to monitor curriculum development and teaching practices" (Davidson: 107). It seems that the "contextual challenge of aligning Arabian Gulf expectations, traditions, and norms with those of knowledge economies" (3) as well as the challenges arising from the fact that there simply *is* no knowledge society have been solved by exalting the theme of abstract excellence.

In general, the education environment in the Gulf is substandard with an education development index putting, for example, Abu Dhabi on place 90 out of 125. The ambition to become a knowledge-based economy also clashes with the fact that, according to the World Bank (2007), the knowledge economy had shrunk since 2005. In 2005, the illiteracy rate in the UAE was still 22 percent (Davidson: 110).

A society of excellence

Technization and "exaggerated measuring activities" are not limited to education and universities but have been implemented in the realms of health, justice, and the police. A graphic example is food. Food has been linked to long-established food cultures, which could be modified and improved. Today we observe a redefinition of "food" in terms of scientifically established components that can be measured and quantified. Food is no longer cultural but has become abstract (calories, carbs, proteins, genes, etc.).

Excellence culture is present even in the police force. Steve Martinot locates "quantification fundamentalism" in urban police culture in the United States, reporting that police departments have initiated a relation to civil society in a (federally) coordinated manner, which he likens to fundamentalism, as the police conceive of the task mainly in terms of "cultural purification." The current police force in the United States sees "civil society as 'de-cultured' with respect to the law (viz. through the principle of equality), and corrupt in its laxness toward criminality," which leads them to "operating through a common hierarchical structure" with common styles of operations, technologies, and ideologies. The result is not a religious society—as required by fundamentalism—but a military society based on fundamentalist standards:

> An essential part of this standardization and purification has been their insistence on the regimentation of society through an attitude of command and an insistence on obedience, as if civil society had been transformed into a military organization in which all police officers played the role of commanding officer. . . . This concrete separation between police culture and civil society (the command / obedience paradigm) becomes an unbridgeable gap as soon as disobedience can be seen as itself criminal. (Martinot 2016)

Lasch detects one of the most obvious manifestations of the deculturation syndrome in sport, which came with the professionalization of sport, which, in return, contributed to the spread of excellence culture in universities. At some point in the 1970s, "trainers, coaches, doctors, and public relations experts outnumbered the players. The accumulation of elaborate statistical records arose from management's attempt to reduce winning to a routine, to measure efficient performance" (Lasch: 120). Today sport is no longer linked to localities or nations, but excellence replaced culture, which has bizarre consequences. In ice hockey, excellence came in the form of violence, which perfectly illustrates the absurd and ethically content-less character of this notion: "The rise of violence in ice hockey, far beyond the point where it plays any functional part in the game, coincided with the expansion of professional hockey into cities without any traditional attachment to the sport" (107).

In parallel with Roy's thesis of secularism-induced religious fundamentalism, Lasch traces the deculturation of sport to secularization. Reminiscing the "sacred" roots of play developed by Johan Huizinga, Lasch concludes that the bureaucratization of athletic careers as well as the preponderance of statistical records led to a "secularization of sport" (119). Lasch's analysis of sport follows the same pattern that Roy describes thirty years later as the condition of religious fundamentalism. Secularization pushes religion into a sphere of purity in which it is not supposed to communicate with the sphere of culture. Lasch quotes the famous sport reporter Howard Cosell: "The attempt to create a separate realm of pure play, totally isolated from work, gives rise to its opposite—the insistence, in Cosell's words, that 'sports are not separate and apart from life, a special "Wonderland" where everything is pure and sacred and above criticism', but a business subject to the same standards and open to the same scrutiny as any other" (124). It sounds as if sport used to be a purist and sacred ritual, and that corporatization introduced sport to the real world. However, the contrary is true. The "sacred" version of sport was separate from work but still a part of culture. Sport as business is work but detached from culture. This is a paradox, but the same paradox underlies the deculturation of religion, which becomes more purist-religious when society no longer recognizes religion as a part of its culture or when religion does not want to be part of this culture.

The overlap of sport with religion is not surprising because both can be traced to rituals and play. However, this is also the reason why both are constantly threatened by narcissism. Narcissism has metaphysical connotations as it often looks for a spiritual dimension of being. In a religious way, narcissism wants freedom beyond this world as well as spiritual elevation; as Lasch explains: "Narcissism in this sense is the longing to be free from longing. It is the backward quest for that absolute peace upheld as the highest state of spiritual perfection in many mystical traditions" (Lasch: 241).

The progressive neoliberal

Excellence culture has sparked an autistic hyperactivity always going for the newest of the new in terms of methods, measuring activities, and standardization. Again, leftist and rightist elements work amazingly well together. Deculturation is not merely the achievement of the neoliberal capitalist eager to earn profit. True, in a globalized world, decultured products sell better, and the deculturation project can be seen as a pro-capitalist measure. However, the progressive liberal influence on this measurement culture is equally important. Deculturation not only is efficient in terms of profit, but also can be considered ethical and socially progressive because decultured education (like many other decultured products) will bring about social justice. Knowledge, once it has been separated from the culture within which it has been produced, becomes accessible to more individuals. Culturally neural knowledge will meet less social barriers. Values embedded in cultures tend to be linked to social classes, which means that value-neutral education makes knowledge more democratic. Deculturation enables social and economic equality, which is why leftists have put it on their agenda.

The results of the educational models proposed by both progressive liberals and neoliberals are similarly disastrous. Teachers are bombarded with new pedagogical methods, workshops, and new teaching techniques, most of which are designed to help the weak. Those innovations can be identified as neoliberal for-profit measures but *at the same time* they are supposed to raise the ethical standards of the university. Of course, the "democratic" university in which teachers have to listen to the students' wishes is also more profitable because students, once they are served like clients, will pay more if they are satisfied. At the same time, pandering to the demands of students can be advertised as ethical because one is helping the weak. This combination of conservative-neoliberal and liberal-progressive ideas has led not only to the lowering of standards but also to cultural desertification in the name of social justice.

Progressive and conservative liberalisms have fused their ideologies and created the strange image of the ruthless capitalist who claims to be humanitarian because her standardization and evaluation methods guarantee social equality. According to Lasch, "in the school, business corporation, courts of law, and authorities conceal their power behind a façade of benevolence" (181). Already in the 1970s Lasch described the soft-footed technocrat stalking universities and drawing down six-figure salaries, whom the *Guardian* would honor in the abovementioned article (Preston 2015). The neoliberal administrator is a profit maker emboldened by his own humanitarian intentions. He engenders not only money but also social justice, and this on a global scale. Globalization is good for you and we will help you to find your place in a global world if you only agree to be converted into a decultured, quantified entity.

The mindless hyperactivity working in the service of excellence can be compared with fundamentalist activities on several levels. Being determined by a naive objectivism, both tend to believe in abstract scientific forms of truth. Furthermore, both developed at the same time and under similar conditions. Both fundamentalism's pure truth and the neoliberal university's excellence are self-referential and self-interested. Both loathe being questioned in terms of culture or what Wilhelm von Humboldt had called "Bildung." And both do not intend to produce well-rounded individuals nurtured by the culture they live in, but prefer to offer training and specialized programs. Finally, both function very well in globalized contexts.

For Roy, evangelism and Salafism, in particular, are modern forms of religion that eschew traditional—and more cultural—forms of religious practice. Instead, truth is formatted and standardized. Categories like "good life" will no longer be established by analyzing centuries of life experience (which is what cultures and traditions actually are), but they will be derived from religious prescriptions alone. This is precisely how the bureaucratic reason of the neoliberal university attempts to establish educative values. The only difference with fundamentalism is that the neoliberal institution does not use religion but the hard sciences, preferably statistics. The result is a "religion of excellence." In a society based on excellence, everything that is "other" than excellence must be banished because it is pagan. Everything is supposed to be "good," a little like in books on the "power of positive thinking." This also means that everything must be explicit and nothing should be implicit. The culture of excellence likes to spell things out, preferably in terms of numbers. The same technique is used in religious fundamentalism. "Negative" and implicit elements of cultures, often only discernable in the culture's subcultures, must be negated though those elements constitute the cultural soul of a society. Roy criticizes this process when writing: "In order to endure, a society cannot rely solely on the explicit, but must build itself on the implicit and the unspoken, even if there is a consensus on the core values (which is not always the case). It must accept and not diminish its marginal elements, deviances, and othernesses—from the brothel to carnival, from homosexuality to drug or alcohol use" (Roy: 110). Instead, those religions exclude "everything from its purview which is essentially unacceptable in human existence." The latter sentence comes from Kundera and he says this about kitsch, concluding that "kitsch is the absolute denial of shit" (1984: 251). In the same vein, theologian John Cilliers writes about religious kitsch that "kitsch cannot endure life's struggles. It avoids theodicy like the plague. It cannot exist in the tension of the quest for meaning. . . . It bypasses reality, also the reality of suffering, poverty and being truly human" (Cilliers 2010).

Political correctness has the same aspirations of purity. Furthermore, both fundamentalism and PC resemble socialist regimes as described by the Polish philosopher and politician Ryszard Legutko: "Those who were ideologically correct 'criticized', 'condemned', 'exposed', 'accused', and 'denounced' what it was proper to criticize, condemn, expose, accuse, and denounce" (Legutko: 12). What both Cilliers and Legutko miss are cultural values of beauty and goodness.

Those values get crushed under the weight of correctness: "Socialists abandoned the criterion of beauty—considered anachronistic and of dubious political value—and replaced it with the criterion of correctness" (Legutko: 14).

Positivism and dogmatism

Normally, in cultures, just like in education, we do not evaluate mere facts (or information) but possibilities. A value is not positively measurable but always a possible choice occurring within a certain context; it has no absolute truth. The problem is that the recognition of values within certain contexts depends on the person's education. In certain situations, an educated person is more likely to recognize what is "probably good" or "plausibly good" while the uneducated person is not. Being educated does not mean being able to recognize absolute truths that have been revealed through religion or checked by science. On the contrary, educated people tend to be critical of absolute truths no matter if they come in the form of statistics or religious revelations. Any form of positivism is deemed to be dogmatic. Instead, facts need to be *understood* within a larger (cultural) context in order to be declared plausible or implausible.

The culture of excellence is dogmatic because excellence is not supposed to be reflected against a cultural screen. The parallel with the most recent development of religions is obvious. What happens is a shift from culturally determined knowledge to belief. Roy writes that "in order to circulate, the religious object must appear universal, disconnected from a specific culture that has to be understood in order for the message to be grasped. Religion therefore circulates outside knowledge. Salvation does not require people to know, but to believe" (6). Also, excellence is not a matter of cultural or intercultural reasoning but of belief. Roy explains that "the word 'conversion' is reserved for changing religion [because] people do not convert to a culture" (34). Nobody will be led toward excellence via a critical thinking process either; one converts to excellence. The reason is that excellence is too abstract and too universal, just like the absolute, revealed truth of fundamentalists. On what grounds would you *refuse* to be excellent? Refusing excellence is like saying that you are a nonbeliever. Critical thinking can lead to the learning and adoption of *certain* cultural values that will probably come in different shades; it can never lead to the adoption of excellence as such. Values—which are always cultural—need to be learned one by one and cannot be acquired through a sudden act of conversion. Cultures offer a "symbolic, imaginary system that legitimates the social and political order"

(110) and communal life is regulated by this system. This has nothing to do with faith or the (blind) belief in some abstract values.

Excellence is a completely different phenomenon. You cannot say: "I want to be a little bit excellent." It's a matter of all or nothing, exactly like what fundamentalists think of religion. When the possibility of critical reflection disappears, the way of thinking is likely to become fanatic. Fundamentalism produces an autonomous reality based on an idea of excellence that constantly refers to itself and loses sight of the social and historical reality that religion and education were originally supposed to serve. The circularity of this structure creates proximities with the model of kitsch. Standardization is one of the major innovations brought about by both neoliberal societies and fundamentalism. Roy devotes an entire section of his book to standardization in fundamentalist religions and detects three main characteristics: "The insistence on the norm rather than on love and compassion; a closed community but a universalist vision of religion; indifference to traditional culture and art but a fascination with modern technology" (8). In traditional religions, "theological reflection is stimulated by contact with philosophy and literature" (6) while in fundamentalism this approach is found inefficient. What fundamentalist religion needs in order to function are standards, norms, and information.

The naive objectivism through which evangelism and Salafism operate is duplicated by neoliberal as well as progressive liberal forms of education that have abandoned any cultural project. Most basically, culture represents a project shared by several people. In order to do so, the people who share the same culture do not need to believe in the same absolute truth. On the contrary, culture as a project is very much about items that can be neither quantified nor spelled out in terms of simple true-false dichotomies: there are emotions, choices, values, desires, perceptions, attitudes, interests, expectations, and sensibilities. To understand and to communicate all those items, cultures need critical thinking, philosophy, and the human sciences. And those items need interpretation and historical mediation. Traditional religions—at least during their modern phases of development—were not hostile toward those critical activities while fundamentalist religions are. Excellence is a similar unmediated, absolute truth. It can be taken away like a hamburger. Fast food is convenient in times of globalization, which is why we have fast food religions, fast food education, and fast food art (kitsch).

To be credible, both fundamentalism and neoliberal education support their ideologies with theories derived from the natural sciences. "An Islamist will speak more easily about the concordances between the Quran and nuclear physics than about those between the Quran and structuralism. Exact sciences, not the human sciences, fascinate the Islamist," writes Roy in *The Failure of Political Islam* (1994: 73). Both religion and education strive to create a unity of life and knowledge. The question is: why do they count on the natural sciences to advance their project? The natural sciences have always had major difficulties creating a unity of life and knowledge. Wherever the natural sciences appear, we observe not a unity but rather a split of knowledge and life. The human sciences have been much more successful in producing this unity. Fundamentalism and neoliberalism *cannot* use the human sciences because fundamentalists have canceled the notion of culture. Therefore they use abstract sciences. Even worse, they use them in a pseudo-scientific fashion.

Another reason why deculturation (Roy) and dereferentialization (Readings) is the preferred approach in fundamentalism and neoliberal/progressive education is that in a decultured world, people can be more easily controlled. The combination of corporatization with the strict application of "scientific" methods creates the "expert culture" of techno-specialists or questionable imams within which increasingly formal methods are absolutized. The absolutization will always be justified in terms of abstract truths. "Objective" measuring methods are linked to the spread of the corporate university because in the capitalist economy, the profitable is most often paired with the instrumental and the technical. Approaches to teaching and administration must be based on "scientific" methods. Our colleagues teaching the humanities often believe that all this is working toward a system of thought control. This is no paranoia if you think of the parallels with fundamentalism. Neoliberalism creates a new reality that everybody is supposed to believe in; those who do not believe are infidels. The problem is that here the "scientific" form has become the reality and that the real world has disappeared behind the form. Reality begins to evaporate through the process of formalization.

Enlightened excellence

Bill Readings has shown that the idea of deculturation was initiated in the United States. In an American context, the idea of culture had to change, which became most necessary in the realm of education. In a democratic context, the relationship between knowledge and tradition differs as tradition is not supposed to influence knowledge or the way of acquiring knowledge. Already Tocqueville saw that "in a democracy tradition is nothing more than information.

With the 'information explosion,' tradition has become superfluous" (quoted in Bloom: 58). In reality, the project started not in America, but the idea of the universalization of human values is present in Western culture since the Renaissance, though America, which began to be settled at that time, played an indirect role already then. Subsequent Enlightenment thinkers faced immense problems when attempting to reconcile the intellectual acquisitions of the new reasonable way of thinking with tradition. Immanuel Kant solved the dilemma most elegantly when formulating an explicit "critique" of reason, explaining that reason cannot be automatically associated with truth. Kant designs particular devices through which abstract reason can function within a concrete "cultural" environment by constantly supervising itself. Reason is limited, but if we know how to handle this limitation properly we will never face a crisis of reason.

In the nineteenth century, the program of deculturation was implemented in a more consistent fashion. The advance of science, together with industrialism and free trade, created what Matthew Arnold would call "industrialism culture" (Arnold: 78). The advent of new middle classes spelled the end of the traditional intelligentsia composed of "generalists," such as philosophers and poets, and replaced them with "experts" who will rely more and more heavily on methods, hard science, and technology. The subsequent development was dramatic. Culture saw science as its enemy and deemed it more and more necessary to limit any scientific invasion into its territory. Also, skepticism toward positivistic and scientistic thinking received an equally enormous push during and after the First World War in Europe when the belief in "progress" was profoundly shattered.

After the Second World War, the "culture camp" saw itself as eternally resistant. Jacques Ellul regrets in his writings from the 1960s that "technique has taken over the whole of civilization. Death, procreation, birth—all must submit to technical efficiency and systematization" (Ellul 1964: xxv). For Ellul, technique in the sense of a "totality of methods" for achieving efficiency in all fields of human activity is a "coupling of rationalistic thinking . . . and a specific cultural value of efficiency" (128). Science was no longer searching for enlightenment that would be able to free humans from ancient constraints but had become a technique working—blindly and presumably value-free—in the service of a restrictive system whose only recognized value was efficiency. An industrialist society treats specialization, quantification, and formalization as an end in itself and reduces culture to a skeleton. Lionel Trilling detects this tendency already in the 1940s and links it to "liberalization": "More and more, as the universities liberalize themselves, and turn their beneficent imperialistic gaze upon what is called Life Itself, the feeling grows among our educated classes that little can be experienced unless it is validated by some established intellectual discipline, with the result that experience loses much of its personal immediacy and becomes part of an accredited societal activity" (Trilling: 10).

Several thinkers describe the confrontation of science with culture in terms of a crisis. Edmund Husserl, in *The Crisis of the European Sciences* (1934–37), explains that the scientific objectivity characteristic of natural sciences (which is a result of the increasing mathematization of nature) is bound to neglect the subjective, historical, and dynamic part of human life from which science once emerged. Culture subsists, but it is affected by a scientific discourse unable to sustain an idea of culture in the Arnoldian sense as "a fuller harmonious development of our humanity" or as the "spontaneity of consciousness." In the 1970s, Jürgen Habermas defines the problem once again by speaking of the elimination of the distinction between the practical and the technical: "The reified models of the sciences migrate into the socio-cultural life-world and gain objective power over the latter's understanding" (Habermas 1971: 113). Habermas claims that the "technocratic consciousness reflects not the sundering of an ethical situation, but the repression of ethics as such as a category of life" (1970: 113). The result is a curious, purely technical concept of excellence that will trace its roots to the Enlightenment, but which has lost the critical input that Kant attempted to enclose to modern reason.

Corporate excellence versus Greek excellence

In philosophical terms, neoliberal excellence is a peculiar phenomenon. The ancient Greeks called excellence *arête*. To some extent the situation described above reflects the difference between two kinds of ethics: virtue ethics attempting to establish concrete and culturally rooted ideas about good and bad, and deontology, which sees the moral world in terms of general rules about right and wrong. Virtue ethics deals with values. Those values can be subjective (like truth, honesty or generosity) or objective (like health or life). However, values are not supposed to be metaphysical entities that are good "as such." It is thus tempting to define the culture of excellence in opposition to virtue ethics as a deontological project establishing the "imperative of excellence" in the same way in which Kant has established the categorical imperative. However, this is wrong for the simple reason that normally *arête* is translated as both virtue and excellence. In other words, in philosophy, there can be no excellence (*arête*) without virtue because excellence *is* virtue.

In ethical terms, "corporate excellence" is a new phenomenon. Virtue ethics, which goes back to Plato and Aristotle, examines the good together with a whole palette of values, while deontology (from *deon*, duty) spells out rules that are right. Virtue ethics is part of the family of teleological ethics (to which deontology is most generally opposed) and defines its values in view of an end or purpose (*telos*) to be achieved. What is good (as opposed to what is right) has to do with benefits. Also, utilitarianism belongs to teleological ethics. However, while utilitarianism wants the greatest amount of happiness for the largest number of people (which it finds "useful"), the other subgroup of teleological ethics, virtue ethics, defines the end in terms of the good or the desirable, which it calls virtue (*arête*). Therefore, the Aristotelian *arête* can be translated not only as virtue but also as excellence or effectiveness. Since virtue ethics is very much dependent on eudaemonist theories about how to achieve individual happiness, the cultivation of moral excellence (virtue) has often been seen as an end to achieve happiness and to achieve this in the most effective way.

The corporate world cannot have borrowed the term "excellence" from the tradition of virtue ethics. Classical moral virtues used to be spelled out in terms of concrete qualities such as courage, temperance, justice, and wisdom (which are rational) or "theological" ones such as faith, hope, and love. Never has excellence been seen as an end in itself; it was always something that is needed in order to obtain concrete virtues.

There is another important difference between corporate excellence and Greek excellence. Though virtue ethics is normative, it never speaks of values as absolutes, but merely indicates what it believes to be desirable *in certain situations*. Plato and Aristotle dealt with values factually, which means that for them a value could never become a rule. In other words, classical virtue ethics integrates cultural components in its evaluation processes, which has an important impact on the definition of values. Values are fluent as they depend on social changes and cannot be summarized in the form of either static rules or principles or of some metaphysical "beyond" dependent on internal states alone. This does not mean that virtue ethics is beyond the reach of all Enlightenment ideals of universality and that it contents itself with debating moral issues in a purely relativistic fashion. Virtue ethics recognizes that values refer to a variety of possibilities of what can and should be done and discusses those possibilities on a reasonable basis. However, it refuses to see the moral world as detached from situated cultural content.

In the corporate world, this cultural content is not discussed: being "efficient" is the only right thing to do. The "rule of efficiency" is implemented by means of evaluation and other technical exercises. In the corporate world, excellence is unrelated to cultural values while for Aristotle, concrete virtues like generosity or honesty were supposed to become character traits. Can corporate excellence become a character trait? Obviously not, it is only possible to be "excellently honest" or "excellently generous."

In antiquity, rules were universal and objective but, very importantly, ethical actions were not viewed through a metaphysical gap between nature and humans. There was no gap between individual striving and universal forces, and consequently there was no striving to overcome those universal forces either. A possible interpretation of (post)modern excellence culture is to see it as a renewed attempt to retrieve the Greek spirit. Excellence culture wants to bring back rules but not in deontological terms as general rules contradicting individual desires. Excellence culture dreams of an ideal world in which the existence of individuals can be spelled out in abstract, generally valid terms. In the perfect culture of excellence there is no gap between individual striving and universal forces. The only possible source for corporate excellence is the Enlightenment. Isiah Berlin, who found that all understanding is necessarily historical and cultural, criticized the "Aufklärer—Gottsched, Lessing and Moses Mendelssohn—[who] not only lack all historical perspective, [but] they tend to grade, to give marks for moral excellence" (Berlin: 263).

Excellence and utilitarianism

Both business and science are given to utilitarianism. Utilitarianism is another branch of teleological ethics and people working in education in the humanities are usually skeptical toward this tendency (exceptions might be made for Bentham and Mill). It is a common wisdom that intellectuals do not like to be inserted into a utilitarian system. The idea of being free from practical considerations is deeply rooted in the tradition of the humanities. Kant distinguished the "class of literati" from disciplines like medicine and jurisprudence because the former may use "their own judgment" (literally, "their own wisdom") when deciding what they want to teach. When Kant speaks of the "free field of self-judgment and philosophy" ("das freie Feld der eigenen Beurtheilung und Philosophie," Kant: 219), he means the entire body of disciplines today called humanities. Looking closer, however, the corporate university is not utilitarian. Utilitarianism considers usefulness as the main *arête*. The frantic striving for excellence is not useful at all, not even when profit is seen as the end of all means. Strictly speaking, the ethics of the corporate university has no place in any tradition. In the best case, it could be characterized as a perverted form of deontology that has established a metaphysical concept of excellence as an absolute rule, detached from local situations and defined in terms of a global standard.

It is perverted for another reason. For Kant, to be free from utilitarian considerations signified academic freedom. This ideal has been continued into the twentieth century. Very often political powers would put the academic freedom of the humanities under pressure, most recently during fascist and communist regimes where many intellectuals perished as they stuck to their ideas. However, the ethical view that intellectual freedom *is* important and should not be strangled by anything would always be maintained and not simply abandoned as a useless fad. After the Second World War, things changed. First, the Cold War shifted the academic focus to the pure sciences, which were merely utilitarian. The humanities were marginalized because corporations required a further shift of focus to the applied sciences. Marginalization did not happen, as it did under totalitarian regimes, because intellectuals formulated opinions unacceptable to the regimes, but simply because they were declared useless. This is not utilitarian. The crystallization of "skills" at the expense of useless "thinking" denotes a shift from utilitarianism to an ethics of excellence.

A part of the humanities curriculum will be reused, like what one does when retrieving car parts from a junkyard. The notion of "thinking skills" symbolizes the predominance of cultureless excellence in philosophy. Philosophy, which is no longer seen as a cultural activity, will be recognized as a provider of skills. And since philosophy thinks, these skills will be named "thinking skills." Those skills need to be measured and quantified to be useful. Thinking skills classes or critical thinking classes are typical examples of how thinking is taught in a decultured fashion in corporate contexts. What matters is not a well-rounded "Bildung" in Wilhelm von Humboldt's sense but "training" provided by specialized "programs."

What is the difference between *education* and *training*? While education generally addresses values and beliefs necessary to make a democratic society function, training is provided in view of professional occupations requiring skills. Some say that this merely corresponds to the students' wishes and that the decline of humanist education is unavoidable. James Traub, former president of the (for-profit) University of Phoenix, writes that "the people who are our students don't want an education. They want what the education provides for them—better jobs, moving up in their careers" (in Donoghue: 136). What will the others do? Those who are still looking for values and beliefs and not merely skills can turn to religion or novels (which now nobody will explain to them in a critical fashion). Or they can simply stop looking and indulge in a consumer society for which values and beliefs have little importance.

Liberal culture developed further in the direction of excellence by generalizing working styles that once used to be limited to business. Both business and science tend to absolutize the methods they are working with. People who are trained for skills and nothing else will necessarily emphasize the formal character of methods. This is why the introduction of "objective" measuring methods is intrinsically linked to the spread of the corporate university. In liberal cultures, the profitable is most often paired with the instrumental and the technical. To advertise approaches to teaching and administration as based on "scientific" methods will have to become the norm. The market methods on which the corporate university relies are more successfully implemented when all aspects of academic life are made dependent on some sort of "hard science" and technology.

Numerous writings criticize the corporate university because it submits the humanities to the laws of the market, which might lead to its extinction. A globalized market lets Western universities and businesses compete with those of China and India. The possibility of competition depends on the conversion of the entire structure of institutions of higher learning to a business model. Humanities departments are targeted most by budget cuts and closures because of their low utility value. Opponents of this tendency criticize that programs have to generate revenue through tuition, external grants, or alumni donations. Donoghue's *The Last Professors* is the most famous example of this critique. However, fewer writings criticize the technization and dubious "scientization" through which the corporatization is implemented. Are the quality measuring methods that attempt to achieve this really scientific? Is it more "scientifically" sustainable to teach usable "skills" instead of educating cultured individuals? And is it more efficient in the long term? Though the general public seems to be thrilled by rankings summarizing the global standing of universities, it is highly questionable *in scientific terms* whether heterogeneous performances can be compressed into a few numbers.

There are reasons why technization and "scientization" have been criticized to a much lesser extent than commercialization. While it is relatively clear why humanities departments are against corporatization, it is less clear why they should speak up against science. Traditionally, the humanities (and philosophy in particular) are skeptical of the claim that science, with its quantification and specialization, is able to organize all aspects of human life. Philosophers often perceive such views as attempts to uncritically recycle an eighteenth-century spirit of reasonableness that elevated empirical and quantitative knowledge, in a naive fashion, over all other forms of understanding. It is also at that time that, through a confrontation of a sweeping "scientific" spirit with counter-Enlightenment forces, the humanities and liberal arts began formulating their own ways of doing things "scientifically." The separation between two camps of scientists ended up as the definite polarization of the Western academic world into two groups that C. P. Snow would later describe in his *The Two Cultures* (1959). The human sciences became a haven for those who thought that the natural sciences are unable to answer important existential questions just *because* they are so much dependent on formalized methods. Still recently, the dean emeritus of the Humanist Institute of the University of Minnesota, Robert Tapp, wrote that "a reliance on the sciences strengthens certain values such as truth telling and integrity, but leaves many questions undeveloped" (Tapp: 152). In a world where more and more thinking activities are confined to machines and where the natural consequence seems to be that, in the future, humans will increasingly be required to think like machines, many humanities teachers see themselves as a bulwark against this tendency. First, because they believe that the technical way of thinking will never be able to grasp the reality of social and cultural life in all its complexity; second, because they think that technical thinking leads to uniformity, especially when excellence is the only "value" permitted. Having most commonly based their identities on the idea of the "intellectual" as a generalist, the humanities experience the confrontation with "experts" deriving their authority from some sort of "hard science" as a clash of cultures. In the present corporate university, the separation can be felt as colonization.

Technical thinking leads to uniformity. Uniformization has always been an intrinsic component of corporatization. Historically speaking, the establishment of norms, limits, hierarchies, and classes has been, since the beginning of capitalism, one of the latter's main concerns. The purpose of any training is to enhance these parameters. One reason why these parameters are implemented in the first place is that a "standardized" society can more easily be supervised. Formalization, quantification, and visibilization provide power to those who formalize, quantify, and make transparent. "Audit culture" must be understood in this context. It represents the new entrepreneurial environment determined by calculative practices such as performance indicators supposed to improve productivity. In the end, it leads to a new "voluntary servitude." *Voluntary Servitude* is the title of Philippe Vion-Dury's book (2016) on algorithm culture. Whenever the university claims to install uniformity, it will receive substantial help from corporate capitalism. Formalized information (especially statistics) is easier to manipulate, which has become particularly obvious in the various financial crises that we have recently witnessed. Rating agencies (the champions of formal reason) should have predicted and prevented those crises but didn't.

By manipulating a reality that has been reduced to numbers beforehand, "science" creates a new, alternative reality. And who would be able to contest this reality composed of infinite sequences of specific details? Certainly not you because you are not an expert! The French psychoanalyst Roland Gori writes that "since the beginning, by emphasizing in its ethics the formal type of rationality and by implementing it through its vice squads, the spirit of capitalism favored, at the cost of all other moral values, the ideals of appearance" (Gori: 217). In other words, the "scientific" form becomes the reality and the real world disappears behind the form. The world of corporate capitalism has increasingly adopted this shape. Can the humanities bring back the real world?

Note

1   The idea of "embedded governance" in which governance is automatized through algorithms is part of this utopia. See the White Book of the Institute for the Future and the chapter "Embedded Governance: Downloading Laws into Objects and the Environment" (Palo Alto 2009).

2

Kitsch: An "Alternative Aesthetic Truth"

A scary form of modern neutrality imposes on all spheres of life what Gillo Dorfles called fifty years ago "right-thinking, good education and the sort of places which have already acquired picture postcard status" (Dorfles: 263). Dorfles speaks about aesthetics and his critique is directed at kitsch. Though Dorfles does not address the neoliberal culture of excellence, he sees "a world made to perfection" thriving within the kitsch world of capitalism justified by "right-thinking." For Dorfles, this is a world imbued with the "superfluity of communication" in which form supplants content and in which "everything has a purely stylistic character." The "self-contradictory technical and formal terms of reference are taken out of context and reoriented towards consumer use pure and simple." In this arguably most fundamental study on kitsch, Dorfles predicts a neoliberal world determined by neutrality, supervision, and deculturation.

Kitsch not only appears in the form of material objects but also penetrates our lives through cellphones, in Twitter updates, in headlines from CNN, or through flash ads displayed on ubiquitous screens constantly vying for our attention. Liberal capitalism does not only concentrate on surfaces and images but also produces an aesthetics of the "too much" in all domains of life. It is thus no surprise that we end up with a world determined by what hundred years ago art historians decided to call kitsch. But what is kitsch more precisely? For aestheticians, kitsch is a product depending on exaggerated sentimentality, banality, superficiality, and triteness. Kitsch has also been defined as "artistic deficiency" (Dorfles 1975: 10), as an overly formulaic aesthetic expression (Greenberg: 10), or as an aesthetic phenomenon contradicting the "law of adequacy" (Calinescu: 257). Baudrillard believes that kitsch is "the equivalent of cliché in discourse" (1970: 165). While there is apparently no classical definition of kitsch, a common understanding sees kitsch as (1) a tasteless copy of an existing style, or as (2) the systematic display of bad taste or artistic deficiency. However, if we want to grasp kitsch not just as a certain type of aesthetics used in art and design but also—in more ethical terms—as a general cultural structure underlying behaviors, economies, and politics, the concept of kitsch needs to be expanded. In this book, I liken kitsch to Harry Frankfurt's philosophically established concept of bullshit. The parallel is plausible. As an "alternative aesthetic truth" kitsch overlaps in ethics with what Frankfurt calls bullshit. Bullshit is not a non-truth (a lie) but a new truth aspiring to coexist with other truths. Both bullshit and kitsch are alternative truths.

Since alternative truths are best produced in situations of relativism, the study of Frankfurt's "bullshit" is related to this book's deculturation theme. Both kitsch and bullshit thrive in situations of deculturation. Both are examples of decultured forms of truths, which is why they can so often be found in contexts of fundamentalism and neoliberalism. Religion is not bullshit as long as it remains embedded in a concrete culture, but it is likely to become kitsch and bullshit when it undergoes processes of deculturation.

Capitalism developed the activity of marketing into a science that can be studied at the university. The marketing specialist is what Lasch called the "master propagandist" who "knows that partial truths serve as more effective instruments of deception than lies" (Lasch: 75). The overlap of Lasch's concept of "partial truth" with Frankfurt's "bullshit" is obvious and will be discussed below. Neoliberalism produces bullshit in the form of "advanced marketing," that is, in the form of value-neutral algorithms, standardization, quantified data, and excellence. What Lasch describes as neoliberal marketing devices is nothing other than Frankfurt's bullshit: "Statements claiming a product's superiority to unspecified competitors, statements implying that a given characteristic belongs uniquely to the product in question when in fact it belongs to its rivals as well all serve to blur the distinction between truth and falsehood in a fog of plausibility" (75). The creation of alternative realities is the next step as those methods give rise "to a pervasive air of unreality, which ultimately befuddles the decision makers themselves. The contagion of unintelligibility spreads through all levels of government. . . . They deprive themselves of intelligible standards by which to define the goals of specific policies or to evaluate success or failure" (78).

My analysis of kitsch as an aesthetic form of bullshit will reveal the pernicious scheme that relatively new social phenomena like fundamentalism and (neo) liberalism have established. Liberalism follows a two-step logic bringing about deculturation through liberalization. First, truth is declared relative because in a liberal society, everybody has the right to have his/her own opinion and his/ her own taste. Next, once relativism has been established as a basis of ethics and aesthetics, alternative truths like that of excellence will be introduced and declared absolute by basing cultural practices on pseudo-scientific approaches. The second step is relatively easy. When truth is no longer rooted in cultural environments, that is, when it has lost its cultural basis, no concrete cultural values can contradict the establishment of pseudo-truths such as the "value" of excellence. Of course, the scheme is paradoxical because, normally, culture represents a relativistic element and scientific truth is considered most value neutral when it is *disconnected* from culture. Normally, the *reduction* of cultural influences leads to truths that are more scientific. Neoliberal-fundamentalist epistemologies function vice versa. Culture is negated and replaced with "absolute" forms of knowledge provided by pseudo-science and religion.

The comparison of bullshit and kitsch elucidates the constellation of some crucial elements. Distorting reality is obviously a matter of ethics, and in that sense, bullshitting *should* be judged in terms of ethics. However, the bullshitter can get away with her distortion because the style with which she commits the distortion aestheticizes the ethical default. What matters in bullshit is the stylistic arrangement, and this turns bullshit into a subject for aesthetics. The easiness, nonchalance, innocence, and—sometimes—naivete with which the bullshitter passes over reality can turn the bullshitter into an artist acting within a playful and merely aesthetically established reality: "Claims are made, judgments cast, arguments presented, all with the unbearable lightness of those free of any responsibility or commitment," writes De Waal (De Waal: 109).

On Bullshit

Harry Frankfurt anticipated a lot of the current neoliberal excellence talk when developing his philosophical analysis of bullshit. His twenty-two-page-long essay "On Bullshit" was published in 1986 in an academic journal and republished by Princeton University Press as a stand-alone book in 2005. The small volume was extremely successful and has sparked many discussions by both academics and public intellectuals. Bullshit as conceived by Frankfurt is a predominantly ethical phenomenon. However, Frankfurt also insists on the aesthetic capacities of the proverbial "bullshit artist" because bullshitting is "not a craft but art" (Frankfurt: 52). The reason is that alternative truths are more easily accepted in aesthetics than in ethics or politics. Furthermore, shifting questions about truth toward aesthetics creates a situation of relativism. "It's just a matter of taste" is a classic device of establishing relativist situations. The aesthetization of truth facilitates the creation of alternative truths.

Frankfurt defines bullshit as the deceptive misrepresentation of reality that remains different from lying because, contrary to the liar, the "bullshitter" does not try to deceive (Frankfurt: 6–7). What matters is not the facts' truth value but the bullshitter's "state of mind." The bullshitter is bluffing but not lying and bullshit is not false but merely fake and phony (47). This means that the bullshitter attempts to establish a new reality, which is an *alternative* reality "not inferior to the real thing" (47). Very importantly, people are typically not *forced* to believe in the misrepresented reality but the "real" reality is often not entirely dissimulated. Bullshit is a prime example of an alternative truth and several authors have defined kitsch correspondingly. Umberto Eco has called kitsch an "artistic lie" (1989: 183) and for Matei Calinescu kitsch is an "aesthetic form of lying" (Calinescu: 229). What both mean is not an aesthetic lie but rather aesthetic bullshit.

Does kitsch exist? Some methodological clarifications

My aim in this chapter is to establish both kitsch and bullshit as ethico-aesthetic qualities able to manipulate truth and reality in environments of deculturation. In globalized, postindustrial societies, kitsch and bullshit have become not only more current but also more diverse and more sophisticated. Since the starting point of this analysis is kitsch, some clarifications concerning the validity of this concept need to be provided beforehand. Can anything be called kitsch at all without running into methodological problems? Does kitsch exist or is it merely a matter of taste and of subjective perceptions? Ethical problems need to be clarified, too. In a neoliberal world of political correctness, the respect of individual tastes is a priority. Kitsch is only what I see as kitsch but what another person might see as the most beautiful art. The assumption that kitsch exists (saying that something *is* kitsch) is incompatible with liberal relativism holding that all (aesthetic) values are alike and need to be respected.

Kitsch and liberalism

The present chapter demonstrates that all of the above positions are wrong. Moreover, the relativism of "kitsch liberalism," which forbids value judgments on the basis of aesthetic relativism declaring that everything is just a matter of opinion, creates an ideal breeding ground for alternative truths. Kitsch liberalism is submitted to a paradox. Holliday and Potts proclaim right at the beginning of their book on kitsch that "we are drowning in kitsch" but quote almost simultaneously Eva London, an artist who published a photo essay on garden gnomes claiming that "it seems pointless, if not impossible to maintain the concept of kitsch" (21). The conclusion seems to be: the more we insist that kitsch does not exist, the more we are drowning in it. Relativism does not make kitsch melt into air but produces new solid kitsch ad infinitum. The relativist annihilation of kitsch (by declaring kitsch inexistent) produces tons of kitsch.

As mentioned above, the relationships between liberalism and kitsch are complex and contradictory. Liberalism is involved not only in economic and political paradoxes but also in aesthetic ones. In principle, the liberal is a kitsch relativist because she defends the liberty of (aesthetic) expression. However, as the successor of the Enlightenment tradition, liberalism has inherited a severe anti-kitsch stance, too. Enlightenment fought against the baroque kitsch that was current before the French Revolution, and liberalism never entirely abandoned this anti-kitsch spirit. Today, as will be shown in the paragraphs that follow, progressive liberalism criticizes the cynical capitalist production of kitsch; even in neoliberalism, an anti-kitsch stance survives in the form of puritanism and the refusal of sentiment (so heavily criticized by Robert Solomon), both of which have become cornerstones of neoliberal management culture implementing "scientific neutrality" in human relations, business, and working life. The problem is that this anti-kitsch produces its own kitsch. Decades ago, Dorfles mentioned varieties of kitsch-like anti-kitsch when describing beatniks who declared traditional family life to be kitsch. Dorfles sees kitsch-like anti-kitsch in the "the kitsch of hippies and long-haired youths, [and in] the kitsch of addicts and beatniks" (Dorfles: 130). Despite their opposition to *certain* forms of kitsch, few cultures produced more kitsch than the hippy culture of the 1960s. Similarly, when today's progressive liberalism and neoliberalism fight against kitsch in the name of value neutrality they produce another sort of kitsch: the kitsch of formulaic technicality or administrative kitsch. Anti-kitsch becomes kitsch when life is formalized via managerial methods in situations where empathy and trust would be more adequate. Kitsch happens when neoliberal value neutrality is implemented for its own sake. This is not only the method of conservative neoliberals. There is an equal amount of kitsch in the sentimental defense of the weak that is regularly enacted by progressive liberals. Those strategies might have begun a long time ago as anti-kitsch projects but must today be classified as kitsch because of their formulaic character, their exaggeration, and their inappropriateness. The development has led to an absurd constellation: while for Enlightenment thinkers, kitsch was bourgeois, and for Kundera, Broch, and Giesz kitsch was even totalitarian, today, in industrialized countries, kitsch can be liberal.

All of this should convince us at least of one thing: that kitsch exists. Of course, it does not exist as an empirically established and measurable entity but as a concept used in language. *In language* it continues being used by people who agree on certain characteristics through which kitsch can be defined. Kitsch exists as an extensional and intensional term referring to a distinct selection of objects having certain qualities. The claim that such a common understanding occurs within some social groups does not need to be substantiated any further, because the fact that the word "kitsch" *can* be used in language within certain groups proves that such a common understanding exists. The profile of these groups is mainly determined by local cultures, class, and education. "Common understanding" is not a misnomer because kitsch is not merely an art-theoretical term but is used by a large number of people also in everyday language. It is even possible to be familiar with the phenomenon of kitsch without knowing the term—for example, when one calls a set of phenomena "cheesy" or "tacky," one is drawing on the idea of kitsch.

I want to be as specific as possible and analyze how different populations deal with the phenomenon of kitsch. Let's assume the existence of distinct groups (A) and (B). If we identify as group (A) the people who adhere to a "common understanding" of kitsch along the lines pointed out above, and who are therefore critical of kitsch, we can identify as group (B) those who do *not* believe in this definition of kitsch. However, we will have to divide this latter group into three subgroups:

(B1) are consumers of kitsch who simply do not know what kitsch is, because if they knew what it was, they would probably not consume it (I say "probably" and do not make a judgment).

(B2) are people who understand perfectly well what kitsch is, but believe that the entire concept of kitsch is irrelevant; they recognize it as a merely subjective construction (produced by an elite) that does not correspond to any "reality" and should therefore be abandoned.

(B3) are people who know what kitsch is, accept its existence, but like it nevertheless. Strictly speaking, they do not like kitsch *as kitsch*. They have an ironical attitude toward it; they do not merely consume it but use it and play with it (most typically in contexts that are alien to kitsch).

The characteristic of (B1) is that they tend to have less education than the other groups. They do not grasp the concept of kitsch and group (A) will probably reproach them for accepting kitsch as "the real thing." (B2) and (B3) most likely are as educated as (A) but differ in their attitudes toward kitsch for reasons of taste as well as for ethical or political reasons. (B3) share certain points with (B2) but are not as relativistic as (B2).

I am spelling all this out in detail because I want to show that something similar applies to bullshit. Bullshit is also not an empirical fact; it is rather a concept used within common language contexts by people who are able to agree on certain characteristics of bullshit. Of particular interest is the (B3) position, because it is based on the assumption that both kitsch and bullshit are not entirely immoral. More precisely, this position holds that judgments of bullshit can be linked to the sort of playful relativism proper to judgments in the realm of aesthetics.

Unfortunately, the methodological complications do not stop here. All that has been said above about (A), (B1), (B2), and (B3) applies not only to the *perceiver* of kitsch but also to the *producer* of kitsch. Usually, in the aesthetics of kitsch, we are as interested in the kitsch consumer as we are in the kitsch producer, while in bullshit we are usually more interested in the act of bullshitting and less in how it is perceived.

If the kitsch *producer* belongs to (A), we might find her cynical because she is selling valueless items for a lot of money. This case corresponds most clearly to that of bullshitting. About a (B1) producer who is producing kitsch or bullshit without being aware of it, we would probably not have much to say except that she is naive. A kitsch producer belonging to group (B2) can be accused of relativism. This relativism can become unbearable if the expression of kitsch becomes "too much."

It becomes clear that a (B2) position is difficult to maintain in the realm of bullshit production and even of bullshit consumption, while it is relatively common in the realm of kitsch. This point makes (B2) very different from (B3). The (B3) producer might be an artist playing with kitsch motives or a politician playing with rhetorical devices bordering on bullshit. The (B3) producer will probably not be submitted to the same ethical criteria as an (A) producer.

A further problem arises because the links leading from producer to perceiver might not retain the initial intention. Something might be emitted by a (B3) producer *as bullshit* but be taken for granted by a (B1) audience, which presents the possibility of the bullshit being interpreted as a lie. But we don't *have* to interpret it as a lie but can also simply say that it is the receiver's fault "to believe such bullshit." In the realm of kitsch such cases are very common: we will not speak of fraud when a consumer buys a piece of kitsch because she has been talked into believing that it is real art. Of course, everything depends on the amount of rhetoric and "free choice" that the consumer has had. If she had been shown some bogus documentation, then we might speak of fraud.

In this chapter, I will approach kitsch and bullshit mostly from the point of view of "common understanding" (which should not be confused with "common sense"). Occasionally I will refer to the perspective of (B2). Of particular interest are possible shifts from (A) to (B3) that might more generally be admitted for kitsch, while the admittance of such shifts for bullshit is rather new. Kitsch exists because certain aesthetic communities share certain ideas and concepts. The "community argument," which is diametrically opposed to the liberal universalism that will be discussed in Chapter 4, does not propagate but oppose relativism. When talking about the existence of aesthetic communities we are not idolizing subjectivity declaring that all communal opinions are equally valid. Nor do we opt for universalism saying that all individual opinions need to be discarded. Liberalism, as the inheritor of Enlightenment, strives to be objective and universal, and refuses purely subjective truths as nonscientific. However, because liberalism cannot apply unequivocally universal judgments in the realm of taste (why should everybody have the same taste?), it reverts to relativism proclaiming that all tastes are equally valuable. Consequently, it becomes impossible to talk about kitsch because by doing so one would necessarily dismiss the taste of a certain community as "bad." For liberals, kitsch does not exist, but kitsch is "just another kind of taste." This taste might be different, but it should not be called bad. I call this point of view the kitsch-liberal-syndrome, and in aesthetics it is represented by authors like Robert Solomon and Celeste Olalquiaga.[1]

Kitsch and bullshit

Bullshit is not a lie and kitsch is not forgery. Both kitsch and bullshit do not hide the truth but, according to Calinescu, kitsch "flies away from reality" (Calinescu: 244). The common understanding of the terms holds that bullshit and kitsch exaggerate and that they are often simultaneously too superficial and too explicit, but that they do not lie. This is true even for propaganda kitsch, which is the form of kitsch/bullshit that comes closest to fraud and which will be discussed below.

An item can be identified as kitsch or bullshit only on the condition that people have the option *not* to believe in its truth or authenticity. Military recruitment advertisements *can* be understood as bullshit, but at the moment they posit a false world for the basis of real-life decisions they become fraud. Once again, the abovementioned methodological problem remains important: *for whom* does it constitute fraud? Only for somebody who does not see through the plot. The person who *knows* that it is fraud might classify the same ad as bullshit or its visual and verbal rhetoric as kitsch.

While the liar covers the truth under a non-truth that he wants to be as substantial and dense as possible, bullshit and kitsch make nonsubstantial claims to create new, less-substantial realities that probably cannot perfectly conceal the more substantial true reality. The *Mona Lisa* printed on the pillowcase is kitsch, as is any tasteless copy of an existing painting, but it is not a falsified *Mona Lisa* that a forger is trying to sell for millions. It is a copy of a famous artwork that acknowledges being a copy and demands to be accepted as such. Another example comes from Dorfles's introduction to his *Kitsch: The World of Bad Taste*, where he writes that kitsch occurs when Chopin's tunes "have been dragged down to the level of sentimental songs." Still, the existence of the real Chopin is not contested.

The above two examples concern only those cases where kitsch imitates existing works of art and the fake/reality dichotomy is easy to establish. However, kitsch most often produces tacky and overdone aesthetic expressions without imitating anything concrete. Is it possible to speak here of falsification? Dorfles holds that kitsch "is essentially the falsification of sentiments and the substitution of spurious sentiments for real ones" (Dorfles: 221). But how can one "falsify" sentiments? Did Hume not, in his thesis on the standard of taste, explain that "the sentiment is always true"? (Hume: 6–7). The sentiment sparked by kitsch is *different* from the sentiment sparked by art, but it is no less true. Dorfles distinguishes the "real feeling" produced by art from the "sentimentality" produced by kitsch and suggests that the latter is a falsification of the former. It seems to me that sentimentality is here produced in the form of a *less-substantial feeling*; however, this is not a false feeling. Kitsch does not consistently transgress the limits that distinguish the authentic from the false, but it alters them—just as the bullshitter's free interpretation of reality follows not the rules of a perfect crime but rather those of creative manipulation.

My view is supported by Robert Solomon who criticized Karsten Harries's idea that kitsch seeks to give the sensations of feelings even when the object that the feelings are directed to does not exist. Are those feelings therefore false feelings? Solomon writes:

> But what is it for an emotion to be false? . . . The fact that an emotion is vicarious (in some sense "secondhand") does not mean that it is not a real emotion or that it is not an emotion of the morally appropriate type. . . . Self-indulgence in an emotion may make it "false" in the sense that one exaggerates either its importance or its effects, but it is not the emotion itself that is false. (Solomon: 14)

It becomes necessary to distinguish between fake and false. Roger Scruton believes that kitsch is faking emotions. The easy and simplistic emotion is fake in the sense that it is "too real to be true"—for example, in music: "The easy harmonic progressions and platitudinous tune take us there too easily, so that we know we have not arrived. The music is faking an emotion, by means that could never express it. Kitsch is pretense" (Scruton 1999). The emotion is still real (and not false), but it is not *the* emotion that should consistently follow from the music played. The composer wants to impose upon us more emotion or another emotion without having the capacity to compose music that "really" engenders those emotions in us. In certain cases, mainly concerning (B3) producers, the manipulation can be playful. But in no cases do kitsch and bullshit falsify the truth. The worst one can say is that they distort the truth through exaggeration, a willful lack of critical activity, or by simply not being serious. Apart from that, both bullshit and kitsch are "conservative" in the sense that they represent closed-minded entities and are rarely eager to absorb new insights (this concerns, of course, only the kitsch and bullshit produced and consumed by (A) and (B1) and is contrary to the way in which they are used by (B3)).

Has a (B3) position ever been outlined *for* bullshit? Maes and Schaubroek theorize bullshit in a way similar to how kitsch liberals theorize kitsch: it can, for example, be "a means to lay contact with others or keep the conversation going, it can be a source of warmth" (Maes and Schaubroek: 178). In the 1907, the Italian futurist Giuseppe Prezzolini developed a provocative theory of "persuasion," claiming that "the lie is for life what the rime is for poetry" (1991: 61). In a Nietzschean way, the lie is aristocratic whereas truth and sincerity are mediocre: "The masquerade, the *nihil mirari*, are aristocratic virtues and the Stoics belong to the family of nobles" (1903: 17). That's as far as it goes. There seems to be nothing like the acceptance of bullshit in the name of pluralism or even as a counterreaction to totalitarian worldviews. There is no real (B2) position for bullshit either.

Kitsch and standardization

According to Philip Crick, kitsch is compact and "final in its quality" (Crick: 50) and the same is true for bullshit. Partly this means that bullshit and kitsch do not falsify but *simplify* realities. This becomes particularly obvious in neoliberal culture and it definitely is an underlying principle of alternative truths. Very often alternative truths are simplified truths even when they have been stylized as complicated by misusing quantifying methods. Kitsch and bullshit prefer standardized, fetishized, and compressed claims and images to the more complex claims and images current in real art and in reality. Correspondingly, when watching a kitschy blockbuster or when hearing a politician utter obvious bullshit we often mumble, "Well, reality is more complicated than that." The simplification patterns work along the lines that Greenberg analyzed as the principal mechanics of kitsch when writing that kitsch limits its presentation to the effect and does not care about the cause. The parallel between kitsch and bullshit becomes particularly obvious as Frankfurt insists that the bullshitter *does not care* about truth (Frankfurt: 17–19). Similar to Greenberg, Tomáš Kulka writes that "for kitsch the 'what' is more important than the 'how'" (Kulka: 82). The kitsch "artist" might work a lot on the "how" but will subsequently present his kitsch as the one and only "what" that no critical thinking should ever dare to analyze. The establishment of alternative realities follows the same strategy. Both kitsch and bullshit tend to be offered as takeaway conclusions. While in real art we often attempt to participate in the underlying creative process and strive to inquire about the "why" (the premises) of some aesthetic choices, in kitsch nobody is supposed to ask "why"; we are simply urged to take the product for granted and enjoy.

In the most typical kitsch cases, the "secret" is a mere exaggeration or an awkward juxtaposition, neither of which requires deeper investigation but tends to overwhelm the consumer. A typical kitsch quality is that of being "hackneyed" and trite. In real art we tend to ask ourselves, "How did the artist do that?" Similarly, when reading a well-argued critical article clarifying claims that were not obvious in the beginning, we might feel the need to examine "how" the writer came to such conclusions. This rarely happens with bullshit, except when we want to prove that it is inaccurate. Reality is complex while alternative realities are simple. Greenberg establishes the difference between non-kitsch and kitsch in parallel: Picasso (non-kitsch) paints the *cause* while Repin (kitsch) paints merely the *effect* (Greenberg: 15).

Interactions between kitsch and bullshit

I mentioned above that bullshit, though being in the first place of ethical interest, has often been dealt with from an aesthetical point of view because it is so closely linked to techniques of embellishment and stylization. For kitsch, the reverse is true. Though kitsch is officially an aesthetic term, Solomon finds that "much of the literature attacking kitsch is political rather than aesthetic" (Solomon: 238). Of importance is the postwar revision of the distinction between mass culture and high art through which kitsch has "suddenly assumed an importance that had as much to do with politics as with aesthetics" (Boyers and Boyers: 197) (more on those postwar developments will follow in Chapter 3).

In the political context, kitsch tends to be discussed in ethical and not in aesthetic terms. Another force that turns kitsch into a matter of ethics is its apparent justification of overly hedonistic expressions. Whenever kitsch is judged harshly, the justification is likely to happen on ethical grounds, that is, kitsch will be diagnosed as a sort of bullshit. In politics, kitsch and bullshit are often twins if we think of propaganda art or of metaphors used in twentieth-century totalitarian discourses. The problem is that in these realms both kitsch and bullshit assume the kind of cynical power that is not part of their initial definitions. True, in most cases, the bullshitter knows what is true and simply says the contrary; however, that alone is not enough to make her a cynic. Propaganda kitsch and bullshit *can* be cynical, but then they are merely particular branches of kitsch/bullshit.

What are the differences between kitsch and bullshit? First, we do not encounter them under the same conditions. Much bullshit is fabricated by people who do not belong to (B1); the producers do not believe in what they say, and this is obvious to many consumers. The position of the kitsch producer is more complicated. She might belong to (B1), in which case condemnations can be expressed on the grounds of aesthetics but not of ethics. But even if she belongs to (A) and produces the most awful kitsch just to make money, she can still say that she likes it, that is, takes refuge in (B1). This creates the false impression that kitsch is morally more acceptable than bullshit; however, with regard to their essence both are the same. Both can be judged on ethical as well as aesthetic grounds.

As a result, apologetic discourses on bullshit will most likely refer to the "merely" aesthetic qualities of bullshit. In a way, they say that their bullshit is merely kitsch. "Unlike the liar, who deliberately obscures what he takes to be true, bullshitters may often be honest and sincere," writes Reisch (2006: 44). Bullshit can indeed easily be explained as a sort of kitsch and—most of the time—kitsch does not cheat because there is no *necessary* link between bad taste and dishonesty.

In a rarer case, kitsch is declared to be "merely" bullshit. Clancy Martin points to Nietzsche's concept of "art as a lie" and finds that what Nietzsche actually means is that artists are bullshitters (Martin: 419). What Nietzsche might have meant in the first place is that all art contains a grain of kitsch in order to please the public. What is worse, being a kitsch artist or a bullshit artist? My guess is that most artists would go for the latter.

Hermann Broch, in one of the most classical texts on kitsch ever written, insists on seeing kitsch in purely ethical terms because kitsch is not art, not even bad art: "The producer of kitsch does not produce 'bad' art. . . . It is quite impossible to assess him according to aesthetic criteria; rather he should be judged as an ethically base being, a malefactor who profoundly desires evil" (Broch: 76). More explicitly, Broch traces the essence of kitsch to "the confusion of the ethical category with the aesthetic category" (71). This last argument is strange in that it evokes the impression that aesthetics, once it is abandoned by ethics and left on its own, *can* only produce kitsch. However, can *only* the right ethics prevent aesthetics from producing kitsch? Are there not intrinsic *aesthetic* standards able to prevent art from becoming kitsch? We cannot discuss here the fundamental problem of whether aesthetics is subordinate to ethics or whether art has its own code of honor. But I believe that Broch's conclusion is hasty as he suggests that everything that is merely beautiful but not also *good* automatically turns into kitsch. This claim is not convincing with regard to art, though Broch seems to have given a good account of what at least (A) and (B3) believe to be the essence of bullshit.

Frankfurt asks why there is so much bullshit, and admits that the answer is difficult to determine. "Why is there so much kitsch?" has been answered by a whole string of commentators. Most answers work along the lines of Kulka's. Kulka points out that kitsch thrives best in a "civilization that is based on excess consumption" (Kulka: 13). The problem is that kitsch also thrives in those totalitarian societies where capitalist-style consumption is nonexistent—though admittedly, over there, it arises in other parts of the politico-social structure (in propaganda). Something similar applies to the distribution of bullshit. The social significance of bullshit depends on whether we are discussing democratic or totalitarian societies.

Is everything relative?

In the contemporary world, both hardline anti-kitsch positions and more "postmodern" relativist ways of interpreting kitsch coexist. The way in which kitsch and bullshit are connected to different social groups determines the significance it has for different people. Hardliners usually assume that kitsch is merely a one-dimensional instrument of oppression and "dullification" of the people. The kitsch liberal position tends to judge kitsch by considering the complexity of pluralistic class structures in contemporary societies or by considering the relativizing power of globalization. Kitsch liberals can belong to (B3) but will most typically come from (B2). Kitsch liberals interpret kitsch as a liberating pluralistic power in the arts or as part of a culture of resistance that can revert to complex rhetorical methods determined by irony. The recent emergence of a "kitsch phenomenon" such as tattoos would be an example of the latter (see Botz-Bornstein 2012).

The question of why there is so much bullshit needs to be answered against this background. Kitsch liberals are here not entirely innocent. True, bullshit liberals are rare: there are fewer statements defending bullshit than statements defending kitsch. (B2) bullshit positions are practically nonexistent and (B3) positions are rare. One reason is that bullshit, like kitsch, has some roots in totalitarian politics but, unlike kitsch, bullshit has been less able to liberate itself from those roots. For kitsch, things were relatively easy: kitsch cannot be *intrinsically* totalitarian because if otherwise, how could we explain that it is so prevalent not only in totalitarian societies but also in liberal democracies (see Boyers: 199)? As a matter of fact, kitsch proliferates in liberal societies even more than in communism and fascism. And as this book attempts to show, since some decades, bullshit thrives very well in liberal societies, too.

So far, in any bullshit speech, we are more likely than in kitsch to hear the voice of a wannabe dictator. If, as Kundera affirms, kitsch is the aesthetic ideal of all politicians (Kundera: 243), then bullshit is their rhetoric ideal. Apart from that, the anti-bullshit stance has even had traditional scientific backing, something that kitsch cannot boast of. According to Hardcastle, logical positivism attempted to eliminate all bullshit from the world (Hardcastle: 141–42). As far as I know, it never spoke of kitsch. Surprisingly, even propaganda (and not just kitsch) has been said to be more prevalent in democracies than in totalitarian societies. Noam Chomsky states in Achbar and Wintonick's documentary *Manufacturing Consent* that dictatorships have simply no need for much propaganda because they can just kill anyone who disagrees. Only in democracies (where people can make relatively free choices) is propaganda truly needed. That said, propaganda is more labor-saving as a method of producing consent, which is the reason why it is current in both dictatorships and democracies. The distinction is blurred for other reasons. While dictatorships need kitsch and bullshit for propaganda reasons, democracies need even more kitsch and bullshit, though mainly for commercial reasons.

Kitsch liberals believe that in aesthetics everything is liberal and that kitsch does not exist for this very reason. I have shown that this argument is weak because kitsch *does* exist as a communal concept. However, another question needs to be dealt with, too: is everything aesthetic really relativist? As mentioned, bullshit counts very much on the relativist judgments that are more common in aesthetics than in ethics. Bullshit rarely proceeds "scientifically" by going from premise to conclusion, but attempts to delude by creating contexts or ambiguous definitions that work in its favor. Bullshit might commit the most outrageous fallacies (red herring, suppressed evidence, begging the question, appeal to ignorance) hoping that people will be blinded by aesthetic and rhetorical devices. Its "focus is panoramic rather than particular," says Frankfurt (52), which indicates a shift of focus from analytical to aesthetic elaborations. However, this does not mean that aesthetics (like rhetoric) is simply relativist. There are certain rules to follow and kitsch skips some of those necessary aesthetic stances—for example, those of adequacy, appropriateness, sophistication, and the necessity of effort and seriousness in art. Most typically, kitsch does so in order to obtain cheap effects of intense emotion. This is similar to how bullshit works in politics, where claims or ideologies often move too quickly toward desired political aims without being backed by critical thought. The answer to the above question is thus that only bad aesthetics is relativist and that kitsch and bullshit refer to deficient kinds of aesthetic procedures when saying that in the realm of aesthetics everything is relative.

Rhetoric

Logic is value neutral and convinces, whereas rhetoric is persuasion associated with the use of power and political aims. Rhetoric can be seen as the contrary of logic or dialectic. Plato was famously hostile to rhetoric, but Aristotle analyzed modes of rhetorical power in his *On Rhetoric*. Until relatively recently, rhetoric had kept this Aristotelian meaning of a reasonable power of argumentation. From the nineteenth century onward, rhetoric gradually lost this status and became identified, with political propaganda, violence . . . and bullshit. The reason was the emergence of larger and less personal political structures in Europe, which were less benevolent for the cultivation of "good" rhetoric. Another reason is the establishment of Enlightenment culture, which prefers straightforward reasonable arguments purified of the more baroque rhetoric. Hans Mayer writes that "the art of speaking (rhetoric) necessitates narrow political and social conditions and a public life that can count on individuals as transmitters of political will in the way in which they existed in the Greek *polis* and the city states of the Renaissance or rural communities in Swiss cantons, and which had its climax in the rhetoric of the national convent of the French Revolution" (Mayer: 125). Today rhetoric is often believed to burst with life but lack reason: it is identified with bullshit. David Tietge, in his essay "Rhetoric Is Not Bullshit" (2006), criticizes this state of affairs and attempts to separate rhetoric from bullshit. He is right in doing so. However, one reason why the confusion of the two could happen in the first place is that rhetoric simply lost control of bullshit.

There is a clear parallel with kitsch. According to Broch, at the time of romanticism, art could still control kitsch more or less successfully because kitsch was "contained within a framework of facades in the neoclassical Biedermeier style (and American Romanticism in the colonial style)" (Broch: 50). However, at one point, it lost control of kitsch, with the result that today many hold romanticism responsible for kitsch (52). Gianni Vattimo even draws the conclusion that after romanticism, any "idealization of beautiful and ethical life" became impossible because the "classically perfect identification between content and form, and the completeness and definitive quality of the work, is anachronistic, illusory and in the end positively kitsch (nowadays only merchandise promoted in advertising is presented in this way)" (Vattimo: 89). Vattimo points to another paradox attached to the postmodern condition: on the one hand, postmodern ways of interpreting kitsch are identified with more relativistic attitudes brought about by the blurring of the borders between high and low art. On the other hand, there is an "increasing remoteness of 'high' art from the perspective of the masses who remain prisoners of the kitsch which for its part seems, paradoxically and in caricature, to be the realization of the 'new mythology' dreamed of by the Romantics" (72). This means that people in group (A) have simply no right to enjoy the "complete and well-rounded [art], boasting the harmonious conciliation and perfect interpenetration of content and form" (Vattimo: 86) that used to be the standard in the classical age. Whoever enjoys such art today enjoys kitsch and is suspected of belonging to group (B).

Can rhetoric and reason regain control of bullshit instead of merely diabolizing it? Can reason reign over bullshit either along the lines of deconstructing rules, or along the lines of ironic but controlled appropriation? This book attempts to formulate such paths. In liberal, globalized, "virtualized," and postindustrial societies, not only kitsch but also bullshit has become more diverse and more pervasive. As a result, hardline anti-bullshit positions are more difficult to assume than ever. Take, for example, the internet and "virtual reality" which is, in some sense, bullshit by definition. In the 1980s, Frankfurt's article could not address the problems of virtual reality. However, Frankfurt clearly declares that "the bullshitter attempts to establish a new reality," which is an alternative reality "not inferior to the real thing" (47). This is in agreement with the definition of virtuality and, in general, Frankfurt seems to believe that our culture is moving away from truth and toward antirealism.

Max Black, in his article on humbug from 1982, is even more explicit when defining humbug as a sort of "virtual lying" based on the definition of the virtual as "being functionally or effectively but formally not of its kind" (Black: 134). Virtual technology works with *immersion*. Immersion is the perception of being physically present in a nonphysical world. "Immersion" is also a metaphor for the loss of the critical mind and, in that sense, virtual reality is bullshit. If anything, it makes clear that the critical evaluation of bullshit is inevitable. We are bound to live with the "bullshit" called virtual reality on a day-to-day basis, just as we are bound to live with kitsch. A critical distance can be established through deconstruction and ironic appropriation. Total elimination is impossible.

Can bullshit be used to fight bullshit? My answer is yes. Much bullshit might *already* be committed out of exasperation with the rigid, administrative universe filled with useless requirements that we are living in. Ranting colleagues who have to hand in their updated CV to the administration four times a year produce tons of bullshit aimed at ridiculing the system and revealing its deficiencies. Neoliberal bureaucracy produces an "efficiency bullshit" that can very well be opposed by producing . . . bullshit. Political correctness, though initially designed to prevent discrimination, can easily go over the top and become a dictatorial sort of bullshit in its own right (see Chapter 3). Again, counterbullshit (such as using the feminine gender throughout academic writings) is arguably an efficient approach. But it is certainly not recommended to go to those extremes suggested by (B2) and declare, as Nelle and Selles do with regard to kitsch, the entire bullshit concept to be obsolete, meaning that bullshit is all right and that anything goes. As a matter of fact, very few people would say this about kitsch either. What I am advocating is rather a (B3) position for bullshit; the (B2) position is too radical.

Note

1   Olalquiaga observes in her *The Artificial Kingdom: A Treasury of the Kitsch Experience* (1998) a "residual aureatic character" in kitsch that could be preserved in a world of intense industrialization. The "paradoxical resistance to and glorification of a wholesale notion of authenticity" (19) that she highlights in nineteenth-century crafts and mass products seems to me more camp than kitsch. The "unfathomable detail—the texture of a paper, an age mark on a certain print, a plastic flower's faded coloring" (98) is not the most typical example of kitsch.

3

Kitsch Liberalism

I have called the "it's just a matter of taste" position kitsch liberalism. Kitsch liberalism is linked to philosophies of relativism of which liberalism is an example. Liberalism wants to liberate *all* individuals economically, politically, religiously, and aesthetically. This is possible only on the condition that political, religious, and aesthetic absolutes are declared *impossible*. Economic absolutes, however, remain possible because the economy can be quantified and calculated. The defense of "the right to individual taste" includes the defense of kitsch. Buying kitsch and liking it is a free individual's fundamental right. As mentioned in Chapter 1, the left-leaning liberal accepts the *production* of kitsch with much more difficulties, but in the end, since "kitsch does not exist" for the kitsch liberal, how can the production of kitsch be a problem at all?

Kitsch liberalism is a relatively new phenomenon. It developed against the background of the Cold War and its sociological contradictions. As mentioned, originally, liberalism, which is the continuation of Enlightenment philosophy, fought against the kitsch culture of pre-revolutionary times, especially against baroque and rococo. Baroque—and to a lesser degree rococo—used exuberance and easy to interpret details, which comes close to our present definition of kitsch. Enlightenment condemned this art as immoral and indecent. The soberer neoclassical style that is vaguely identified with the Enlightenment period is thus opposed to kitsch. The reasons for these differences of taste were also political. Baroque civilization was associated with the period of absolute monarchy, a period that had to be overcome also aesthetically.

Despite temporary kitsch temptations occurring in romanticism and in art nouveau, an anti-kitsch mindset based on Enlightenment values has been continued in Western elitist culture into modern times. The later eighteenth and nineteenth centuries were not exempt from this rule because even in romanticism and art nouveau it was possible to say *that* something is kitsch. Nobody would contest the *existence* of kitsch. Enlightenment anti-kitsch values were defended for the last time by Theodor Adorno who held that an enlightened human being should be able to distinguish between art and kitsch. Far from the arguments of postmodern liberals, Adorno saw kitsch not as popular taste that needs to be defended against bourgeois attacks. On the contrary, he saw kitsch historically, as the symbol of bourgeois values.

The liberal successors of Enlightenment philosophy changed the game. Liberalism became pro-kitsch in the name of freedom, relativism, and tolerance. This can be observed everywhere—not only in the realm of aesthetics. The freedom that kitsch liberals want to attain is twofold. Kitsch liberalism strives to obtain not only the liberation of those who are oppressed by the dictatorships of (bourgeois) good taste; the kitsch liberal also prides himself to be value neutral and free of all prejudices. Contemporary liberalism entirely changed the kitsch/anti-kitsch coordinates in place at least since the early nineteenth century and put Enlightenment upside down. The latter would now be seen as a force stifling creativity; peoples' tastes had to be liberated from all reasonable limitations. In this sense, kitsch liberalism harks back to pre-Enlightenment positions, that is, to monarchist points of view. According to Rémy Saisselin, a monarchist could hold "that neoclassicism, in retrospect, was the taste of the upstart nouveaux riches" (Saisselin: 2). Before the revolution, rococo could be seen as progressive, modern, and revolutionary, and neoclassicism could pass as reactionary and kitsch because it had been invented by the nouveau riches. For the monarchist, Enlightenment aesthetics was reactionary because it had abolished the more progressive rococo art.

The Cold War

Those changes prepared the stage for radically relativist positions of kitsch liberalism. Most of those positions crystallized during the period of the Cold War, which offered a particularly relativist scenario to progressive liberals. Since during that period none of the two opposing blocks (East and West) were willing to make any concessions, relativism became the liberal's common wisdom: "Both of you are right, and now stop arming yourself." Passionately fighting for the insight that everything is relative and that everybody's point of view should be respected (if not, the Cold War would most likely turn into a hot war), the liberal began advertising relativism as the most enlightened political activity since Enlightenment. Critiques of that position like those of Allan Bloom were formulated at that time. Bloom explicitly recognized the kitsch input in this kind of pacifism and called this new politics a "saccharine moral": "We should all get along. Why fight?" (Bloom: 35). Relativist positions caught on particularly well because fighting for political aims other than tolerance and correctness had become almost unnecessary. In the 1950s, incomes had become higher for all classes in the Western world, and in the 1970s, feminists came close to achieving their aims of equality. What was there to fight for except for the eradication of remaining prejudices about politics, culture, education, and art?

Paradoxically, the new leftist liberalism received a relativist push from the right. In the early 1980s, leftist thought took a capitalist turn as in most Western European countries leftist politics ceased defining itself as incompatible with capitalism. All that was left for the left was the fight against racism, intolerance, and the exclusion of minorities. Political correctness originates here. If societies would only terminate the last misconceptions about the superiority of their own culture and the inferiority of that of other, the world would be an ideal place. In an era where the utopias of communism and socialism had slowly collapsed, the liberals' foremost goal would become the destruction of all "absolutisms." The new relativism was rocked by another capitalist theme, which emerged in 1971 when Richard Nixon canceled the direct international convertibility of the dollar to gold. Contrary to what some might have expected, this measure would close the chapter of illiberal capitalism and a new chapter promoting the liberal world as we know it could be opened: now capitalism was "open, fluid, without order or reference, and dynamic." This is how the French conservative thinker Eric Zemmour describes the new economy dominated by the powers of finance (Zemmour: 10). In this new liberal world where the contrast between left and right had almost disappeared (compared to the harshness of past battles), political correctness became the new universal ethical yardstick that would soon be fetishized.

All this was reinforced by the fact that the improvement of salaries had also led to different attitudes toward class structures. True, people continued having different incomes, but to spell out those differences in terms of class had become politically incorrect. Holliday and Potts observe that today "class seems to have disappeared from the view of cultural analysis" and that it is "distasteful to talk about class at the present moment despite economic polarization reaching unparalleled depths" (Holliday and Potts: 27). Talking about kitsch as the art of the lower classes became inappropriate at the same time. The attribute of classes is that they are structured vertically and not horizontally next to each other. Since class includes not only money but also style, speaking of kitsch means to put the taste of a certain class down. Apart from that, any class talk can lead to the enclosure of persons within classes or even to their essentialization, which is ethically unacceptable.

At the same time and paradoxically, in the real world of Western societies, social distinctions have become clearer than ever. First, those distinctions are the results of neoliberal economic policies, and second, of immigration. Still it remains more appropriate to spell those distinctions out in terms of ethnicity than of class. Even *if* kitsch exists, it should not be mentioned as a matter of social distinction. Political correctness reinforced this kitsch taboo.

The new relativism could be advertised as a new Enlightenment project. Did Enlightenment not fight against absolutism? Did it not emphasize tolerance? A new relativist liberalism creates its own utopia in the form of a world without absolutes. Society will be entirely based on tolerance, mutual acceptance, and correctness. Beginning with the 1970s, this new spirit of relativism had moved into the realm of aesthetics, especially into fashion. A purified form of elegance was still the standard and an aesthetic landmark in the 1960s. From the late 1970s onward, we note the multiplication of irony, humor, and "second degree" significations. The notion of style, which up to then had kept a link with dandyism and the life of a rather conservative prewar upper class, loses its authoritarian connotations and becomes simply "a style." By the 1980s, style turns into an entirely relativistic game, which made Gilles Lipovetsky say that "fashion has become desubstantialized [as] it has neither stake nor challenge" (Lipovetsky: 217).

Aesthetics becomes playful, which does not mean that it has become trivial and unimportant. On the contrary, liberals continue taking questions of style very seriously, especially when it comes to the defense of kitsch. Ironically, until today, liberals are more affected by kitsch prejudices than members of the upper class and even members of the working class. The working class does not care whether somebody might think that they are kitsch or not; they probably do not even know what kitsch is. In contrast, the liberal middle class lives in a state of permanent kitsch anxiety. The upward striving liberal middle class is constantly afraid of being declassified, and the safest way to decline this aesthetic status anxiety is to declare that kitsch does simply not exist.

The denial of kitsch

The cultural situation of Western countries is permeated by a further paradox. Since the end of the Second World War, the Western world and Japan have seen the dramatic disappearance of old customs and institutions. Standards have been loosened in various domains. At the same time, cultural items from regions representing the cultural "other" were massively imported. Much kitsch is produced in cheap labor countries like China, and much of it can be found not only in regular malls but also in the ethnic quarters of Western cities. Denying the existence of kitsch has become more absurd than ever, yet many liberals see denial as the only solution. Some engage in the other extreme as Vittorio Gregotti noted already in the 1960s. By consciously and conspicuously affirming that "kitsch is alright,"[1] kitsch liberals seem to practice a sort of "kitsch exorcism": "Current cultural trends regard kitsch as a form of exorcism of the world of industry and mass consumption; we feel a wave of sympathy for those products which, by their philistine quality, demonstrate at one and the same time the blindness of industrial production and the assumed indispensability of the intellectual" (Gregotti: 256). Engagement with kitsch becomes a social critique mocking those who stick to the old standards of style.

Following the end of the Cold War, liberal attitudes become more radical through the propagation of a cultural attitude that will soon be called "postmodern." Postmodernism has marked its arguably most distinctive achievements in the realm of aesthetics. Postmodernism is the playful continuation of a *certain kind* of modernism. The relativist mixing of high and low culture will now be considered progressive and will soon become fashionable and cool. It is wrong to attribute this phenomenon to the fact that aesthetics became relative: relativism has been aestheticized. Aesthetization becomes a pervasive paradigm implying that nothing is serious because it is "merely" aesthetic. In the 1980s, class conflicts and revolutionary appeals had become history, which does not mean that they had entirely disappeared from peoples' minds. On the contrary, the afterimages of class conflicts and revolutions inspired a playful reenactment of formerly serious fights. Che Guevara T-shirts worn without knowledge about the actual person are examples of such attempts to aestheticize politics. In the end, politics becomes desubstantialized in the same way in which fashion had become desubstantialized two decades earlier. Or politics becomes a sort of desubstantialized fashion. According to Lipovetsky, in the 1980s even "democracy becomes merely an ambiance" (187). The main reason is that most values that former revolutionaries had fought for will no longer be recognized as such. Few people are willing to fight for communitarian values or class values. In a liberal world, values should be either universal or individual. Postmodernism continues the modern project of individualization. The result is a sort of relativism contained only by some abstract, universal values such as human rights, tolerance, and correctness.

Liberalism holds that in a real democracy, taste should play no role. The end of kitsch (or the interdiction to say that kitsch exists) signifies the end of taste, but it also has a political dimension. The "end of kitsch" signifies what Holliday and Potts have called the "new bad taste democracy" sporting an "anything goes ethos" and the "affectation of indifference" (Holliday and Potts: 26). This indifference can easily be confused with democracy though, in reality, it is enacted as a constraint. It imposes uniformity of views, behavior, and language upon people. Political correctness is the direct result of the above developments. At the turn of the millennium, the playfulness will be dramatically accelerated by the loss of (political) reality through the internet. Modernity represented the era of production and revolutions while postmodernity represents the era of information and expression. During the entire process of "derealization," kitsch liberalism consolidates its position.

The beginning of this era's kitsch liberalism is best symbolized by American architect Robert Venturi's dictum that "high street is almost alright" (Venturi et al. 1972: 3). Venturi speaks about aesthetics, and he is ready to fight for the acceptance of kitsch in all domains. His statements are not mitigated by irony. But by propagating kitsch he is propagating neoliberal commercialization and brainwashing through advertisements. Had those disturbing facts ever crossed his mind? A new pro-kitsch culture becomes the norm of the progressive liberal. People who oppose kitsch will be declared snobs steeped in the bloodless, antiquated high culture of the upper bourgeoisie.

The reversal of older paradigms is remarkable. Enlightenment had held that kitsch is bourgeois, stupefying, immoral, and indecent. In Enlightenment philosophy, aesthetics and economics could be seen as being wrapped together into one progressive package. The "progressive" structure leading from rococo to the French Revolution, that is from kitsch to less kitsch and, finally, to anti-kitsch, was supposed to be reflected by the liberation of the economy. "Everything moved toward Adam Smith and free trade . . . and it is possible that the nearly parallel rise of aesthetics and economics somehow represents a linked development," writes Saisselin (1). Who would still, in a free and democratic economy, stick to the heavy bourgeois aesthetic values of rococo? Free people want a purified aesthetics. That's the spirit of Enlightenment. From the 1980s onwards, things begin working the other way. Neoliberal liberations of the economy will be accompanied by the "liberation" from oppressive anti-kitsch prejudices. In democracies people are allowed to buy and like whatever they want. And: the more they buy, the better it is for the economy. This is the new policy of liberalism, and its economic aspect will soon be called neoliberal. However, neoliberalism receives plenty of help from progressive liberals as the latter declare that critics of kitsch recede to old models of repression. Had not Bourdieu analyzed the symbolical violence of taste? Is the entire concept of taste not based on old-fashioned class distinctions? Or maybe those anti-kitsch people are simply puritans because they cannot accept the sensual exuberance attached to kitsch expressions? Even worse, kitsch has feminine features and is also more current in homosexual circles. Are opponents of kitsch thus anti-feminist and homophobic? It must be concluded that refusing kitsch is politically incorrect.

What liberal defenders of kitsch forget is that kitsch is primarily totalitarian. When kitsch and politics unite, the result is non-liberal authoritarianism. Kitsch liberals are not aware of this contradiction. If liberalism had really listened to the Enlightenment heritage that it claims as its own, it should have been anti-kitsch because kitsch was originally conceived as anti-modern. Echoes of this Enlightenment anti-kitsch appeal were still audible in modernism, but the pull became weaker and weaker as styles moved toward the postmodern universe of relativism. In the Cold War context kitsch could become the symbol of freedom. Again, this went in parallel with economic developments. Enlightenment philosophers found that anti-baroque aesthetics was linked to the progressive structure of Adam Smith's liberalism; postmodern neoliberalism would reestablish the same parallelism between aesthetics and economics, but it would present it like seen through a mirror image. Suddenly it was possible to say that kitsch is liberal because it democratizes consumption.

Gert Selle and Peter Nelles are kitsch liberals who present kitsch as a new "anti-snob device" and defend it on the grounds that it is simply real—at least more real and less pretentious than much of the so-called high culture. Kitsch is *not* based on lying while high culture, with its "false" and imaginary norms, most often is: kitsch "is not founded merely on deceit; it is not an 'as if' culture, it is 'lived' culture, and whoever calls it kitschy is making an absolute of a position based on educational tradition and normative interest" (Selle and Nelles: 41). This argument, a classic (B2) case, defends kitsch because kitsch is able to fight the bullshit of high culture. Consequently, the entire "kitsch as kitsch" concept will be declared obsolete: "The parvenus know themselves what is suitable, and their measure of suitability has, as a new standard taken the place of temperate restraint. There is no kitsch, only design" (41).

Progressive and conservative forces work hand in hand. Kitsch liberalism can also come from the conservative-religious side. Paul Griffiths, author of *Decreation: The Last Things of All Creatures*, writes that "every human creature's formation in the discernment and delight in beauty is different, and because each of us is badly damaged with respect to our capacity to make reliable judgments about the presence and nature of beauty." Whatever hierarchy of beauty there may be, it isn't "obvious to all, or even most, human creatures" (Griffiths 2014: 324). Griffiths defends kitsch because it is able to transmit an immediate truth, a process that gets lost in intellectualist approaches:

> Christianity—Catholic, Protestant, and Orthodox—has been and remains among the great generators of kitsch, and that is because Christianity is and always has been a religion of peasants and proles. Most Christian art is and always has been kitsch: that's what most Christians like, and they like it exactly because it has the principal identifying mark of kitsch, which is to be free of nuance, lacking in subtlety. A kitschy artifact leaves those who interact with it in no doubt about how they should respond. The Stations of the Cross, present on the walls of every Catholic church, are not subtle and are not supposed to be. They are there to conform you to the bloody sufferings of Christ. (324)

Similar to Selle and Nelles, Griffiths resents "the connoisseur's hushed, museum-trained gaze" that "values subtlety, complexity, ambiguity, and irony" (324–5). Further down I will compare this view with other statements on religious art.

Managerial kitsch

The loss of utopias in the postmodern era sparked the development of a branch of liberalism called neoliberalism, which is often seen as the opposite of the leftist branch, though both have a common root. Like neoliberalism and progressive liberalism, the managerization of the economy and working life (and even of culture and of education) developed in the late 1980s. Since politics was, in the eyes of the liberals, no longer determined by ideologies, value-neutral methods such as evaluations and statistics had to be introduced in every domain of life. Concrete cultural values had lost their importance. What mattered was the right management based on universal prescriptions. Political correctness would take care of the rest. Since the end of the Cold War we observe the rise of a managerial class creating a decultured world of excellence. The methods are based on science as neoliberal managers work with quantified data, algorithms, and standardization systems. The economy, administrations, schools, and everything else are run by specialists. Through its naive exaggeration and formalization, the new manager culture becomes kitsch. Scientific values that had once revolutionized production in the factory are now supposed to revolutionize education and even private homes. Holliday and Potts mention the "Rational Household Movement" of Lillian Gilbreth, who suggested submitting private housekeeping to scientific management (89). The rationalization of work leads to a frantic overproduction of form with a lack of cultural content. If we insist on the parallels between economics and aesthetics, the phenomenon can be described as the kitschification of economic culture, of education culture, and of everything else that once used to be cultural. This analysis follows from the original definition of kitsch. According to Dorfles, kitsch "augments the variety of forms . . . and at the same time substantially reduces their significance" (Dorfles: 276).

Equally in the name of freedom, postwar liberalism produces rigid ideologies of tolerance and political correctness. As a result, the progressive liberal joins the most conservative chorus of neoliberals. Inscribed into the agenda of relativization through aestheticization is the idea that "marketing is almost alright." This concept is related to Venturi's "high street is almost alright" but now it is not kitsch but bullshit that is invited to the liberal feast. "Bullshit is almost alright" because it is not lying. In a neoliberal world, half-lies will be called marketing, which must be accepted as an expression of capitalist freedom. In a liberal society, anything goes, at least as long as it can be disguised as an innocent search for freedom. This is an act of aestheticization conceived in proximity with the concept of kitsch. "It's *only* marketing" and "it's *only* aesthetics" are similar strategies. Dorfles had pointed to the fallacious character of this argument already in the 1970s when writing that "this kind of styling, or 'face-lift', is applied to industrial design products exclusively for marketing reasons" (Dorfles: 32).

Kitsch humanism

Liberalism attempts to amend one sort of kitsch through another sort of kitsch. Kitsch liberals like to put forward the humane dimension of kitsch as a counterreaction to excessively rationalistic worldviews because kitsch helps us to "come to terms with an increasingly abstract and non-intuitive understanding of reality" (Kalisch: 50–51). The kitsch supporter thinks he is fighting the bullshit of modern culture with its boastful rationalization and its pretentious scientification with kitsch. The "humane dimension" argument is found particularly pertinent when kitsch adopts the shape of cuteness. A "Hello Kitty" sticker on the fridge makes everyday life more bearable for stressed-out modern people. The argument partly overlaps with Adorno's idea that art is a "pleasurable escape from the drabness of modern quotidian life" and that therefore kitsch can sometimes be justified. It is also similar to Gregotti's observation that kitsch can be "a kind of exorcism of the world of industry and mass-consumption" (Gregotti: 256). Of course, those thoughts cannot be entirely discarded. Even if we assume consumer culture to be at the root of most of the world's kitsch productions, two mechanisms need to be distinguished: (1) consumer culture produces kitsch and markets kitsch in a cynical fashion, but (2) kitsch *can* also arise as a counterreaction to consumer culture. However, we need to see the contradiction that this produces: can kitsch, which makes us unfree, become the symbol of freedom? The problem is closely linked to that of kitsch relativism. Kitsch, which used to be a symbol of bourgeois oppressive taste, can also be seen as a liberating force in a free economy. The problem is that this kind of liberation also frees us from culture, which is dangerous. Greenberg was very lucid when writing in 1939 that whenever plebeians become dissatisfied with culture, the resentment "is to be found where the dissatisfaction with society is a reactionary dissatisfaction which expresses itself in revivalism and puritanism, and latest of all, in fascism" (Greenberg: 17). Pro-kitsch liberalism or humanism is constantly threatened by precisely this danger, just like economic neoliberalism is constantly running the risk of turning into a non-liberal economic system.

All these are reasons why, in most recent times, liberalism has made huge efforts to appear as predominantly innocent. To achieve this, liberalism does not use kitsch but a subcategory of kitsch: cuteness. Cuteness is the most innocent strategy of deculturation. When kitsch is cute, it is excusable. Even more, kitsch can be disguised as the innocent search for freedom. This is one reason why the internet has been submerged cuteness. The strategy is also typically liberal: one sort of kitsch is used to amend another sort of kitsch. The relationships between neoliberal excellence and innocent cuteness will be explained in Chapter 5.

Militant kitsch

I want to conclude this chapter on kitsch liberalism by presenting a more sophisticated pro-kitsch argument, which is Robert Solomon's much noted defense of kitsch. Solomon praises kitsch in an article on emotions in art (Solomon 2004, originally published in 1991) and gives it the provocative title "Thank Heaven for Little Girls: In Defense of Kitsch." Solomon's critique of exaggerated anti-kitsch attitudes in modern culture employs several of the arguments mentioned above. However, his critique is not based on simplistic liberal-relativist convictions stating that all art—good and bad—is alike. Solomon simply doubts that sentimentality necessarily has a negative effect on art: "What is wrong with sentimentality, and sentimentality in art in particular? . . . The heart of the problem lies in our poor opinion of the emotions in general, and in particular the 'softer' sentiments" (Solomon: 236). Taking the representation of innocent little girls as a typical example of kitsch, Solomon does not deny that kitsch is also Las Vegas and horror movies, and that the entire kitsch phenomenon cannot be grasped by concentrating on the display of emotions in painting. He simply dislikes the modern identification of sentimentality with a naive or even unethical way of thinking. He finds those identifications fanatic.

Solomon does not strive to establish a philosophy of art in the sense of Karsten Harries, who sees aesthetics as immediately linked to value judgments. Harries holds that "if a philosophy of art fails to provide criteria by which to distinguish the good from the bad, it is inadequate" (Harries: 74). Solomon simply doubts that emotions and rationality are antagonistic (Solomon: 251), which has nothing to do with good or bad art. Yes, bad art exists: "Bad art, like falsehood, comes in many varieties and is subject to different kinds of objections" (235). Solomon keeps his pro-kitsch theory separate from the theory of taste. According to him, problems linked to good or bad art can be temporarily excluded from discussions of sentimentality in art. Sentences like "kitsch is art (whether or not it is good art)" (251) appear repeatedly in his article. Solomon grants that kitsch "may show poor taste. But my question here is why it is the sentimentality of kitsch that should be condemned [and] why it is thought to be an ethical defect and a danger to society" (239). All those premises provide a high degree of sophistication to Solomon's discussion, which cannot simply be summarized as kitsch liberalism.

It is not a liberalist-relativist whim that drives Solomon into the pro-kitsch camp. Like Kalisch's, Solomon's critique of anti-kitsch attitudes can be read as an anti-bullshit statement directed at a liberal political correctness attitude eagerly trying to eliminate all direct and authentic feelings in art. It is a critique of a culture that standardizes and flattens all expressions. Only because liberals think that "cuddly just isn't cool" (242), this does not mean that all art should be conceived as emotionally neutral in order to be recognized as such. What makes those modernist liberal puritans think that emotion needs to be combated in every field of aesthetics? There is a dictatorship of ambiguity and sophistication out there that is just as kitsch as the kitsch it is trying to combat: "How much macho paranoia, under the guise of sophistication and moral superiority, underlies the attack on kitsch and sentimentality?" (252). Emotions are good and ethical and do not undermine a work's artistic value only because modernists have universalized puritan standards. While Broch declared "the fiction of innocence" a "universal hypocrisy" (251), Solomon believes that the real hypocrites are the kitsch haters. This strategy is refreshing and provocative and I would attribute it not to the liberal but on the anti-liberal agenda. Still I am not sure if Solomon wanted it to be there.

As Solomon's reasoning moves from the critique of politically correct anti-kitsch liberalism to the advocacy of a full-fledged kitsch liberalism (and thus from one liberalism to another), the argument begins playing with fire. Another person who was walking a similarly dangerous line was Venturi. Venturi attacked the "simplistic progressivism" of modern capitalist society represented by a mixture of progressive liberals and conservative neoliberals who manage to unite progressive anti-kitsch and neoliberal kitsch in a paradoxical combination. Venturi found that the best way to provoke those well-meaning "always-right" and "always-ethical" utopian liberals is by saying that kitsch—which is not a utopian theory but merely the concrete expression of a social reality—is fully acceptable. In a famous passage on the high street aesthetics of Las Vegas Venturi declares: "The commercial strip, the Las Vegas Strip in particular, the example par excellence, challenges the architect to take a positive, non-chip-on-the-shoulder view. Architects are out of the habit of looking nonjudgmentally at the environment, because orthodox Modern architecture is progressive" (Venturi et al.: 3).

Like Solomon, Venturi presents opponents of kitsch as hypocrites; however, by abandoning kitsch as a legitimate aesthetic value altogether (we do not have the right to say that something *is* kitsch) he opens the door to relativism. Venturi's and Solomon's provocative pro-kitsch gestures are admirable as slaps in the faces of all those who think that art must be restrained, controlled, and politically correct. However, declaring that any kind of kitsch is acceptable *is* relativist because, contrary to what Solomon believes, the "emotion is alright" attitude *cannot* be entirely separated from the question of taste. In the end, Solomon brings forward some typical kitsch liberal arguments comfortably enclosed in the postmodern aesthetics of the 1980s from which also Venturi's architecture emerged. Even more, Solomon cannot avoid joining the regular kitsch liberal choir—above represented by Selle and Nelles—when critiquing the class bias and the gender bias of anti-kitsch. Solomon maintains that refusing kitsch denotes a class bias. Nobody should tell poor people that their art is kitsch as they must be allowed to have their own taste. The disdain of kitsch "surely has much to do with economic class distinctions and manufacturing values rather than aesthetic evaluation as such. Much of the literature attacking kitsch is political rather than aesthetic" (238). "Cheap" means "low-class," (264) and the lower classes should be defended and not despised only because they do not have the irony and the skepticism of the intellectual: "One cannot understand the attack on kitsch without a sociological historical hypothesis about the fact that the 'high' class in many societies associates itself with emotional control and rejects sentimentality as an expression of inferior, ill-bred beings" (264). This argument very much overlaps with the above-presented pro-religious one by Griffith. Furthermore, so Solomon continues, in a globalized society, the anti-kitsch attitude also denotes racism: "I am tempted to suggest that the attack on sentimentality also has an ethnic bias, northern against southern Europe and West against East, with only a few geographical modifications for ethical and aesthetic prejudice in North America" (264). Next on the list is the sexist prejudice. Kitsch is feminine and those anti-kitsch males are suppressing women's emotions: "Male society has long used such a view to demean the 'emotionality' of women" (264).

I cannot follow Solomon along that path. It *is* the path of liberal political correctness. But was he not against it? Solomon's path is tortuous. A minute ago, Solomon slapped the politically correct liberal's face (whom he believed to be an anti-kitsch person), and a little later he is patting his back by reinstating kitsch in terms of political correctness. We need to tolerate kitsch for matters of equality, otherwise we are snobs: "In a society that strives for political equality, can we afford to tolerate such snobbery? ('Some of my best leftist friends . . . ')" (246). The mysterious "some of my best leftist friends" contained in brackets and put right behind the bland equality statement begs the question what his "leftist friends" are actually thinking. Are they ethically minded pro-kitsch people who are afraid of any direct and heartfelt expression and never dare say that something *is* kitsch? Solomon refers to this possibility when writing: "Though ironically much of [anti-kitsch] comes from Marxists and their kin who despise the mass-marketing origins of kitsch at the same time . . . they would defend the people who are most likely to purchase such objects" (238).

Solomon's and Venturi's writings are built around a paradox. Like human rights and algorithm culture, anti-kitsch philosophy is an Enlightenment project, and like all Enlightenment projects, this one too can become just as totalitarian and formulaic as the kitsch it is trying to combat. Kitsch is irrational and cannot be tolerated in a modern world, except if we define kitsch in terms of minorities, feminism, and lower-class culture. Then it needs to be defended. Solomon quotes Mary Midgley and Mark Jefferson, who find that kitsch distorts reality through self-deception or that it distorts reality because sentimentality involves attachment to a distorted series of beliefs (16). Midgley and Jefferson are Aufklärer and Solomon tells them politely that he has the right to enjoy any art he likes, even when it is irrational. Solomon criticizes a self-righteous puritanist anti-kitsch culture holding that we should "never have a nice thought without a nasty one as well" (251). He opposes a liberal dictatorship of taste, which is laudable. However, Solomon is throwing the baby out with the bathwater. Yes, "progressive" anti-kitsch puritanism is a nuisance, but in a globalized world invaded by kitsch, kitsch liberalism is even worse. "We're on the point of drowning in a sea of kitsch," write Holliday and Potts (2012: 2), and the capacity to develop critical attitudes toward kitsch has become more necessary than ever. True, easy emotions can be nice, but we don't want to be forced into them. This does not mean that "we are too timid about or embarrassed by even the gentlest sentiments" (Solomon: 247). Advocating kitsch to promote emotions is like advocating pornography to promote sexuality. In the end, and disappointingly, Solomon joins the progressive liberal chorus that he himself and Venturi had criticized. In other words, Solomon fully settles on a liberal (B3) position.

Note

1 I coin this expression with Venturi's sentence that "high street is almost alright" (see next page).

4

A Culture of Narcissism

Like Salafist religious values and neoliberal excellence, kitsch abounds when concrete truths rooted in cultural environments are no longer available. In the worst case, the aesthetic reference will be self-enjoyment. Like alternative truths, such as religious truth current in fundamentalism and quantified truths based on a culturally empty idea of excellence, "kitsch truths" are not dialectically derived from confrontations with concrete cultural realities, but they establish themselves autonomously by narcissistically affirming their own truth. Frankfurt had precisely this in mind when developing his definition of bullshit starting with Max Black's concept of humbug. For Black, Humbug has a "whiff of self-satisfaction and self-complacency" (Black 1983: 121). We should therefore not speak of misinformation, which is the holding back of an existing truth, but rather of the kitschification of truth, which leads to the total loss of truth.

The narcissist lacks inner *cultural* resources and cannot sublimate her desires in the form of culture. Therefore, she is basking in kitsch. The narcissist needs to validate her sense of self. Unable to achieve satisfying sublimations in the form of love and work, she wants to be admired for her beauty, charm, celebrity, or power-attributes (see Lasch: 189). Accordingly, many kitsch theories highlight an intrinsically narcissistic impulse. Broch (1933) and Giesz (1969) depict kitsch as linked to self-indulgence, and Kundera holds that kitsch is not just enjoyment but "self-enjoyment" (Kundera: 251). For Giesz, kitsch is the self-enjoyment in which the "enjoyer enjoys himself" (Giesz: 65), and for Dutton kitsch is about narcissism because it contains "a strong sense of self-congratulation and attempted selfjustification" (Dutton 1992). For Broch, the kitsch person uses a "highly considerate mirror so as to be able to recognize himself in the counterfeit image it throws back of him and to confess his own lies (with a delight which is to a certain extent sincere)" (Broch: 49). The narcissist tends to exaggerate expressions of himself and is therefore a typical example of Giesz's "kitsch-man."

Kundera expresses the narcissistic pattern through the scheme of the "two tears" which constitutes the aesthetic experience of self-enjoyment: "The first tear says: how nice to see children running on the grass! The second tear says: How nice to be moved, together with all mankind, by children running on the grass! It is the second tear that makes kitsch kitsch" (Kundera: 251). Even if it is not plausible that *all* kitsch is narcissistic, it is obvious that narcissism leads to kitsch when consistently practiced. Repetition, self-confirmation, exaggeration, stating the obvious, sublimizing banalities and banalizing subtleties—all these items are in the narcissist's toolbox, and they are also written in the recipe for kitsch.

Harries establishes a structural link between kitsch and narcissism when explaining that the consumption of kitsch is based on a self-reflexive emotional saturation: "When objects cannot elicit desire, man desires desire. What is enjoyed or sought is not a certain object, but an emotion . . . even if there is no encounter with an object that would warrant that emotion. Thus religious kitsch seeks to elicit religious devotion without an encounter with God, and erotic kitsch seeks to give the sensations of love without the presence of someone with whom one is in love" (Harries: 80). Also Lipovetsky speaks of the "gadgetisation of what used to be superior, which characterizes narcissism" (Lipovetsky: 20). Dragging high art into the sphere of commercialization is kitsch and Lipovetsky finds this narcissistic.

We tend to see in kitsch mainly the explosion of emotions, but one should not neglect another aspect of kitsch, which is its self-enclosure as well as the self-enclosure of consumers, which *reduces* emotions. It recycles the same emotions. Harries writes that "kitsch creates illusion for the sake of self-enjoyment. It is more reflective than simple enjoyment in that it detaches itself from the original emotion in order to enjoy it" (80). Kitsch is monological self-enjoyment and any art theory that reduces art to self-enjoyment reduces art to kitsch.

Solomon contradicts Harries' anti-kitsch discourse diabolizing self-indulgence. Instead he suggests, in a liberal fashion reminiscent of Venturi, that narcissism is almost alright: "The enjoyment of the seeing and not just of the seen? What is wrong or self-indulgent about enjoying our emotions, even 'for their own sakes'? Again, I suspect a deep distrust of and disdain for the sweet emotions as such, and the ethical innocence of kitsch and its enjoyment thus becomes a suspected vice" (Solomon: 248). Solomon believes that self-indulgence has become "a code word for unearned or untutored enjoyment" (249). Would Solomon today advocate selfies saying, "What's wrong with taking a photo of yourself and posting it on the web?" Is self-indulgence really "nothing other than the fact that one is enjoying one's status as a viewer"? (250). In the end, indulging in a feeling and having a feeling are not the same. The critique of indulgence is not against emotions. When I have a feeling I simply state it. Indulgence refers to a sentimentality that is proper to kitsch. Steinvorth writes: "In such sentimentality I enjoy feeling myself; the sentiment may be painful but as it agitates me; I like it because I enjoy feeling myself, or rather my subject, the passive side of the person whose active side alone should be called self" (Steinvorth: 210).

Nor are the above anti-narcissism statements anti-narcissistic because they dislike the freedom offered by narcissism and selfies. The problem is rather the circularity and the self-sufficiency of the action: it has to be done because it has to be done. The lack of reflexive distance represents a big problem in the contemporary use of electronic media of which selfies are the most blatant consequence. In social media, narcissism and self-enjoyment have become principal driving forces. But the pattern persists everywhere—for example, in administrative activities. Accumulating information or creating complex administrative schemes whose only purpose is to feed these schemes with work is based on the same narcissistic structure. That's what is behind the above "false emotions" claim: narcissists are indulging themselves in items (emotions, information, etc.) that are not justified. It has been shown above that emotions cannot be false. However, the problem with narcissism is that here emotions get blown up to unrealistic dimension, which makes narcissism kitsch: "Kitsch art is *pretending* to express something, and you, in accepting it, are pretending to feel," writes Scruton (1999).

Kitsch and bullshit: Wittgenstein on Fania Pascal's "Narcissism"

In Frankfurt's book *On Bullshit*, the narcissism theme is developed by means of an analysis of Ludwig Wittgenstein's remarks on "Unsinn." Frankfurt bases a great deal of his descriptions of bullshit on an analysis of the Austrian philosopher's reaction to a friend called Fania Pascal who claimed, after having undergone throat surgery, that she now feels like a "dog who has just been run over." Wittgenstein dismisses her words as "nonsense" because she cannot really know what "a dog who has just been run over" feels like. Frankfurt believes that Wittgenstein interprets Pascal's statement as bullshit. The term "*Unsinn*" (nonsense) used by Wittgenstein, just like the stronger term "*Schwachsinn*", is indeed one of the most likely words that any German speaker would use to designate bullshit in German. However, Pascal is not simply talking nonsense. What disgusts Wittgenstein is rather that she "is not even concerned whether her statement is correct" (31). This permits its classification as bullshit. We can also say that her statement is kitsch because, as Frankfurt suggests, "her characterization of her feeling is too specific; it is excessively particular" (29). Kitsch is overly particular. Kitsch makes the shoes red until we see only their redness; it overemphasizes a few sentimental details in a film until we no longer care about the film's other cinematographic aspects. Dorfles's analysis of kitsch as an aesthetics that has "isolated one single aspect of the artistic phenomenon" (Dorfles: 35) and which it will subsequently exaggerate provides one of the most pertinent definitions of kitsch. The description of Pascal's state like that of a "dog who has just been run over" is simply too concrete, which dramatizes the situation in a strange way. Frankfurt says that Wittgenstein probably found the particular character that Pascal attributes to her feeling inappropriate, which is another characteristic of kitsch: "Hers is not just any bad feeling but the distinctive bad feeling that a dog has when it is run over" (Frankfurt: 29). The fact of providing inadequate words, feelings, or images is a feature of kitsch. That said, not everything inadequate is automatically kitsch. Kitsch often places wrong metaphors into wrong context. This happens in Pascal's statement. Still not every badly placed metaphor is kitsch. What is important for kitsch is *how* things are placed. When the aesthetics works apparently carelessly, by boldly disregarding reality though it is there right in front of our eyes, then the result is likely to be kitsch. Or it will be kitsch when it disregards the minimum requirements generally believed to be necessary to qualify as art.

All this also concerns bullshit, and Frankfurt's explanations make this very clear. Despite the "mistakes" that Pascal might have committed, neither Pascal nor producers of kitsch are lying. Wittgenstein seems to hold her accountable for making a false statement and the "fussiness" of this attitude appears inappropriate because he confuses an aesthetic mistake with an ethical mistake. Though Pascal might indeed have made a kitsch or a bullshit statement, most people would find that Wittgenstein has been unusually harsh in criticizing her for this (and Frankfurt believes this, too). Pascal is not pretending to give an accurate account of her situation. She simply feels like she has a full body blow, like an encounter with a large object, and so she gives an analogy. It is therefore more or less appropriate to the situation and Wittgenstein seems to be grasping at straws. Pascal's only mistake is that she puts "too much" into her statement and that she places it into an inadequate context. She indulges in her feeling.

Is there an ethical problem? Normally, a kitsch producer will be judged in terms of aesthetics rather than of ethics. Even Wittgenstein says that Pascal's statement is neither false nor unethical but simply that it is "nonsense." He does not criticize her in terms of aesthetics either. So what is he criticizing? His bullshit reproach offers a peculiar ethico-aesthetical criticism. Imagine a poet who has written a line that goes "I felt like a dog who has just been run over." Can we call this bullshit? No, because here it does not matter that the poet cannot really know what that dog feels like. As a matter of fact, a poet does not have to be overly concerned with reality. Would it then be kitsch? No, because the poet has the right to describe feelings in a particular fashion and the phrase is not hackneyed or overused. The bullshitter, however, acts like a poet but within a situation where she is not supposed to act like a poet, and this is a particular ethico-aesthetical mistake. Pascal is doing exactly this. Like a poet, she does not care about the contextual reality, but still she pretends to give Wittgenstein a more or less accurate account of her situation. This is also the reason why those same words can be understood as kitsch: their poetical content is inappropriate in this particular context. The situation can be compared to somebody reciting Stéphane Mallarmé's "Dame sans trop d'ardeur" in a business meeting and who will subsequently be accused of producing a kitsch-like setting. Mallarmé's poem is not kitsch, but the way in which it is used is kitsch. It is like hanging an authentic Rembrandt in an elevator.

Pascal's mistake can be summarized as self-indulgence. The person who recites Mallarmé's "Dame sans trop d'ardeur" in a business meeting and the person who is hanging a Rembrandt in the elevator are self-centered and narcissistic because they disregard the environment in which they are acting and want to show off a culture that they have probably misunderstood. Their acts disregard larger contexts; they are, as Frankfurt said about Pascal's statement, too particular. We find a trace of self-indulgence or self-enjoyment in Pascal's statement, and this might have disturbed Wittgenstein in the first place. Frankfurt sees the same kind of self-sufficiency and narcissism (the fact that she is concerned only about her own nature and not that of the context) as essential for bullshit (65). The bullshitter enjoys his bullshit in the same way in which the kitsch lover enjoys kitsch. Kitsch and bullshit are most likely to happen not when ethics is bluntly abandoned but when aesthetics is misused to make inappropriate statements in a real-world context by shifting the focus to one's own person.

Self-deception and pretentiousness

The pretentiousness of bullshit has recently received academic attention in a study of "pseudo-profound" bullshit in management. Pretentious bullshit is the target of the online software called the New Age Bullshit Generator (http://sebpearce.com/bullshit/), which detects pretentious religious (or pseudo-religious) bullshit. Among other things, the authors state that vagueness of meaning typical for pseudo-profound bullshit has been propelled by the Twitter limitation of messages to 140 characters (Pennycook et al. 2015). Not only garrulousness but also forced succinctness creates bullshit.

Self-indulgence easily becomes self-deception and pretentiousness. Those uncritical forms of kitsch and bullshit consumption and production can be subsumed under the heading of narcissism, too. Pretentiousness and self-deception are particularly present in neoliberal cultures of excellence. A pretended feeling is similar to a false feeling. As can be expected, when it comes to "pretense," Solomon disagrees and suggests that "pretended" feelings cannot be false: "One prominent suggestion is that sentimentality yields 'fake' emotions because the object of the emotion is not what it claims to be. It is displaced. A sentimentalist only pretends to be moved by the plight of another; he or she is really reacting to a much more personal plight" (Solomon: 14). Feelings might be inappropriate without being pretended: "A man, angry with his boss at work, comes home and yells at his misbehaving kids. His anger is displaced, but it is nevertheless not the case that 'he isn't really angry at his kids'" (15). This might be true about the feelings, but should we conclude that it is therefore impossible to be pretentious? Anger might be a bad example. But what about pretending to be happy without being so? Scruton mentions "the attempt to appear sublime without the effort of being so" (1999). This must be called pretentious.

Pretentiousness was already the topic of Kundera's kitsch examinations. In *The Unbearable Lightness of Being*, Kundera advances the concept of kitsch as the "denial of shit," which corresponds to the idea of pretentious bullshit: saying that we are the best though obviously we are the worst (thus denying the "shit" around us) is pretentious. What does Kundera mean more precisely? Kundera's understanding of kitsch might appear as unusual because kitsch has often been called trash or "artistic rubbish." Dorfles explained this most famously when insisting on the German linguistic connection with "collecting rubbish from the street" (Dorfles: 4). Also Greenberg emphasized that kitsch uses "for raw material the debased and academicized simulacra of genuine culture" (Greenberg: 10) (it seems he was criticizing the neoliberal university culture *avant l'heure*). Thus, given the parallelism with bullshit, how can Kundera characterize as "shitless" the very element that carries shit in its name? Kundera's focus is on the perfectionism of kitsch. The shiny productions of kitsch are often the elaborations of minds that leave nothing to chance. Those minds are also the minds of quantifiers and pseudo-scientists who are trying to convince us producing bombastic cascades of numbers, but who seem to be losing contact with reality (shit) by doing so. The mathematician Nicolas Bouleau has recently shown how the extreme mathematization of finance has made markets unstable because they have lost contact with reality (Bouleau 2018).

For Kundera, kitsch negates reality by excluding "everything from its purview which is essentially unacceptable in human existence" (Kundera: 243). The problem is that Kundera does not make any effort to review his "kitsch as a lie" pattern in a more complex context provided by the particular ethico-aesthetic status of bullshit. Kundera belongs to the group of people who equate kitsch (which is for him mainly a propaganda phenomenon) with brainwashing. Like Broch before him, Kundera thinks that kitsch is inalterably evil. An ironic production or consumption of kitsch (or bullshit) is unthinkable for him because the communist kitsch world that Kundera experienced was presented as a utopian world from which all irony had been banished (Kundera: 245). In communism, kitsch and bullshit became as serious as religious fundamentalism, a state of affairs that has been perpetuated in Korea. When Korean leader Kim Jong Il died in 2011, North Korean papers reported that a Manchurian crane was observed flying three times around the Kim family monument. The unusually cold weather was also ascribed to the leader's death. This is pretentious bullshit (working with images of kitsch), but it becomes fraud should the population really be brainwashed enough to believe in it. The government was addressing a public that had perhaps no choice but to really believe in it. In other countries, political bullshit tends to be taken with a grain of humor and will not follow the strict rules of brainwashing. In the postmodern situation of relativism and tolerance, bullshit—most likely coming in the form of fake news—can be presented as an opinion, but it should be subtle enough not to be identified as brainwashing.

In the cases of the North Korean propaganda, we detect a solid amount of pretentiousness. The Wittgenstein-Pascal case is different. Though Pascal pretended to give a more or less accurate account of her situation and in the end, she was not, her statements are not pretentious. But we can detect self-indulgence and self-enjoyment in Pascal's statement, which is precisely what Wittgenstein found appalling. He found it appalling in the same way in which many people find kitsch and bullshit appalling; but it was not pretentious.

To make the point about the pretentiousness clearer, it is necessary to spell out more precisely what it is that people can find appalling in pretentious bullshit and kitsch. The main problem with kitsch and bullshit is that often they do not enrich our (social, aesthetic, and so on) experiences in a meaningful way. We dismiss them not because they have misled us; we dismiss them by saying that this is *simply* kitsch or *simply* bullshit. However, this alone could merely make us indifferent toward kitsch and bullshit. But sometimes we get annoyed. Why? If we find kitsch and bullshit appalling it is not necessarily because we feel that kitsch and bullshit are at the root of an unfair treatment. Most typically we feel "bullshitted" when somebody is trying to talk us into something by using obviously false conclusions while hiding the premises. What we dislike is the pretentiousness. In this sense, Wittgenstein was overly sensitive because the slightest trace of self-indulgence present in Pascal's speech reminded him of pretentiousness.

It has been established in the preceding chapter that there are three ways of dealing with kitsch and bullshit: a) to reject them because one has recognized them as kitsch/bullshit and one does not want to deal with them; b) to accept them because one does not realize that one is confronted with kitsch/bullshit but believes them to be true claims or true art; c) to accept them though one has recognized them as kitsch/bullshit but one finds the illusion they purport pleasant and enjoyable as long they remain confined to certain quantitative limits. Let's take a typical example from neoliberal culture of education. The engineering department of a minor college in the United States has lost its accreditation and when it finally gets it back after three years of tense struggle, the college's president announces in his speech that the accrediting body simply had to give the accreditation back, because "how can they not accredit the best engineering department in the whole country?" Everybody in the room knows that what the president is saying is false, even ridiculously false, but he is not lying. It is even possible to sympathize with him because he wants to encourage the department and perhaps make them feel less embarrassed about having lost the accreditation in the first place. A pragmatic analysis will also state that people who sympathize with the speaker's political position in general will forgive the bullshit more easily. But they will not believe it. The pragmatic goals of the bullshit will be recognized and the speaker will not be held to account for the accuracy. In its hopeless exaggeration, in its naive simplicity, as well as because of its vibrating self-indulgence and narcissism, the president's claim is not only classic bullshit, but comes close to kitsch. His statement has the effect of moral reassurance that is a common feature of kitsch. But in some cases, even bullshit and kitsch are permitted. Solomon points to "old soldiers [who] fondly remember the camaraderie of a campaign and try hard to forget the terror, bloodshed, and death that surrounded them. But unless such nostalgia is used as a dubious defense of the 'glory' of war, why should this be cause for indignation? One can 'sentimentalize war'" (Solomon: 18). Of course, we can bear the president's words only as long as they are used sparingly. Should he repeat his claim on a weekly basis, we might accuse him of brainwashing and manipulation of the students' sense of reality and of producing an alternative truth.

For Kundera, kitsch negates reality by excluding "everything from its purview which is essentially unacceptable in human existence" (Kundera: 243). This is the meaning of the "denial of shit." The college president presents the same "shitless bullshit" because: is there anything more "shitless" than a world in which the country's worst department still remains the country's best? In the end, the college president was guided by monetary motives because he did not want engineering students to leave the department. But those motives were not too obvious, he did not appear greedy and, as explained above, he did not insist too much on his false claim. Here pretentiousness remains secondary.

Excellence@tfu.edu.com

Pretentiousness is linked to narcissism. Pretentiousness occurs when the bullshitter herself appears to believe, at least halfway, in her own bullshit in order to feel better; and this state of mind manifests itself as narcissism, which most probably will come along as self-indulgence and self-enjoyment. Kundera's "shitless word" as well as Pascal's case are therefore examples of *narcissistic* self-indulgence. True, Pascal is not *very* pretentious because her self-indulgence and self-enjoyment are not very strong (though still strong enough to annoy Wittgenstein). Let us look at a better example from the corporate world of neoliberal education. The college's email address is excellence@tfu.edu.com. There was really no reason to put the word "excellence" into that place. Throwing around the word "excellence" like this makes it meaningless and trite. The value of real excellence has been debased, which is a typical feature of kitsch. Excellence must be worked for and not merely mentioned in the most inappropriate places. The college might defend itself by saying that for them excellence is so important and primordial that they decided to use it in their email address. We cannot refute this, but it seems unlikely. We would claim that this is bullshit and ask:

"Do you really believe in what you are saying?" The problem is that they do believe in it and at the same time they do not believe in it—and this precisely what makes it pretentious and also narcissistic. What the college is doing is not merely boastful. If they were boasting, we could hold them morally accountable for breaking a cultural code of modesty. Here we are put into a much more complicated situation that comes closer to the task of explaining why a certain work of art is bad and not good. Pretentiousness shifts lying from ethics to aesthetics, which creates bullshit.

This is precisely what happened to the term "excellence". The meaning has become extremely vague, which was the intention from the beginning. At the same time, the college is not lying nor does it affirm something in which it does *absolutely* not believe. It simply effectuated an aesthetic embellishment of a non-truth. It decided to believe *in this embellishment alone*, but it does not necessarily believe in the reality itself. So, what can it be accused of? It can be accused of narcissism and of pretentiousness, which brought about a confusion of aestheticized image and reality. Certain things got out of control during the frantic search for excellence.

Frankfurt attaches much importance to pretentiousness as a motivation of bullshit (Frankfurt: 11). It is what distinguishes, in his opinion, bullshit from humbug (as defined by Max Black), though Frankfurt also recognizes that "it must not be assumed that bullshit always and necessarily has pretentiousness as its motive" (12). First, not everybody who pretends is pretentious. For example, the real estate agent who cheats me into signing up for a hyperreal loan scheme by pretending that the loan system is entirely safe when it is not is not pretentious but simply lying. In some instances of pretentious bullshit, the bullshitter is really lying (consciously or unconsciously) but without taking care to dissimulate the truth properly. This is unintentional pretentious bullshit, which is different from unconscious bullshit where the bullshitter believes she is telling the truth. In unintentional pretentious bullshit, the bullshitter is trying to lie but her lies remain on the level of bullshit. Unconscious bullshit happens relatively often because bullshit has an intrinsic illusionist component and often settles in the area of self-hypnotization. Should the bullshitter really not be aware at all of her own bullshit, she strikes us as naive, but not as pretentious because there is no motivation (either good or bad) behind her act.

Then there is the liar who desperately tries to become a bullshitter by saying, "But I thought that this would not matter." She is not pretentious but simply defending herself. In any case, pretentious bullshit (which Frankfurt identifies as a stock phrase, 11) is worse than regular bullshit because it annoys us, but in moral terms, it is not as bad as regular lying. Kitsch works along similar lines. When bullshitters and kitsch people boast about their (nonexistent) capacities or about the (imaginary) artistic value of their latest "art" purchase from the tourist souvenir stand, we can either see them as victims of a reality scheme that has kept them in the dark for whatever reason or we can find them annoying because they are trying to talk us into something. In the latter case, kitsch and bullshit lose their playful input and become pretentious because they start becoming serious strategies. What is annoying is the believe/not-believe state of mind of the person who talks about kitsch. When she is pretentious, she "somehow" knows very well that it is kitsch but she does not want to admit it, possibly not even in front of herself. The creation of alternative realities very often follows this scheme.

Sometimes kitsch and bullshit are guided by monetary or political motives and they become particularly pretentious and annoying when those motives move to the foreground. Of course, this concerns the kitsch producer and not the kitsch consumer, who will rather be a victim of those strategies. We are annoyed that the real estate promoter presents the gorily decorated apartment that is obviously tuned to the taste of his nouveau riche clientele as tasteful and up to high-class standards. We are also annoyed when looking at the apartment's price because the tons of marble and fake gold have made it unnecessarily expensive. However, the kitsch items themselves are not annoying but might even evoke our pity. What is annoying is the fact that here kitsch is sold as non-kitsch or, in other words, that bullshit has moved closer to a lie (without really being one). We find the promoter pretentious because she takes kitsch for the real thing (or pretends to do so) and imposes her false judgments upon us in the name of profit. Still we remain in the realm of taste and aesthetics and a remnant of the matter's playfulness prevents us from calling this fraud. The following example, on the other hand, is not pretentious because here we are dealing with false facts. The politician's declarations about the existence of weapons of mass destruction in Iraq might merely strike us as a typical bullshitting discourse aiming to gain the sympathy of voters; everyday politics abounds with such declarations. However, when the bullshit is taken seriously enough to serve as a reason for invading a country, then bullshit has become a lie incurring a crime against humanity. Alternative realities are often created by following this blunt strategy, which makes them distinct from bullshitting. The "facts" have assumed a reality status without anybody having made an explicit effort to declare them to be real: "I am only asking to see President Obama's birth certificate, I am not saying that he was not born in the US," said Donald Trump. Despite the indirectness of the strategy and the attempt to make the lie look less serious than it actually is, such statements remain lies and should not be confused with bullshit. Correspondingly, in those cases we are not dealing with kitsch either. There is nothing kitschy in those statements apart from the indirect link with overly patriotic expressions of the love of the country.

Self-deception

Harries argued that self-enjoyment can easily be transformed into self-deception (Harries: 80). Self-deception is closely linked to narcissism. We have already talked about half-belief as a marker of pretentiousness. The pretentious person does not *straightforwardly* believe in what she is saying. As soon as the bullshitter *really* believes in her own bullshit she is not pretentious but simply naive. In the ideal cases of kitsch and bullshit, the "real" reality should never be entirely dissimulated. This distinction is also important for the receiving side. Some people decide to believe in bullshit to some degree, that is, they do not "really" believe in it but temporarily enjoy it like a fiction or a computer game. The narcissist teenager who posts forty-five selfies per week on the internet is not necessarily convinced that her looks are as good in real life as what is shown on the photos. She might want to believe it, but she is not necessarily engaging in this half-belief because she is pretentious.

Commercials are typical producers of bullshit as well as of kitsch, but normally their images enter our minds not in the form of an accepted reality, but rather as pleasant illusions that we like to entertain within certain limits. Social media have even invested in this limitation. A considerable part of photos posted by teenagers appears on snapchat, which displays pictures only for a very limited time. The vagueness of information or of pictures themselves is part of a marketing concept that *eludes* pretentiousness and acquits its users of accusations of narcissism.

I might choose to "believe" in the authentically German craftsmanship of my dearly paid car though I know perfectly well that most of the car's parts were made in China. However, nobody would classify this as a serious act of self-deception or say that I am producing an alternative reality. The point is that I *honestly* do not exactly know what percent of my car should be considered

German and what percent Chinese, and it is this blurred state of reality that invites a playful acceptance of bullshit. In those cases, we join the bullshitter or producer of kitsch at least temporarily in their "indifference to how things really are," to put it in Frankfurt's terms (34). It is important to express these convictions about my car as the result of my indifference, and not of my fanatical adherence to another reality. Otherwise there would be the desire to deceive myself, which is the same desire that is at the root of narcissism. I must be ready to give up my illusions without difficulty and at any moment. Otherwise I am really the victim of bullshit or, technically speaking, of fraud. If I know that my car is Chinese but frantically proclaim that it is purely German made, then I am pretentious. If I draw a monetary benefit from it, I engage in fraud.

Max Black attempts to prove self-deception impossible because if humbug (or fraud) requires concealment of a deceptive intent, the speaker and the audience cannot be identical: "The following argument for the impossibility of self-deception seems to be conclusive: Humbug requires concealment of a deceptive intent; but if the speaker and the audience are identical, as in soliloquy, there can be no such concealment; so there can be no such thing as self-deception" (Black: 138). However, Black admits that all this is only true for straightforward situations in which real concealment took place, that is, for "first-degree humbug": "For second degree humbug, produced by a self-deluded speaker or thinker, the unsatisfactory reference to thoughts and so on would need to be replaced by something like 'thoughts . . . that might be revealed by candid and rational self-examination'" (143). Black would probably call the case of the German-Chinese car "second degree humbug" (143). Unfortunately, the limits that separate self-deception from the mere play with partial deception are flimsy. In general—if at all—bullshit and kitsch can blur the distinction between reality and non-reality or between art and non-art only slightly; but just because the limits are only slightly altered, the alteration can be rather consistent and durable. This is why Frankfurt concludes that "bullshit is a greater enemy of the truth than lies are" (61). The point is that the bullshitter "does not reject the authority of the truth, as the liar does, and opposes himself to it. He pays no attention to it at all" (61). It is less likely that proofs will be searched for and that falsehood will be detected. Bullshit can last longer simply because it has declared that truth is not otherwise but merely unimportant. Through this device bullshit can even engage our participation or enjoyment. And this enjoyment factor is, of course, also very important for kitsch. It can be concluded, in parallel with Frankfurt's statement, that kitsch is a greater enemy of art than fake art.

Cheating

Cheating is different from fraud. "Cheating" sounds less severe than "deceiving." Cheating takes advantage of the fact that the limits between bullshit and lying (or kitsch and fraud) are often difficult to establish; they are fluid and manifest various degrees. The perception of cheating shifts from the ethical to the aesthetic. The junior high school student who has cheated on the math exam might believe that she is "cool" because she managed to delude an authoritarian school system and got away with it. Moral concerns do not affect her as much as they would were she told that this is fraud. The German and French languages use special words for cheating on exams (*pfuschen, tricher*) to distinguish this act from that of normal deception. *Pfuschen or tricher* is a lighter form of deception. Unlike deception, *pfuschen and tricher* are intransitive verbs, which seemingly cancels a part of their ethical implications. One cannot pfuschen/tricher somebody, but one does it on one's own, which sounds very much as if there is no victim. There is a parallel with bullshit. I can say "he has cheated me" but will I say "he has bullshitted me?" I cannot be considered a victim.

Where do we draw the line between fraud and cheating? Some people think that religion is bullshit but they would not hold the "bullshitting" priest accountable for fraud. The leader of a sect, on the other hand, will more commonly be accused of deceiving and lying. The same goes for religious fundamentalists who insist on the absolute character of some absurd dogmas and turn religion into a sort of science-based ideology. Creationism, for example, turns from bullshit into fraud when it is no longer presented as a culturally/religiously determined worldview but as a scientific theory. George Reisch has doubts whether creationism fits Frankfurt's definition of bullshit because advocates of creationism "are plainly not indifferent to truth" (Reisch: 37). The bullshitter can or cannot be indifferent toward the truth, but she invites *us* to be indifferent toward truth though she knows that, at least theoretically, the truth is present and accessible to everyone. She invites us to ignore the elephant in the room. Because, in most cases, this strategy cannot be carried out along the lines of a perfect brainwashing, bullshit will remain bullshit. If, however, serious attempts are made to negate reality throughout, then creationism turns into fraud. Fraud happens when creationists attempt to publish their intelligent design theories in serious scientific journals or create their own journals for that purpose and advertise them as academically sanctioned (the reality of creationism promotion is obviously more complicated than can be dealt with in this short space, but it has been well analyzed by Reisch). How does this work with regard to kitsch? There are examples where kitsch has been advertised as science. Ugo Volli mentions the case of a piece of pornography (which he sees as an example of kitsch because it is too explicit) that has been declared to be merely a scientific study of sexuality (Volli: 226). If people really believe this, kitsch becomes fraud. There are numerous other cases where kitsch is advertised as non-kitsch, though the strategy is less obvious. The quasi kitsch religion that invades contemporary brains in the form of a mind-numbing television culture is acceptable as long as people are left the choice to watch other programs and see other realities. Television as a media is different from cinema because through its permanency, it pervades peoples' minds in a more "brainwashing" fashion. Through television, kitsch (and bullshit) is often forced upon people in such a consistent manner that they simply cannot escape. Here kitsch becomes fraud. The kitsch painting sold in the local mall, on the other hand, remains kitsch because the seller is merely bullshitting. Kitsch as fraud can also happen when kitsch is systematically employed in architecture. Wherever kitsch takes over too much of reality (the media or the built environment), it turns into the exclusive kind of reality that is similar to the reality offered by sects.

Seduction

Many negative things have been said above about kitsch and bullshit. So why are so many people attracted by them? Kitsch is boastful, exaggerated and "not quite true"; it can still be attractive when it is aesthetically pleasing. Both kitsch and bullshit play with what Baudrillard has called "weak signifiers." It has been shown that both kitsch and bullshit maintain strong relationships with narcissistic impulses such as pretentiousness and self-deception. In all those cases, ethical and aesthetical perceptions of kitsch and bullshit overlap. A more straightforward case is seduction. Despite its predominantly negative connotations, kitsch and bullshit are able to evoke a considerable amount of sympathy among the public. Most bullshit is blunt, but in particular cases we might like the bluntness, be it only because its production obviously required a considerable amount of intelligence. In commercial slogans bluntness can almost become an art. Very often bullshit expresses secondary claims (which Frankfurt observes with interest) with which we can sympathize; and sometimes those secondary claims could hardly be expressed otherwise than through bullshit. Here we have seduction.

Unfortunately, both bullshit and kitsch tend to follow certain repetitive patterns that provide novelty value only on rare occasions. Apart from that, the ethical evaluation depends on the audience that has been addressed. Take the example of the university president lauding the engineering department. The students who listen to him are educated people and the president knows that most probably they will not take his words for granted. But the same action will become morally abject when carried out in front of an entirely uneducated audience. Scott Kimbrough notes that "we sympathize with the liar's victim but not with the bullshitter's" and judge that the victims of bullshit "allow themselves to be mentally lazy and blinded by desire" (Kimbrough: 6). In the above case, anybody who takes the college president's words for granted is naiver than even the president expected; the bullshitting technique was too obvious and nobody was forced to believe in an alternative reality.

The example works in parallel with the perception of kitsch. Some people find the sporadic presence of kitsch acceptable as long as it does not interfere with their critical distance toward kitsch. They are not disinclined toward seduction but do not want to be overwhelmed. They want to know that it is kitsch and remain able to draw the limit between kitsch and real art. They want to keep a "cool" distance toward what they identify as kitsch. Then they might decide to enjoy a sentimental song, a funny but tacky commercial, an eccentric armchair in their living room that is "normally" too colorful but still interesting. Only when they appreciate kitsch *as* kitsch are they able to play with certain kitsch motives in a "cool" fashion and might appreciate them in the form of "self-conscious subversions [or] as part of irony" (Kulka: 9). In other words, paradoxically, just because they see kitsch as kitsch, kitsch no longer functions as kitsch. The enjoyment is controlled by an aesthetic sensibility that is not merely dependent on kitsch. Camp is very much based on this ironical attitude toward kitsch, as are "postmodern" ways of using kitsch motives attempting to challenge official aesthetic standards. The above consumers of kitsch do not want to be overwhelmed by kitsch. The pattern corresponds to Milan Kundera's concept of self-conscious kitsch, that is, the fact of "knowing that kitsch is kitsch"—which, for Kundera, makes kitsch not kitsch at all: "As soon as kitsch is recognized for the lie it is, it moves into the context of non-kitsch ... becoming as touching as any other human weakness" (Kundera: 256). The latter option is unique to bullshit and kitsch, and it is based on the assumption that both kitsch and bullshit are not entirely immoral or, more precisely, that their existence is linked to the sort of playful (though not complete) relativism that is proper to judgments in the realm of aesthetics. Kundera is even more radical because for him, the fact of "knowing that kitsch is kitsch" is a reason to exempt kitsch from ethical requirements altogether.

That's how kitsch and bullshit can be seductive. Fraud or the act of convincing operate with strong signifiers while kitsch and bullshit operate with weak signifiers. Somehow we know that it is false. We can be seduced by the college president's statements only *because they were not too strong*. He was not insisting too much. The pattern is in perfect agreement with the scheme that Baudrillard describes as the principle of seduction. Seduction always "lies with the annulment of the signs, of their meaning, with their pure appearance" (Baudrillard 1990: 76). Strong kitsch and bullshit will not seduce but annoy. Some might embrace strong kitsch and bullshit, but in that case, they do not embrace it *as* kitsch and bullshit but rather as art and reality. Though kitsch and bullshit are strategies of exaggeration relying on the completeness of signification, they do not violate but seduce. To be effective, they have an intrinsic weakness: "To seduce is to appear weak. To seduce is to render weak. We seduce with our weakness, never with strong signs or powers. In seduction we enact this weakness and this is what gives seduction its strength," writes Baudrillard (83). Accordingly, we can be seduced by kitsch or bullshit when it is "weak" but are repelled when it is "strong." Baudrillard classifies seduction as a ludic activity because of "the capacity immanent to seduction to deny things their truth and turn it into a game, the pure play of appearances, and thereby [to] foil all systems of power and meaning with a mere turn of the hand" (8). The president of the college was playing with the truth and therefore his bullshit *could* seduce some listeners. Further exaggerations about the quality of the university would have been perceived as annoying. Baudrillard calls this the "principle of uncertainty" that rules in seduction (12). It applies to kitsch and bullshit, which can exercise a "power of attraction and distraction, of absorption and fascination" (81) only as long as some uncertainty subsists. They seduce best when the persuasion remains incomplete and when the process appears mobile and diffuse. When kitsch and bullshit can be constructed as an "exhausted meaning" or as the annulment of signs, they can have "the beauty of an artifice" (76).

Coolness

Seduction can also happen through coolness. Can kitsch and bullshit be cool? The principle of the week signifier can indeed make kitsch and bullshit cool. The reason is that kitsch and bullshit provide "weak" types of information. Long before Baudrillard, Marshall McLuhan called this type of information not weak but cool. McLuhan's idea of coolness is useful for further clarifications of the functions of kitsch and bullshit. For McLuhan, "hot" is any kind of information that is highly defined or that "leaves not much to be filled in" (McLuhan: 37). Hot media favor analytical precision, quantitative analysis, and sequential ordering while cool media leave the transmitted information open to interpretation or even partly unexplained. Speech is thus cooler than highly defined images. The cool signifier is a "weak" signifier because it lacks some information and is more seductive for that reason.

McLuhan's concept of coolness will most probably be viewed today through another idea of coolness, which has been developed in the form of a behavioral attitude practiced by black men in the United States at the time of slavery and residential segregation. Here "to be cool" means mainly to remain calm even when being under stress. While blacks were not allowed to enter certain areas of the city at certain times, a cool attitude made it possible for them to walk streets at night or at least to deal with their oppressors in a dignified fashion. This coolness depended to a large extent on pretending. However, whenever it appeared as pretentious, the behavior would not be recognized as cool. Then it was just "bullshitting."

If we accept this idea of bullshit as a lack of coolness, Fania Pascal's problem might turn out to be a simple "coolness" problem. She did not stay cool, lost control, and started talking bullshit. Her behavior was uncool just like that of somebody who recites Mallarmé's "Dame sans trop d'ardeur" in a business meeting, or somebody who hangs an authentic Rembrandt in an elevator. Those are not seriously ethical errors but ethico-aesthetical mistakes. In spite of this I would insist that bullshit can be cool in certain cases. Some facts concerning the cool *perception* or consumption of kitsch/bullshit have been pointed out above. However, the *production* of bullshit can also be cool. The student who has cheated on the exam might believe that she is cool because she managed to delude an authoritarian system. The "doing away" with moral concerns brings this action close to bullshit. Yes, bullshit can be cool, but in that case, its existence will depend very much on its aesthetic arrangement. Most probably, bullshit will then come closer to cool kitsch. The bullshitter might get away with her distortion of reality because the style with which she commits the distortion aestheticizes the ethical default. This can be cool because "to be cool" means to remain calm even when taking considerable risks. The easiness, nonchalance, and feigned innocence with which bullshit often passes over premises that should be obvious to everybody makes the bullshitter a risk taker. And anybody who takes risks without losing control is cool. Even more, we can say that the higher the risk the cooler the bullshit (provided that she can get away with it). This does not mean that the bullshit is entirely hidden under the aesthetic and that nobody recognizes the bullshit as such. But the aesthetic arrangement urges us to pass over the bullshit occurrence because the person can be described as "bullshitting with style."

This is closely related to another point: the cool bullshitter *does not care* whether people believe in her claims or not. Not to care about what others might say is cool by definition. Coolness is here not a matter of ethics but of aesthetics. A bank robber can be cool while the most ethical person might be uncool. What matters is not the content of the speech or action but the bullshitter's style or what Max Black has called the "stance" of the one who produces humbug. Black means by stance "the speaker's beliefs, attitudes, and evaluations" (Black: 118), and we have identified the stance of the bullshitter not only as the intention to not lie or to bluntly conceal the truth, but also as a complex mixture of negligence, boldness, and nonchalance. The weighting of all those qualities is decisive for deciding whether bullshit is cool or not. This highlights the contrast with the negative qualities that have been analyzed above: pretentiousness, self-deception, and cheating make any attempted bullshit immediately uncool. Of course, bullshit becomes also uncool when it moves too close to blunt lying. The liar cannot be cool because she clearly hides the truth and is not ready to take any risk. Compared to lying, bullshitting appears more like a game (even as a game of hazard) and games are cool by definition. Bullshit is coolest when it stimulates a playful attitude toward itself, and this attitude is normally excluded from lying. Lying is simply too serious.

Cool kitsch (which is arguably rarer than cool bullshit) is inscribed in the same logic. Normally, kitsch is conservative and hostile toward risk taking. The kitsch producer takes no risk but is eager to please. However, should she nevertheless get away with impressing an art-educated public with kitsch because there is "something" in it that is cool—then the kitsch artist is indeed cool. Strictly speaking, this is then no longer kitsch but kitsch art. It is cool because she was taking a maximum risk but kept the situation under control.

The last possibility for kitsch being cool is when it is produced in the form of "self-conscious kitsch" (though Kundera would not recognize this as kitsch at all). Lebensztejn and Cooper affirm that by "appreciating kitsch and collecting its objects, the supercool amateur assures for himself a certificate of good taste and distinction" (Lebensztejn and Cooper: 76). Here kitsch can be freely combined with bullshit. A good example is the work of Jeff Koons, who is one of the most virtuous artists employing kitsch for the purpose of art; and he is also a master of bullshit, as is demonstrated by his declaration that Cicciolina (an Italian-Hungarian porn star and politician formerly married to Koons and featured in some of his work) "is the eternal virgin [because] she's been able to remove guilt and shame from her life, and because of this she is a great liberator" (Koons 1992: npn).

Baudrillard confirms that belief or make-believe "employ signs without credibility and gestures without referents; their logic is not one of mediation, but of immediacy, whatever the sign" (Baudrillard: 75). Kitsch and bullshit are among the most obvious examples of such techniques of make-believe. Both try to outwit the critical mind. When this act of outwitting is playful it might be cool, but it becomes annoying when it is pretentious, which is one of the contraries of cool. One reason is that the pretentious person is no longer in control of the situation but believes (at least partly) in her own kitsch/bullshit. Then there is the case of the consumer who insists on the real value of kitsch and bullshit; she might also be classified as pretentious and not merely be pitied as a victim.

In neoliberalism, kitsch and bullshit are on the increase, be it only because of the importance that social media have taken. Horkheimer and Adorno pointed out that liberalism can be criticized for its lack of style (Horkheimer and Adorno: 131). Today things are more complicated. Kitsch is not only determined by politics, but politics can be determined by kitsch. Kitsch is more than a spontaneous neoliberal whim, but the occurrence of kitsch is linked to comprehensive cultural systems fostering certain political behaviors.

As long as bullshit knows that it is bullshit (and everybody else knows it as well), bullshit can be used to challenge orders. Kitsch is kitsch and bullshit is bullshit. There is nothing intrinsically annoying about them except when they become pretentious—in other words, when they become pushy and move closer to lies. Just as kitsch has increasingly come to be seen as an artistic device, bullshit could be seen as a rhetorical device, playfully—but while still controlled by reason—deconstructing existing rules. This is no kitsch liberalism à la Solomon, but it calls for an enlightened form of self-control.

Frankfurt names the general retreat from correctness to sincerity as one of the more obscure sources of bullshit, and that's where I see a major problem with Frankfurt's analysis: "Rather than seeking primarily to arrive at accurate representations of a common world, the individual turns toward trying to provide honest representations of himself" (Frankfurt: 65). What Frankfurt means and what he criticizes is that once we have acquired the image of an honest person, we can bullshit as much as we want. Correctness and accuracy—which are, for

Frankfurt, the only powers able to fight bullshit—will no longer be standard in a world in which we are looking *only* for honesty. I do not agree. Today it is very much possible to understand "honesty" (just like bullshit) as a counterreaction to exaggerated requirements of correctness or pseudo-correctness. It seems to me that Frankfurt, when saying that "the individual turns toward trying to provide honest representations of himself," confuses honesty with "personality," which is very often a *pretended* honesty and thus bullshit. However, honesty is precisely what we should use in order to fight bullshit.

Marilyn Motz, in her analysis of Douglas Lurton's 1950s bestseller *The Power of Positive Thinking*, explains that in a world where everybody thinks positively, "personality [will have] replaced character as the primary measure of one's worth. Positive thinking is what Broch called sweet kitsch. A pleasant smile, a well-groomed appearance, self-control and conformity replaced honesty" (Motz: 134). Positive Thinking, which asks us to adopt a radically positive attitude toward everything even when reality looks completely otherwise, carries many qualities that justify its classification as typical bullshit. It also accords with the curious ethics of excellence that has replaced Greek character ethics (virtue ethics) in the twenty-first century. The radically positive-thinking person is a "bullshit personality" whose pleasant smile is, in the final instance, dishonest. Though positive thinking is always "correct" (not necessarily in the sense of political correctness though distantly related to it), it is dishonest because it lacks self-criticism, is narcissistic, and leans toward auto-hypnotic self-aggrandizement. In other words, it is mere excellence and therefore kitsch. And like the bullshitter, the positive thinker pretends not to be aware of this. Is "honesty" here not the best remedy? A (B3) position of bullshit includes honesty and it can be reached by thinking about parallels between kitsch and bullshit.

5

Cute, Excellent, Sublime, Interesting

In the last chapter, kitsch and bullshit have been considered from both the receiver's and the producer's points of view. The difference between both needs to be made clearer to point out a paradox. While kitsch can appear as cool to some people (the receivers), it needs to be clarified whether kitsch can also be produced as cool. The kitsch-cool relationship is paradoxical. Kitsch prefers all that is sentimental, round, warm, soft, and fluffy, and everything that is associated with slightly warmer temperatures. Normally, kitsch cannot be cool. However, when kitsch manifests the same innocence (and perhaps even nonchalance) as bullshit, one might detect traces of coolness. Most of the time one would not call this cool but cute. Kitsch has been said to have a natural affinity with cuteness. Rosenberg points out that "when kitsch first began to spread in European cities, the liveliest poets found it cute" (Rosenberg: 264). Cuteness is not only the helplessness sparking exuberant emotion. "This is so cute" can also signify recognition in terms of coolness similar to the world "charming."

Can bullshit be cute? It is difficult to think of examples, but the possibility exists. Since the production of kitsch is not a serious ethical mistake, the producer of kitsch or the kitsch lover might get away with their kitsch for the same reason we pardon bullshit when it is committed by children. "But I only wanted to . . ." is a child's excuse for having transformed the kitchen into a wetland and it comes across in the form of bullshit (the case where the liar desperately tries to become a bullshitter has been discussed above). Bullshit is cute when the bullshitter is trying to lie but she simply can't. In general, kitsch belongs to the universe of children and bullshit must have some affinities with the childishness of kitsch expressions. It is no coincidence that the *Oxford English Dictionary* equates the meaning of "bull" to the word "trivial" (though Frankfurt does not agree with this definition) (34). Bullshit and kitsch can be cool when they take risks without losing control of the situation; and they can be charming and cute when they appear to be innocent. In all other cases they are most probably neither cool nor cute.

The cute, the excellent, and the innocent

Cuteness appears in cases where kitsch manages to seduce in a particularly straightforward fashion. Anthropologists Morreall and Loy define cuteness as "a group of features that evolved in mammalian infants as a way of making them attractive to adults" including "a head large in relation to the body, eyes set low in the head, a large protruding forehead, round protruding cheeks, a plump rounded body shape, short thick extremities, soft body surface, and clumsy behavior" (Morreall & Loy 1989: 68). Innocence and helplessness are the most important character features of the cute. Cuteness sparks human instincts provoking spontaneous reactions. The cultural concept of cuteness as it is known in the West emerged around 1900 when the "bubbling enthusiasm of the child" (Cross: 43) could be interpreted as charming. The initial meaning of cute as "shrewd" would be replaced with that of "wondrous innocence."

The preceding chapter has shown that kitsch liberals defend kitsch by putting forward its humane dimension to contradict the excessively rationalistic worldviews of modernity. A "Hello Kitty" sticker on the fridge makes modern everyday life more bearable. Kitsch might be an art suited to passive people with a short attention span looking for immediate gratification; however, it also mediates modern life dominated by technology and impersonal rationalization. Through kitsch we "come to terms with an increasingly abstract and non-intuitive understanding of reality," writes Kalisch (50–51) and this is even truer for cuteness. Cuteness can function as a "softener" of modern life, as Hannah Arendt noted already in her *The Human Condition* (1958) when being intrigued by the modern enchantment with small things. Cuteness is also the perfect example of "seduction through weakness." The Japanese kawaii has been said to be so prominent in Japan after the Second World War because the emperor had been weakened and because Japan had become militarily weak (Ngai: 3). Warm kitsch and cuteness are used to amend the excesses of cold modern rationalism. At present, images of cats and kittens make up some of the most viewed content on the web. In 2016, the Museum of the Moving Image New York organized an exhibition titled *How Cats Took Over the Internet*, and a study of Indiana University found that viewing cat videos "boosts positive emotions and decreases negative feelings" (Indiana University 2015). Cuteness can revoke the abstract reality fostered by the decultured type of modernity and excellence. Cuteness can help to overcome a world in which human-guided sensation is replaced with automated productions. Cute objects can be touched and provide an authenticity that is getting lost in industrial societies. Cuteness can effectuate a familiarization of mass-produced items like cell phones. Images of cute animals represent a cure for people who are under pressure of a merciless modern machine forcing them to adhere to more and more universal standards of excellence.

Living in a modern rationalized world can be difficult, but is cuteness the antidote? If yes, we are destined to end up with a world plastered with cat stickers. Of what, exactly, are the images and videos of cute animals supposed to be the remedy? Seeing the cute gives us a few seconds of relief from an industrial world of measurements and evaluations. The cute is individual and exists beyond globalized standards. The cute does not care about the world around, it exists just for itself. In that sense, cuteness is opposed to excellence. Cuteness is concrete, and excellence is abstract. Cuteness is used to contradict the rationalist or pseudo-rationalist worldviews of modern culture thriving in the cold neoliberal world of enforced excellence. The problem is that here one sort of kitsch is used to amend another sort of kitsch. By taking refuge in cuteness, one does not introduce concrete elements from a certain culture into the decultured world of excellence-driven modernity. Cuteness is just as decultured as excellence. The cute kitten posted on Facebook might represent an attempt to establish a community of like-minded people in a globalized world. However, this "community" will not be a *cultural* community but it remains based on an abstract and cultureless perception of cuteness "as such." Cuteness is a puff of oxygen enabling us to survive for a few more seconds in the world of excellence-driven modernity. By combating cold quantitative excellence with warm qualitative cuteness, one does not combat deculturation through an act of acculturation but stays in the realm of deculturation. Cuteness is excellence reversed. Cuteness is everything that excellence isn't. Excellence is strong and cuteness is weak. The seductive cute is the opposite of the absolutely non-seductive excellence. Cuteness is overly concrete and excellence is abstract. Sianne Ngai has called cuteness the "erotization of powerlessness" (Ngai: 3). Conversely, excellence stands for the de-erotization of the powerful. Cuteness is submissive, transgressive, and feminine while excellence is egalitarian, politically correct, and ungendered.

Despite these contrasts, excellence remains just as cultureless as cuteness because it partakes in the same process of cultural neutralization that we encounter in neoliberal civilization. Content-wise, excellence does not signify much more than cuteness. "How cute!" and "How excellent!" are emotionally unidimensional "ah" reactions similar in punctuality and spontaneity.

Cuteness and excellence thrive particularly well in neoliberal environments. They are appropriate ideals in environments in which cultural values are frowned upon as premodern and anti-modern. Consequently, the only legitimate way to counter the values of excellence is to refer to expressions of cuteness. However, though cuteness is employed to make a decultured modern world more livable, those cat campaigns do not suggest concrete cultural values and expressions able to improve the situation.

The cute versus excellent confrontation can also be interpreted as an approval of more relativist standards. Cute relativism is a counteraction to absolute excellence. Lasch mentions the contemporary glorification of "amateurism, equating spectatorship with passivity, and deploring competition" and believes that "recent criticism of sport echoes the fake radicalism of counterculture" in sport (107). Amateurism thrives via the contempt for excellence as it proposes "to break down the 'elitist' distinction between players and spectators" (108). As amateurs contradict the absolute values of excellence, they are moving toward cuteness. By taking refuge in the relativism of the "merely adorable" they escape the competitiveness of neoliberal society. Elise Godart detects a similar pattern of self-cutification in the fact that more and more famous people are taking selfies (Godart: 110). Normally stars have their photos taken by photographers and only anonymous people need to take selfies. The selfying star steps out of the excellence machine and attempts to behave like the public. In a world of imperative excellence, it feels good not only to watch the cute, but to be cute. Cuteness is not just about cats; it's a matter of politics when "becoming cute" becomes a strategy of resistance. Self-cutification through (duck-faced) selfies, self-infantilization, enforced amateurism, and self-victimization represents an effective strategy to gain status.

The self-cutification reflex has serious social consequences as it has led to the mechanics of self-victimization in neoliberal societies. David Green describes modern society as a victim culture in which too many people desire to be classified as victims. The quest for preferential status is so massive that in Britain "the officially protected victim groups are no longer in the minority but add up to 73 per cent of the population" (Green: 1). Self-victimization is nothing other than "self-cutification" desperately searching to escape a culture determined by the imperatives of excellence. However, like excellence, it is driven by a good portion of narcissism. Green quotes the American lesbian feminist writer Tammy Bruce, "who began to see some of the flaws in the intellectual positions she had earlier defended, has shown how many activists were motivated by what she calls 'malignant narcissism'" (41–42). Further, Green draws a link with the increasing medicalization of life (23). When conditions of stress are diagnosed, one becomes a victim and can take advantage of the system. Of course, in excellence-driven modernity those conditions need to be overcome with expert therapy or counselling. Western societies are driven by an excellence-cuteness syndrome. In the past, cultures and religions could provide stable sources of transcendental, cosmic meaning. Today, all we have is excellence and cuteness. Green presents the state of self-victimization as a force undermining liberal culture. This is true but, paradoxically, self-victimization is also—at least indirectly—the *result* of liberal culture.

The excellent and the sublime

What is the contrary of the cute? Sianne Ngai designates in her *Our Aesthetic Categories: Zany, Cute, Interesting* (2012) the sublime as the direct opposite. However, the sublime is also related to the excellent and the remainder of this chapter will examine the relationships emerging from those constellations. Let's first look at the sublime. The sublime is an aesthetic category prominent in Western philosophy inspiring greatness or even a sort of sacredness that transcends mere beauty. It can be experienced in the form of violent storms or huge mountains. The sublime is not just beautiful. The distinction between the sublime and beauty is important for Western aesthetics and has been established in modern times by Burke and Kant. In sublime experiences, something unreachable and immeasurable instills astonishment, reverence or terror.

Sianne Ngai contrasts the sublime with the cute. This is correct, but I also see some similarities. We can be "taken away" by the cute as well as by the sublime. One reason is that both categories have affinities with kitsch. Both can be kitschified or both have a strong kitsch potential. This is clearest for the cute (which represents a major part of kitsch aesthetics), but it also applies to the sublime. In the nineteenth century, sublime landscapes were mass produced. Albert Bierstadt's paintings are good examples, but even the sophisticated paintings by Caspar David Friedrich could land as reproductions on the living room walls of petty-bourgeois German clients who exalted and kitschified this art's "romantic" feelings. This is surprising in the light of the fact that Kant opposes the sublime to kitsch-like qualities and even believes that the sublime can *combat* kitsch. Still, the sublime *does* have kitsch potential, and this is not only due to its "romantic" tendencies.

The links between the sublime and the kitsch are multiple. Edmund Burke associates the sublime with terror, and both Lyotard and Adorno believe that when sublime qualities are transposed into politics they will support fascism or terrorism. Lyotard describes the sublime as "an emotion, a violent emotion, close to unreason, which forces thought to the extremes of pleasure and displeasure, from joyous exaltation to terror" (Lyotard 1991: 228). For Adorno, the pathos-laden discourse of Napoleon is "a result of a disproportion between its high claims and its pedestrian reality" (Adorno 1997: 198) and is comical at best but also close to kitsch. For Adorno, the proximity between sublime and kitsch is determined by the history of the twentieth century, as he explains in his *Aesthetic Theory*. After fascism and Auschwitz, the idealist concept of the sublime has lost its actuality and validity and must be reconceptualized. After fascism and Auschwitz, the sublime will probably appear as kitsch.

It remains correct to oppose the cute to the sublime, but the above parallels and interferences are important, too. Indirectly, an amount of cuteness is attached to the sublime because the sublime is experienced by the "small" individual when being overpowered by the fearful forms of nature. Whenever there is extreme greatness there is also extreme smallness. Though it was probably not Friedrich's intention, in his painting *Monk by the Sea*, the monk can look cute.

The cute and the sublime are simultaneously similar and different. The paradox is reinforced when considering the link between the sublime and the excellent. From the beginning, the sublime contained the "genes" (metaphorically speaking) of the excellent because, etymologically, the sublime was predestined for a shift toward excellence. The Latin root of sublime means "to go beyond the limit" as the *limes* is the boundary, the limit, or the door threshold. *Excellere* means "to leave." It comes from the Latin *ex-* (out, beyond) and *celsus*, which means lofty, high, tall, and proud. The linguistic parallel with the sublime is thus very strong. We experience the sublime when we attempt to go beyond. What is beyond that mountain range? What is below the ocean? The sublime is transcendent, and excellence follows the same pattern. However, there is also an important difference: excellence is not driven by Eros. It is nonerotic and therefore more similar to another concept that emerged in romanticism: the interesting.

The interesting and the excellent are linked, though they can—like the other two terms—also be opposed to each other. What emerges is a square of oppositions enabling relationships between four terms (Graph 1).

The top axis features aesthetic concepts, whereas those on the bottom axis are scientific (in the broadest sense). However, all concepts *can* be used in the context of aesthetic judgments. I divide the square into four areas: the left side features decultured phenomena, and the right-side phenomena that depend on culture. It has been explained above why the cute and the excellent should be

Deculturation   Culture

CUTE   **SUBLIME**

EXCELLENT   **INTERESTING**

Deculturation   Culture

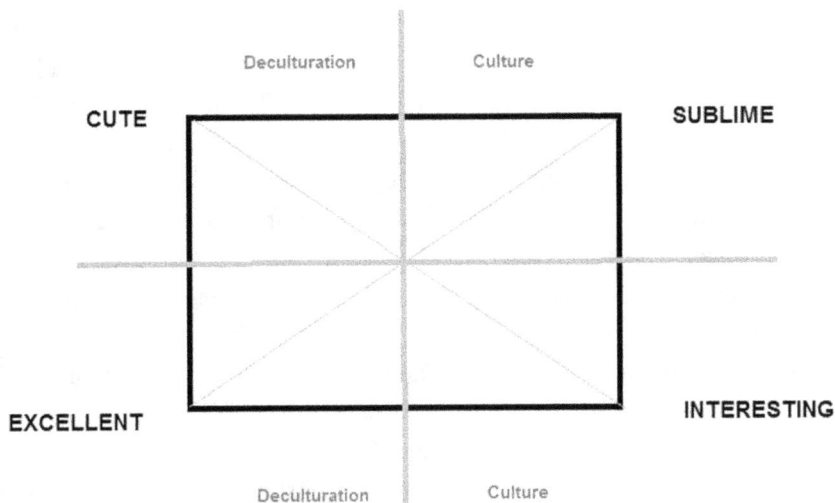

Graph 1 Deculturation, culture.

seen as decultured or noncultural notions. The sublime might not be an artistic notion in the first place (it is not used by Kant for the analysis of artistic practice), but it remains a cultural notion, even if only because Kant links it to dignity and virtue.

The cute and the sublime

The present considerations of the sublime follow partly from Kant's early writings on the sublime in which he explains that women predominantly have feelings for all that is beautiful and decorated whereas men have mostly feelings for the sublime (*Observations on the Feeling of the Beautiful and Sublime*, Section 3). The sublime can be experienced in the form of violent natural phenomena. Often the sublime is accompanied not only by awe and admiration, but also by discomfort or even fear. In spite of this, the sublime is thought of as a pleasurable experience. The pleasure results from aesthetic distanciation, which establishes another major difference with the cute. In experiences of the cute, the distance between the object and the subject are diminished.

The differences between the sublime and the cute are obvious. Great versus small, *unheimlich* versus familiar, male versus female, respect versus love, and so on. Cuteness effectuates a familiarization of objects and makes them more personal whereas the sublime moves even natural objects toward the abstractly metaphysical and infinite. The sublime sparks a melancholic longing whereas the cute is not melancholic but stands for instantaneous gratification. One of the reasons is that the sublime remains a cultural notion. The virtues of the sublime can only be understood through acts of acculturation. This does not mean that the sensation of *any* sublime quality is dependent on culture. In parallel with beauty, we find the sublime in nature *and* in culture. However, the virtuous sublime linked to respect is clearly on the cultural side. Kant believes that men have it, most probably because they are more educated whereas women (beauty) are closer to nature.

Still, there remains an ambiguity. The sublime and beauty are cultural and noncultural at the same time, which makes both relatively complex. Sublime things are not merely interesting (in terms of culture) but through its connection with nature, the sublime can also appear as an instinct or a drive that is not merely rational but supported by Eros. Here lies also the danger. Because the sublime is "half-natural," it can easily abandon culture and shift toward the deculturation area presented by the left side of the square (Graph 2). The sublime can be cultural but it is not cultural *by definition.* This means that whenever the sublime loses its cultural interest it slides down on the square toward the excellent. If it maintains its cultural input but merely abandons its erotic driving force, then it will turn into the more matter of fact interesting. And when the interesting becomes "merely interesting" and no longer operates in terms of cultural enrichment, it will approach the excellent.

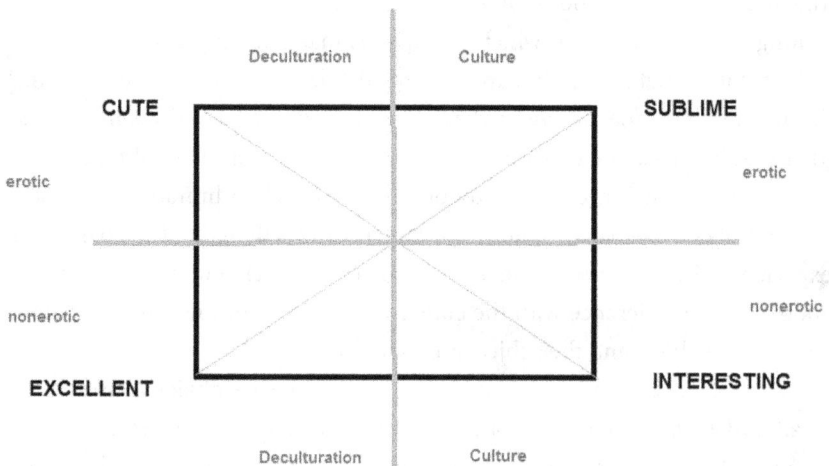

Graph 2 Erotic, non-erotic.

Contrary to the cute, the sublime is serious and has even moral connotations. Big things tend to overwhelm us, and for Kant the sublime is linked to respect (*Hochachtung*). Ethical matters can be judged from the point of view of the sublime: "Among moral qualities, true virtue alone is sublime" (Kant 1965: 22/ German: 215). This makes the sublime cultural. We need the sublime if we want to judge moral actions. The Platonic link between the good and the beauty is not sufficient because in beauty we do not find respect. Kant is convinced that beauty inspires "merely" love: "The sublime qualities inspire esteem, but beautiful ones inspire love" (1965: 18/211). Beauty comes closer to cuteness. Beauty can reach into the realm of politeness, but it has no impact on questions of respect.

Ngai's main project is to establish the sublime as the contrary of the cute. However, I believe that the excellent is, next to sublime, *the other* contrary of the cute. The sublime overwhelms us with enormity and vastness whereas cuteness "underwhelms" us. Cute is weak and sublime is strong. This finding is also significant for an analysis of excellence in neoliberal culture and I will show in this chapter that the postmodern concept of excellence is related to its Enlightenment ancestor, which is the concept of the sublime. Excellence is the decultured, de-eroticized version of the sublime. Excellence preserves the sublime's strength whereas the interesting plays the role of the weak counterpart of the excellent—just like the cute is the weak counterpart of the sublime. Seductive elements (that can be both weak and strong) are located on the upper axis; and non-seductive elements (weak ones as well as strong ones) are located on the bottom axis (Graph 3).

Though the cute and the sublime are opposed to each other, they have one thing in common: both function through seduction. This is very clear for the cute, but

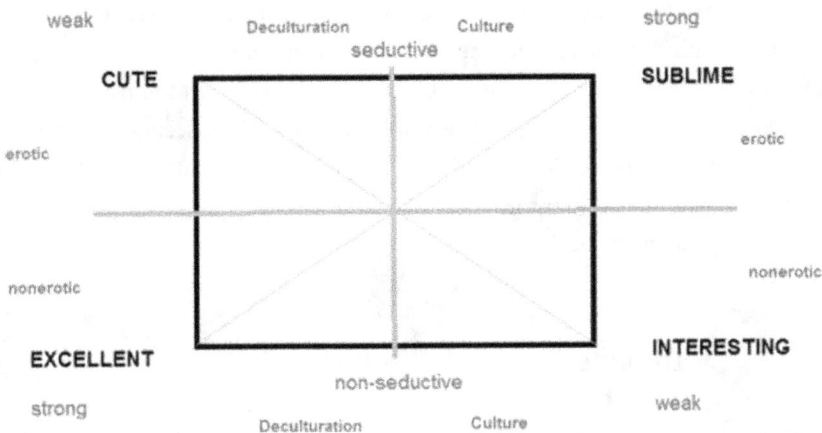

Graph 3 Seductive, non-seductive.

it also applies to the sublime. The importance of the Platonic Eros for the sublime (and even for the interesting) has already been addressed earlier in this chapter. The sublime is driven by an erotic force that pushes the contemplator to go beyond. What is beyond that mountain range? What is below the ocean? Experiencing the sublime always means to go beyond. This is why the sublime is not a subject of mere interest. We are not "interested" in the sublime object, but we are curious, and curiosity is linked to Eros. The sublime is therefore similar to cuteness, which seduces through Eros, sensuousness, warmness, and a promise of reward. On the other hand, a cute object will never seduce us because it appears as interesting.

In the age of Enlightenment, the sublime used to be—similar to excellence today—a substitute for God, able to provide a purpose for an otherwise meaningless life. Like excellence, the sublime is highly abstract. In the eighteenth century, like today, it was important to "ex-cel." The post-Copernican world was experienced as frighteningly limitless, but through aesthetization, the "beyond limits" could be equipped with meaning. The sublime served this purpose. Through the sublime, the rationalized universe became inhabitable again. The infinite universe with its eternal "beyond" was no longer meaningless and a symbol for the absurdity of the human condition. An aesthetically invested beyond became a limitless "sub-lime" and brought meaning to a senseless universe that was constantly going "beyond."

Today the world is limitless through globalization and virtual reality. C. G. Jung wrote that "our fearsome gods have only changed their name: they now rhyme with ism" (Jung 1967: 203). Therefore, in neoliberal culture, God is represented by excellentism. Both excellence and cuteness attempt to constitute values and meaning in a world that is constantly going "beyond." However, neither the compact image of cuteness nor the heroic narrative of sublime excellence can imbue life with *cultural* significance. All they can offer are empty, self-referential notions of excellence lacking concrete cultural references. In the past, cultures (just like religions) used to provide stable sources of transcendental, cosmic meaning. In the age of deculturation, cultures are less available and cannot provide transcendental, cosmic meaning. In a meaningless world, meaning is provided by cuteness and excellence.

The cute, the interesting, and the sublime

Ngai attributes much importance to the comparisons of the cute with the sublime as well as to comparisons of the cute and the interesting. I develop those comparisons further and complement them by introducing the element of the excellent. The confrontational character of the cute and the excellent has been explained above. What about the cute and the interesting? The interesting is not cute but cool by definition. At the end of the eighteenth century, Friedrich Schlegel, representative of Jena romanticism and major theorist of the German romantic school, created a philosophical aesthetics of the interesting. Schlegel insists on the component of detachment necessary for the experience of the interesting. Ngai even associates Schlegel's aesthetics of the interesting with the "coolly regulated aesthetics" promoted by the fictional character Adrian Leverkühn in Thomas Mann's *Doktor Faustus*. "*Kühn*" means "bold" in German, and it is also similar to "*kühl*" (cool). Leverkühn's cool detachment exemplifies modern scientific and aesthetic ideals.

The "cool interesting" is opposed to the Eros-driven cute, which remains close to intrinsically "warm" and overwhelming kitsch. But it is also opposed to the equally overwhelming sublime that makes us lose control; and losing control is incompatible with cool. Both the cute and the sublime are opposed to the interesting. We will not be "taken away" by the interesting but the interesting relies on a "relay between pleasure and cognition" (Ngai: 129), which means that the interesting is not even a purely aesthetic quality but shifts between the aesthetic and the non-aesthetic. In contrast, the cute does not appeal to cognitive faculties but merely to sentiments. The same is true (though to a lesser degree) for the sublime. Normally, the interesting is cool. Some reasons have been presented above, but there is still another explanation. The existence of the interesting depends on the rules of probability, which create a link with risk taking. Mikhail Epstein explains that things are more interesting when they are less probable (Epstein: 81). When a fact is highly unlikely but still possible, we will find it interesting. Of course, there must be a reasonable chance that the interesting *is* true. Should it turn out to be false, then the fact immediately becomes uninteresting; and the interesting factor increases when the probability is low though still possible. This means that the interesting has a coolness factor. Betting on the less probable is cool—on the condition that I win. Risk taking is cool by definition—on the condition that I win. The more unlikely the fact, the cooler it becomes. When the highly unlikely fact turns out to be wrong after investigation, then the gambler is "uncool."

The interesting seduces, but only in a very indirect way *through coolness* whereas the cute and the sublime follow direct, "hot" principles of seduction. The interesting is determined by irony, which was particularly important in romanticism. The interesting is incompatible with "hot" expressions such as the cute and the sublime.

I derive the present hot-cool distinction from Marshal McLuhan's "hot and cool" frame that the sociologist developed in the early 1960s in the context of media studies. According to McLuhan, "cool media" display detached objectivity and disinterestedness while "hot media" favor analytical precision, quantitative analysis, and sequential ordering. Cool media "leave the transmitted information open to interpretation or even partly unexplained" (McLuhan 1964: 37). Can the interesting be kitschified? Yes, in which case it will become excellent. This process will be explained below.

Aesthetics of the non-beautiful

Before continuing the comparison of cute, excellent, interesting, and sublime, it is necessary to specify the relationship that this study maintains with Ngai's study of zany, cute, and interesting. Ngai investigates three "non-beautiful" aesthetic concepts, all of which are different from the sublime. Her perspective is not comparative, but aims at elucidating those under-investigated aesthetic notions. My approach is different. By excluding the zany and by adding the excellent and the sublime, I create a symmetry. Just like zany, cute, and interesting, the sublime is different from the beautiful. In parallel with Ngai's approach, I contrast the sublime with the cute. However, the excellent is not an aesthetic, but *primarily* an ethical concept (the sublime is also ethical but not primarily so). By introducing the excellent into this discussion, the analysis no longer revolves exclusively around aesthetic questions but describes more general developments in modern civilization. Still, the excellent is not a mere intruder. Strictly speaking, the interesting is not an aesthetic concept either, but it has been turned into an aesthetic quality in romanticism that would be consolidated later in modernity.

The sublime is contradictory because it refers to nature but is extensively used in the realm of ethics. In *Observations* Kant explains that true virtue is achieved when we raise the feeling of humanity's beauty and dignity to a principle. One can be "sublimely virtuous." The sublime thus settles between culture and nonculture, which explains the dynamic behavior it can adopt on the square. Most important, it can shift from right to left and become excellent.

Kant, in all his descriptions of the sublime, draws on nature more than on art. Still the sublime is linked to art, and this to an increasing degree in post-Kantian philosophy. For Hegel, the sublime is an absolute idea that "places itself above nature" (sich über Natur erhebt) as well as above the "determinedness of appearances" (die Bestimmtheit der Erscheinungen) (Hegel 1986: 394). Hegel substantializes the Kantian sublime by turning it into a property of art, a development that continued so that Lyotard could write that "for the last century, the arts have not had the beautiful as their main concern, but something that has to do with the sublime" (Lyotard 1991b: 135). However, the sublime is used in the context of art not because it signifies natural beauty. The sublime is a *cultural* phenomenon that can be experienced in *nature* in moral terms in the form of powerlessness that we feel when facing the forces of nature. For all those reasons the sublime appears on the graph in the "culture" half.

Each of the two fields on the graph can be divided further into two parts: the erotic and the nonerotic (Graph 4). As explained above, the expressions on the upper half depend on an erotic impulse mainly because they are able to seduce. The cute and the sublime seduce whereas the excellent and the interesting are nonerotic. The mentioned hot-cool distinction (vaguely derived from McLuhan's media theory) applies in this context.

There is a hot-cool bipartition (upper versus lower axis), but hot and cool can be expressed in both personal and impersonal ways. This means that the hot/cool distinction does not overlap with the personal/impersonal distinction (Graph 5). There is the hot-personal (cute) and the hot-impersonal (sublime) as well as the cool-impersonal (excellent) and the cool-personal (interesting).

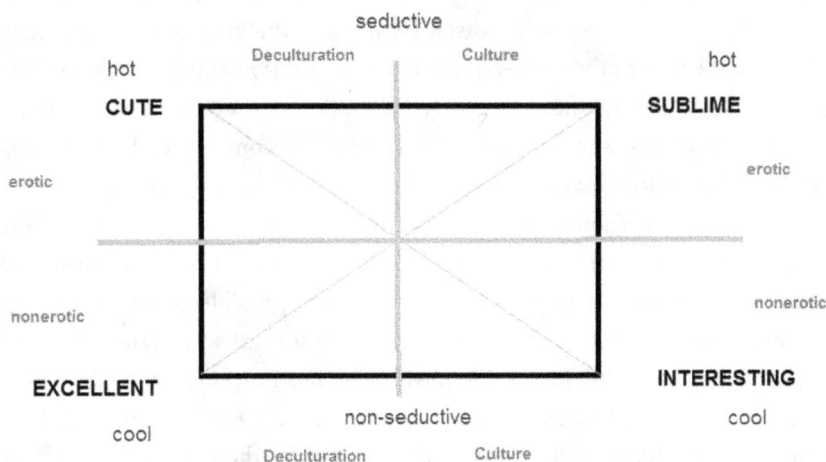

Graph 4 Hot, cool.

personal   Deculturation   Culture   impersonal

CUTE   **SUBLIME**

erotic   erotic

nonerotic   nonerotic

EXCELLENT   **INTERESTING**

impersonal   personal

Deculturation   Culture

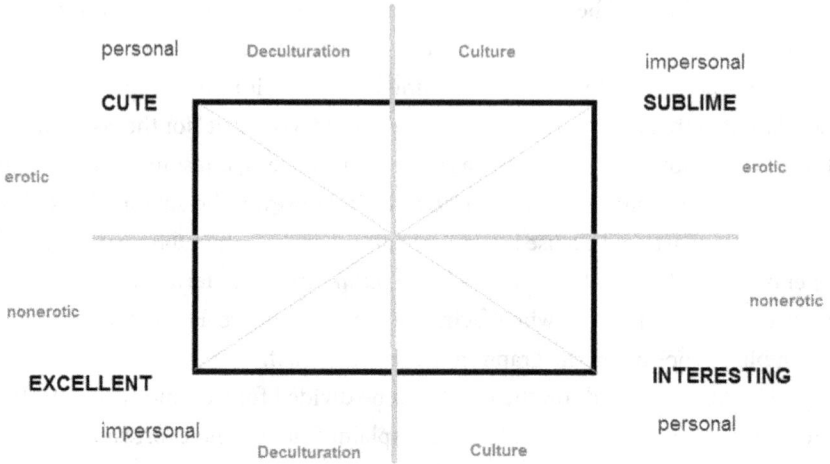

Graph 5 Personal, impersonal.

Kitsch

The square is dynamic. All four concepts can be defined in purist ways as absolute oppositions; however, they also constantly attract each other. All concepts can move toward each other and create hybrids. The main purpose of this chapter is to show how the concepts on the right side can get corrupted by those on the left side. However, the right-left shift is not the only possible corruption. Erotic elements can become nonerotic and vice versa. The square is dynamic because all four notions have one thing in common: they maintain some sort of relationship with kitsch (Graph 6). The cute and the excellent, which are the decultured concepts given to exaggeration and particularization, are close to kitsch by nature. However, the other two concepts, the cultural ones, can become kitsch, too. The interesting will become kitsch by becoming narcissistically self-reflexive and interesting "as such." In that case it approaches the excellent. The sublime can be kitschified through an emphasis on the sentimental (romantic) or in ways that have been pointed out by Adorno and Lyotard (see above). Even Kant was aware of the possible corruption of the sublime through kitsch. The sublime can move toward what Kant calls "the magnificent" (1965: 29/German: 64), which is "*das Prächtige*" in German and comes relatively close to our modern notion of kitsch. For Kant, the *Prächtige* is only a gloss (*Schimmer*) of sublimity, which hides the inner content of the object or the person. It enforces the superficial attributes of the sublime but

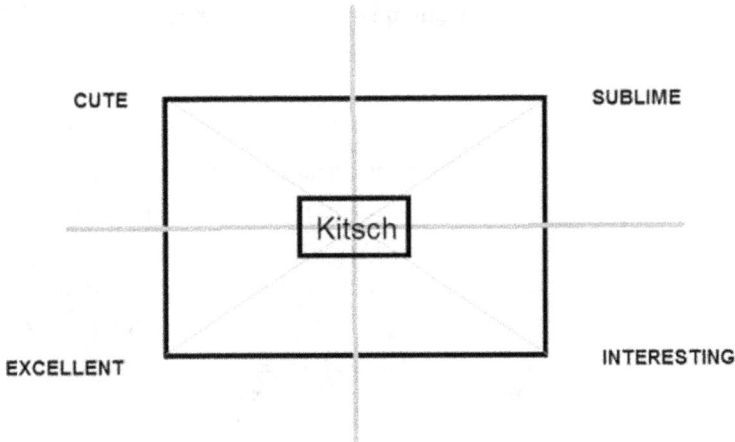

Graph 6 Kitsch.

neglects the object's or person's moral (or cultural) significations. Kant is very outspoken about this boastful aesthetic expression explaining that

> just as an edifice makes just as noble an impression by means of a stucco coating that represents carved stones, as if it were really made from that, and tacked-on cornices and pilasters give the idea of solidity although they have little bearing and support nothing, in the same way do alloyed virtues, tinsel of wisdom, and painted merit also glisten. (1965: 29–30/German: 223)

The interesting and the excellent

In Ngai's book, the interesting is mostly understood in the sense laid down by Schlegel, as the "merely interesting." Schlegel first criticized and later (ironically) defended the interesting. Being first a purist and opposed to the interesting as a sort of modern fad, he later reevaluated his judgment under the influence of Kant's aesthetic relativism. In his *Fragmente*, Schlegel develops the idea of "'romantische Poesie' out of the earlier concept of 'interessante' literature, leaving behind his purist tendencies and embracing a non-objective, relativist aesthetic" (Wheeler 1988: 177; see also Ngai 125). We observe a shift from the individual to the general as Schlegel celebrates "Die romantische Poesie" as a "progressive Universalpoesie" (1986/1991: Fragment 116).

The excellent becomes kitsch because it trivializes the interesting. Mikhail Epstein describes this process as a "thought that relies solely on facts without rising above them": "in scientific inquiry, thought that resists facts and despises evidence is as trivial and boring as thought that relies solely on facts without rising above them. The interesting is what comes in between two mutually exclusive and equally indispensable aspects of the phenomenon" (Epstein: 84). First, the excellent and the interesting are similar because they are cool and more or less scientifically determined concepts maintaining contradictory relationships with the concepts located on the upper axis. However, the excellent and the interesting mediate their scientific characters in different ways. The excellent likes regular and general expressions, while the interesting is irregular, individual, eclectic, and ambivalent. Schlegel (in his earlier phase) sees in romantic poetry "nothing but interesting individuality" (2001: 20/220), enchaining content after content without caring about the general form. Of course, Schlegel has in mind the "merely interesting," but the irregular, individual, eclectic, and ambivalent *can* also be interesting in a positive sense.

Ngai is thus right when defining the interesting as the antipode of the cute. However, cuteness has still another opposite that must be considered as the decultured version of the interesting: excellence. Excellence pretends to be interesting, but its operational mode is symmetrically opposed. The excellent has no cultural content, but it exalts the quantitative, general form. Excellence is the decultured version of the interesting, which makes it *not* interesting. Schlegel himself establishes in his *Fragmente* a link between the interesting and the excellent (*das Ausgezeichnete*) by half critiquing and half praising—in an ironical fashion—the new aesthetics of the interesting: "If you happen to be an interesting philosophical phenomenon and an excellent [ausgezeichneter] writer as well, then you can be quite sure of gaining a reputation as a great philosopher. Often one gets it even without the latter prerequisite" (Fragment 343).

The shift of the interesting toward the excellent can be analyzed as follows: first, the interesting decultures itself by becoming "merely interesting" in the earlier Schlegelian relativistic sense. Subsequently, it will be taken over by excellence. Excellence, which conceives of itself as a remedy of relativism, establishes general, scientific, absolute truths. This does not mean that excellence has any cultural truths to offer. In reality, it is just another symptom of postmodern deculturation unable to reestablish truth in the form of cultural contents. Both excellence and the "merely interesting" pretend—in a narcissistic fashion—to be interesting simply because they are supposed to be interesting—which means that they are not interesting.

The excellent can also be seen as the cutified version of the interesting. There is a parallel between the excellent and the cute because both are inward-oriented and are narcissistic whereas the interesting and the sublime are outward-oriented. Both the sublime and the interesting (when it is not the *merely* interesting) move on toward new horizons. When the interesting turns inward and becomes narcissistic, it approaches the excellent. Both the cute and the excellent concentrate on details and are interested only in themselves (see Graph 7).

Excellence will never be interesting, cool, or cultured. The "interestingly excellent" is like the celebrity who is famous for being famous. She is not famous because she has enriched the world's cultural life with concrete cultural contributions. Her celebrity is decultured and refers to itself as the only source of celebrity. Excellence is similar to the selfie which might provide a momentary sense of identity in a labyrinthic world of the virtual and the inauthentic. However, though the selfie-ing self desires identity, the selfie will normally not anchor the self in a concrete cultural context. Instead, the picture offers a moment of glowing brilliance inside the formless space of virtual reality and it will most probably disappear in this virtual reality as quickly as it had appeared. The selfie only gives the semblance of an identity without providing concrete *cultural* impacts or references from which the subject or the subject's environment could benefit. The selfie's self remains as fluent as the internet itself, which is why Godart calls the selfie a "new form of hybrid subjectivity" settling between a real subject and its internet avatar. As a "virtual subjectivity" it is a subjectivity without subject (Godart: 73), which establishes a parallel with excellence. Excellence, too, is suspended in an "in-between" as it is unable to strive toward

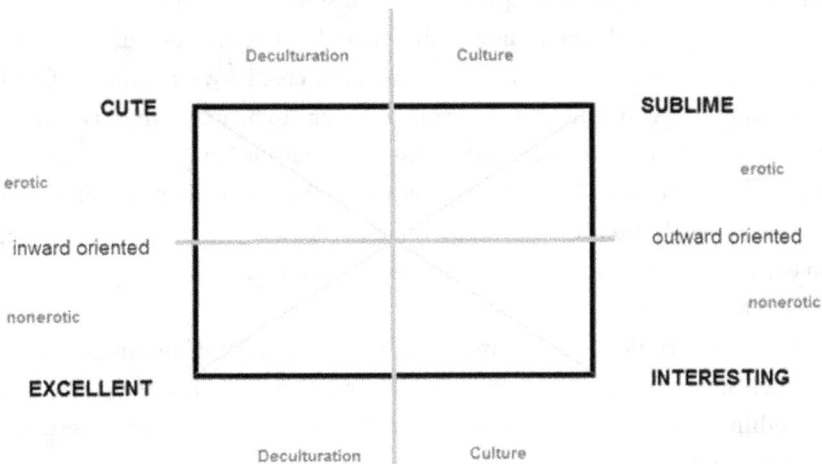

Graph 7 Inward oriented, outward oriented.

concrete cultural values such as identity or the beautiful. Excellence avoids those values (see Chapter 1).

As mentioned, in Ngai's book, the interesting is mostly understood in the sense laid down by Schlegel, as the "merely interesting." In some way, this is misleading because the interesting adopted features of the "merely interesting" only at a later stage. Seeing the interesting as the "merely interesting" creates a partial overlap of the interesting with the excellent. Epstein finds that "while in the past a literary or scholarly work was generally valued for its truthfulness and beauty, usefulness and instructiveness, in the twentieth and twenty-first centuries it has been a work's primary evaluation as interesting that paves the way for any further evaluation, including critical analysis" (Epstein: 75). What Epstein describes is the foundation of excellence culture. "Interestism" is for Epstein the "contortion of the interesting, a quick discharge of its resources, an intellectual coquetry, a spasm" (85). This is also a good description of "excellentism."

In spite of all this, the "merely interesting" is not part of the *intrinsic* definition of the term "interesting"; it is rather due to a perversion of the term's original meaning. The shift from the interesting to the excellent signifies a shift from culture to deculturation. Initially, the fact of "being interested in" had to be directed toward a concrete content. The word "interesting" comes from the Latin *interesse*, which means "to differ" or "to be important" and it is composed of *inter* (between) and *esse* (to be). *Inter-esse* denotes the process emerging between an interesting object and a subject trying to approach this object. An interest *in* exists only as long as there is a final object that the subject is interested in. One cannot be just interested, just like an object cannot be just interesting. The object must be interesting with regard to something that goes beyond the state of being "merely interesting." I find a book interesting because it teaches me about human nature, cultural environments, creativity, etc. I do not find it interesting simply because it is interesting. When "to be interesting" is used on its own, or when "to be interested" is used without the "in," the interest is not directed at a "beyond" but at the "in between" (the *inter*). Then the interesting becomes "merely interesting." Interest is then no longer a means for approaching an object, but the interest has become an end in itself. The interesting has moved toward the excellent.

By narcissistically looking at itself, the "merely interesting" becomes a matter of interest in the form of excellence. The excellent, too, is not excellent *for* something, but it represents an end in itself. Normally, "interesting questions" are questions that have some importance. Via the "inter" (between) we move toward those important matters because we believe that the knowledge we obtain when answering those questions is beneficial *for something*. In a Platonic sense, the acquisition and transmissions of knowledge is supposed to have an "erotic" basis because we are attracted. Though the interesting—as opposed to the curious and the sublime—is not erotic, we still need some Platonic "love" for the object that will be transmitted through a specifically affective relationship with the person who arouses this interest (in Plato's dialogues it is Socrates). In the case of the interesting this love is not erotic (as it is in the case of the cute and the sublime), but it becomes manifest in the form of fascination. Fascination is unique to the sublime and the interesting and it does not occur in the cute and the excellent. The interesting can have a "fascinating" attraction similar to what we experience in the sublime (though to a lesser degree). For Kant, the sublime is more fascinating (*bezaubernd*) than the beautiful: "All emotions (Rührungen) of the sublime are more enchanting (bezaubernd) than the deceptive charms of the beautiful" (1965: 27/1764: 220). The interesting resembles the sublime in this respect; as Epstein writes: "The interesting usually sparks and glimmers rather than shines brightly and evenly" (85). The excellent and the cute do not spark and glimmer but they shine so brightly that it is impossible to be fascinated. Therefore, they are closer to kitsch. The fascination attached to the interesting and the sublime is related to the interplay of the individual and the general. In the sublime, the contrast between the small contemplator and the overwhelming mountain, or between what used to be small, and what is big now, is fascinating. The interesting (if it is not the "merely interesting") establishes similar relationships between individual facts and statements about general rules: "How is it possible that within this larger context a certain particular thing can arise?" Those large-small relationships are fascinating. The excellent and the cute are not fascinating because they are either overly particular (cute) or overly general and universal (excellent). Graph 8 shows those relationships.

At the end of the eighteenth century, Schlegel embraces a relativist philosophy of the interesting. In his earlier work *On the Study of Greek Poetry*, he was still very critical of this new aesthetics. In the preface (not translated) to the book, he describes the interesting as an intermediary stage, which should only have temporary validity ("provisorische Gültigkeit," 1797: 214). We should "go through" the interesting on our way to the knowledge. The "merely interesting" that Schlegel attacks in modern poetry neglects this objective. It has either "not attained the goal towards which it is striving" or "its striving has no established goal, its development no specific direction, the sum of its history (Masse ihrer Geschichte) no regular continuity, the whole no unity" (2001: 17/1797: 216).

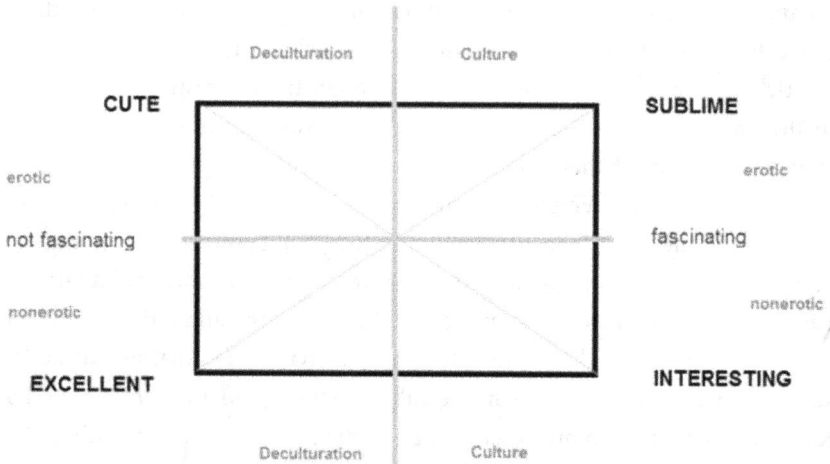

Graph 8 Fascinating, not fascinating.

Schlegel's descriptions of naive poetry overlap with what we would today describe as kitsch. It knows no striving, it aims at no beyond. However, it does not need to be kitsch, but it can also be "merely interesting."

The sublime is not "merely" interesting; it also maintains a link with the erotic fascination of beauty. Schlegel speaks of the "restless, insatiable striving after something new, piquant, and striking despite which, however, longing persists unappeased" (24/227). The sublime is seductive and fascinating while the cute is seductive but not fascinating. Therefore, those two terms can be opposed to those on the lower axis: the excellent is neither seductive nor fascinating and the interesting is not seductive but still fascinating.

Another problem is that in our contemporary world, knowledge has been reduced to information, which can even be transmitted by machines or in other highly impersonal ways. Platonic eroticism is no longer needed. This, too, contributes to the culture of excellence. By denying the affective, human, and *cultural* basis of knowledge, knowledge ceases being an intermediary process leading to concrete values. Interests are no longer motivated through culture. As a matter of fact, a lot of interests will never arise in the first place. The person who reads Heraclitus' sentence "You cannot step twice into the same river" will find this statement only interesting when reflecting it against a certain cultural and philosophical background. The connections that this statement *could* have with certain insights must be guessed beforehand. In a culturally dull world this statement will be perceived as dull and uninteresting.

Another factor impacting the evolution from the interesting to the excellent is capitalism. Capitalism and the rise of a liberal economy enabled a flagrant tautology. Already in early capitalism, profits ceased being exclusively the results of production. As capitalism evolved, profits and benefits became more and more dependent on speculation, which means that the abstract "interest" became more important than the concrete product. Now it became possible to say "I am interested in the interest," which makes no sense if we consider the original meaning of interesting. The economy became more liberal in the sense of "rational" as it spelled out human motivations as interests. Now economics could lift itself up on the same scientific level as Newtonian physics. As a result, humans became social atoms motivated by interests.

The shift of the interesting toward the decultured "merely interesting" or even toward excellence was preprogrammed by the notion's early roots in financial culture. Further, in parallel with this "virtualization" of interest, aggressive marketing methods valuing the "merely interesting" became part of modernity. Packaging and the visually enhanced wrapping became more important than the content. These marketing methods have been accepted as normal in modern capitalism and they apply not only to merchandises, but also to people. Lasch points out that real skills that were still valued in the periods of preindustrialization and industrialization are no longer primordial; today, "men and women alike have to project an attractive image and to become simultaneously role players and connoisseurs of their own performance" (Lasch: 78). The legitimization of a lack of substance emphasizing the "interesting" wrapping more than the "virtuous" content has brought about the "bullshit culture" whose philosophical examination Harry Frankfurt began in the 1980s. Frankfurt's analysis of bullshit is almost identical with Epstein's analysis of the interesting when Epstein writes: "The interesting is constituted not merely in opposition to truth, after all, but in its juxtaposition of the truthful and trustworthy with the improbable and wondrous" (78).

Modern marketing has imported another element from Schlegel's romantic aesthetic of the interesting: detachment. The problem is that in modern marketing this detachment is often artificially produced by imposing upon items a pseudo-scientific air of neutrality. The interesting is cool, and we should incorporate scientific detachment into commercial items if we want them to be interesting. More than ever the interesting comes close to Frankfurt's "bullshit." Pseudo-scientific detachment is common not only in retail, but also in the administration. Lasch writes about the language that "surrounds the claims of administrators and advertisers alike with an aura of scientific detachment. More important, it is calculatedly obscure and unintelligible-qualities that commend it to a public that feels informed in proportion as it is befuddled" (Lasch: 77).

Romantic artists were the first to legitimate the "merely interesting." In romanticism, the interesting adopted the superfluous, detached meaning that Schlegel first criticized and then theorized. Romanticism has also been held accountable for the invention of kitsch (see Calinescu 237–40 and Broch: 56). Like kitsch, the "merely interesting" strangely connects with our postmodern situation: the relativism resulting from Schlegel's defense of the interesting (which Schlegel himself sees as "a general store of aesthetics" ["ein ästhetischer Kramladen"] 20/221) opened the door to a loss of truth that excellence culture would later try to retrieve in its own decultured fashion. When Deleuze and Guattari declare in 1991 in their *What Is Philosophy* under Kuhnian influence that "philosophy does not consist in knowing and is not inspired by truth [but] it is categories like Interesting, Remarkable, or Important that determine success or failure" (1994: 82), there are reasons to conclude that this celebrated "freedom from truth" has opened the doors to Frankfurt's world full of bullshit. Epstein is right in dismissing the French philosophers' liberal attitude as "overly romantic [and] as narrow, in its own way, [just] as the rationalist conception of truth" (Epstein: 78).

The overly rationalistic (or better pseudo-rationalistic) conception of truth would soon become the main feature of excellence culture. In principle, excellence is a weapon invented to fight Deleuze's and Guattari's relativist "Interesting, Remarkable, or Important" by constructing absolute, scientific values. However, what the "merely interesting" as well as excellence would really need in order to establish truth is a cultural foundation providing real values based on impersonated identities.

Schlegel, when establishing the interesting as an artistic style, effectuates a shift from the interesting to the excellent, which becomes most obvious when he advocates a rapprochement between art and science: "The more poetry becomes a science the more it also becomes art" (Fragment 255). Later ideologists of excellence and champions of evaluations developed this rapprochement in the most consistent fashion. The excellent is the interesting, minus some important features. According to Epstein (78), the interesting is used by the rational mind to come to terms with probabilities that we encounter in real life. The interesting can bridge a gap between reason and surprise. However, in reality, the interesting should not entirely rationalize the improbable, but rather extend the limits of rationality. There should always be the remainder of a risk, otherwise the interesting ceases being cool. In the culture of excellence, the risk factor is lost together with fascination, eroticism, and outward-oriented interest. In the worst case, everything is calculated through algorithms.

Ngai states that the interesting establishes a relationship between individuation and standardization or between existence and doctrine (Ngai: 7). It has been said above that the interplay of the individual and the general provides the particular "fascinating" input. Ngai also holds that the interesting mediates between cognition and pleasure and accomplishes what the other three terms on the square are unable to do. This shows that the interesting and the sublime have unique functions as they unite qualities that appear as isolated next to the other two terms (Graph 9).

As long as the object or the situation are found interesting, the relationship between pleasure and cognition is determined by a tension. However, when the interesting becomes excellent, the tension is sublated and everything will follow the rules of standardization. In excellence culture, individuation is impossible. Surprises are not permitted because facts are no longer probable but necessary (calculated by algorithms). In excellence culture, the uncertainty and the eclecticism that Schlegel designates as necessary ingredients of the interesting are neutralized. Excellence culture describes the world in terms of certainty and regularity.

Excessive standardization and the loss of individuation entail a loss of playfulness (see Graph 10). Irony, which was so important for romantics like

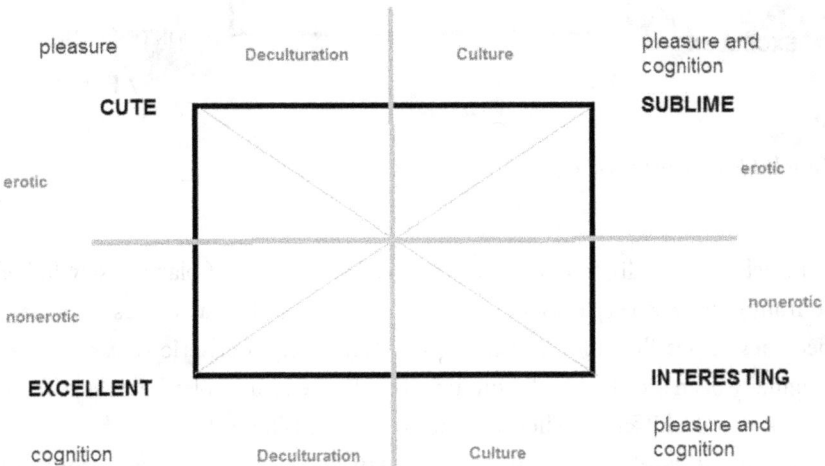

Graph 9 Cognition and pleasure.

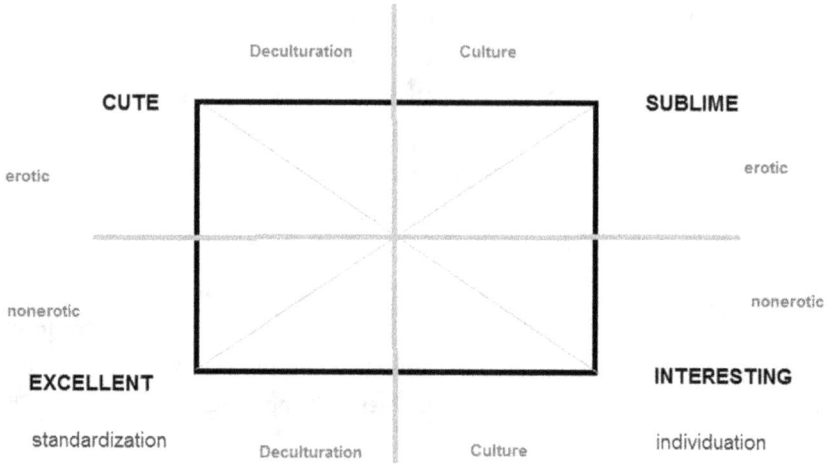

Graph 10 Standardization and individuation.

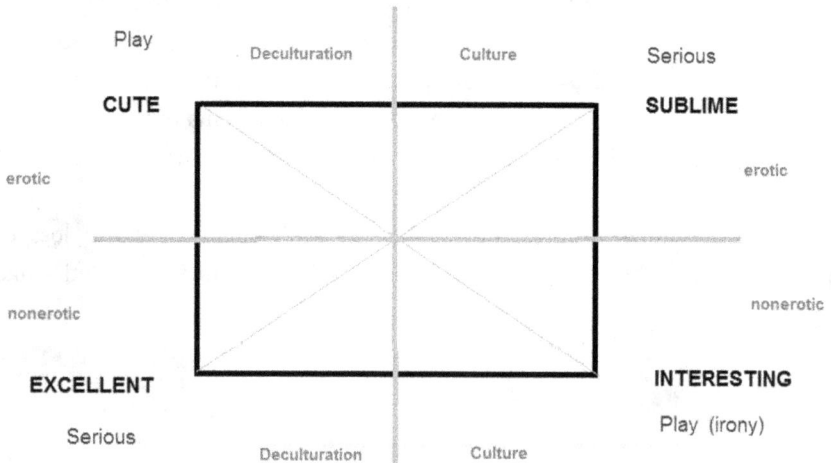

Graph 11 Seriousness and play.

Schlegel and Novalis, becomes impossible. The element of play (closely linked to irony) that was very present in the romantic interesting as well as in the cute becomes impossible, too. Excellence relies on the kind of seriousness that had originally been attached to the sublime. Excellence refuses play because it wants authority. Like kitsch, excellence wants to impress (Graph 11).

The negation of play overlaps with pretentions of absoluteness that we find in excellence but also in the sublime (from the Kantian moral sublime to the relative   Deculturation   Culture   absolute

CUTE   **SUBLIME**

erotic   erotic

nonerotic   nonerotic

EXCELLENT   **INTERESTING**

absolute   relative

            Deculturation   Culture

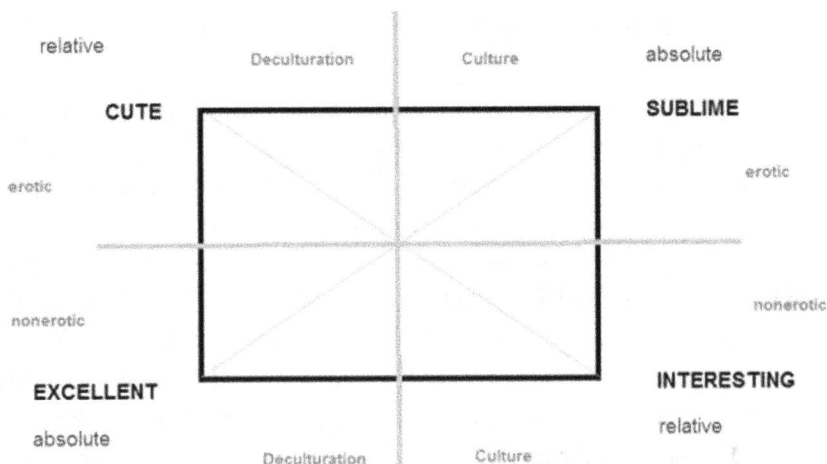

Graph 12 Absolute, relative.

"totalitarian" sublime used in propaganda). Excellence culture rationalizes the postmodern relativism initiated by Schlegel's concept of the interesting and advertises itself as absolute. Therefore, it can consider itself as sublime. In other words, excellence reissues the ironic interesting in the form of a pseudo-scientific concept of absolute truth. It can do so because excellence is the "merely interesting" without cultural content (Graph 12).

The cute and the interesting

The relationships between the cute and the interesting have been addressed above. Normally, the terms are diametrically opposed and apparently incompatible. The "cool interesting" is opposed to the Eros-driven cute. The cute appeals merely to sentiments and not to cognitive faculties like the interesting. The interesting seduces, whereas the cute and the sublime follow direct, "hot" principles of seduction. The oppositions of the cute and the interesting are multiple and will be addressed in the remainder of this chapter: inward versus outward, fascinating versus not fascinating, trivial versus important, available versus fleeting, whole versus part, pure versus diverse. However, there are also similarities between the cute and the interesting. Both are relative, and both have a positive attitude toward play. Further, both are personal, though the cute is hot-personal whereas the interesting cool-personal.

The interesting, the cute, and the excellent

Vice versa, "to be interesting" does not have particularly erotic connotations. The interesting expresses a matter-of-fact attraction. Freud distinguishes in his essay "The Libido Theory and Narcism" (in Freud 1920) between libido and interest, explaining that interest is directed toward certain facts or events in a non-libidinal way. Only the "energy which the ego directed towards the object of its sexual striving" can be called libido whereas all others, "which proceeded from the instincts of self-preservation," are called interest (361). Ngai adds that "interest is less eroticized than its feminized cousin curiosity" and supports this with Hans Blumenberg's characterization of curiosity as the "libido of theory" (Ngai: 131). Interest is directed toward certain facts or events. However, those facts and events need to be cultural in the largest sense. The "really interesting" will never be interesting "as such" but must refer to some sort of content. That's what distinguishes the interesting from the cute and the excellent. The cute kitten does not attract us because of its cultural connotations; we simply like it because it is cute. For the same reason people go for excellence. Excellence is desirable simply because it is excellent.

The interesting, the sublime, and the cute

The sublime is not detached from the beautiful, but shares with the beautiful a similarly "erotic" attraction. Jacques Derrida notes:

> One can hardly speak of an opposition between the beautiful and the sublime. An opposition could only arise between two determinate objects, having their contours, their edges, their finitude. But if the difference between the beautiful and the sublime does not amount to an opposition, it is precisely because the presence of a limit is what gives form to the beautiful. The sublime is to be found, for its part, in an "object without form" and the "without-limit" is "represented" in it or on the occasion of it, and yet gives the totality of the without-limit to be thought. Thus the beautiful seems to present an indeterminate concept of the understanding, the sublime an indeterminate concept of reason. (Derrida 1987: 127)

The interesting, if we do not see it as the "merely interesting" but as a subject of interest directed toward something concrete, is cultural, too. Unlike the cute and the excellent, the interesting is not merely formal and emptied of cultural contents. However, the interesting does not have the erotic function that is attributed to the sublime (or much less of it). The sublime depends on the Platonic Eros that pushes us forward toward the mysterious unknown. Freud defined "sublimation" as the process of deflecting sexual instincts into cultural achievements or at least into acts of higher social valuation. The driving forces of those acts are sexual instincts, which become "sublimated" under the influence of civilization. This establishes a connection between the sublime and the erotic, a connection that the interesting does not have. An "interesting girl" is not primarily interesting because of her erotic attributes but because of certain cultural connotations. A "cute girl" has completely different connotations.

Trivial versus important

The large-small dichotomy has been explained above with regard to the sublime and cuteness. The same dichotomy can be applied to the interesting and the excellent. Interesting questions become *more interesting* when they are "big questions" while excellence tends to deal with trivia. As excellence is quantity driven, it collects data and goes more and more into details. Evaluations are detailed, and the entire apparatus of the increasingly excellence-oriented human sciences develops toward empiricist particularization. Technical details become more important than a holistic *Bildung*. Administrators have little use for *general* education. The whole idea of the generalist is alien to the defender of excellence and neoliberal economies rarely finance generalist projects but work toward professional compartmentalization. The neoliberal economy, from which excellence emerges, prefers the expert and the specialist. One result is trivialization. Graph 13 shows how the square can be divided into a "trivial" and an "important" area.

Though cuteness is excellence reversed, both share the same preference for the trivial. The excellent becomes kitsch because it trivializes the interesting. For Ngai, the zany, the interesting, and the cute are trivial because, in contrast to the "moral and theological resonances of the beautiful and the sublime and the disgusting," zany, interesting, and cute do not express big ideas (Ngai: 18). Excellence might come along in the form of "big ideas"; still it is trivial because it is culturally empty. The big ambitions of universities' "Centers of Excellence" are not supposed to be pursued as projects of acculturation. Excellence

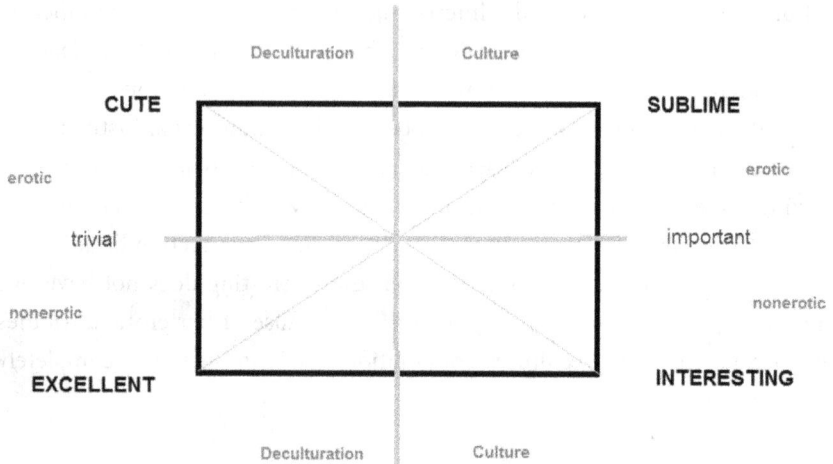

Graph 13 Trivial and important.

projects tend to refer to technicalities. No "erotic" impulses are supposed to lead toward an improvement of culture. Instead excellence concentrates on information and minimal differences between bits of information and insists on scientific precision in cases where the appreciation of bigger cultural ideas would be more inspiring. This deficiency is particularly obvious in the human sciences. The wonderment or, as Epstein says, the fact to "be puzzled by ourselves, to experience something in ourselves that is, as yet, unknown and undiscovered" (Epstein: 87) is still present in the interesting (and much more in the sublime), but it cannot be found in excellence. Excellence establishes certitude and a belief in absolute truths that exclude all wonderment. Earlier educative philosophies had visions rooted in traditions and cultures. Excellence has no real vision, first, because it has no culture from which it can derive visions; second, because excellence is inappropriate to apprehend any totalities. Lasch explains how the loss of visions coincides with the above-described "information glut, with the recovery of the past by specialists, and with an unprecedented explosion of knowledge" (Lasch: 151). Knowledge is no longer seen as a big project leading to a well-rounded *Bildung*, but knowledge is split into small bits of information. Lasch cites the example of psychology. Freud tried to answer big questions that were often already discussed in ancient myths, but psychology moved "from the challenge of Freud into the measurement of trivia" (xiv). The world of excellence is dominated by specialists specializing in "special" questions. Educational, cultural, and even scientific ideals cannot be maintained. Lasch attributes the particularization to political changes in the Western world: "After the political turmoil of the sixties, Americans have retreated to purely personal preoccupations" (4). The fascination with the particular is directed at the own self, which Lasch noticed long before the invention of selfies. The culture of psychic self-improvement launched in the 1960s duplicates this inward-turned tendency: "Getting in touch with their feelings, eating health food, taking lessons in ballet or belly-dancing, immersing themselves in the wisdom of the East, jogging, learning how to 'relate' . . ." (4). Here we also approach kitsch. The fascination with the particular can become pathological, in which case we speak of narcissism. Or it can become a neurotic compulsion, some idée fixe, or a "magnificent obsession" (99).

Of course, kitschification is not limited to the level of the individual. Universalist kitsch exists, too, which brings us to the "sudden blazing" Lyotard speaks of when describing the sublime (Lyotard: 55). This too exists in modern civilization. The conquest of nature and the search for new frontiers that Lasch mentions as another manifestation of narcissism culture (25) is a kitschified version of sublime. However, it remains strongly linked to its particularistic counterpart because the aim of such universalist striving is self-fulfillment.

The above considerations show that the excellent can look cute when it deals with the small and the trivial. The difference with the cute is that it has a pretention toward the absolute and wholeness. The excellent does not want to be "merely interesting" and submit to relativism. Though the "merely excellent" shares much with the "merely interesting," the propagator of excellence will always insist that she has access to absolute and "total" truths. Again, there is an overlap with the cute. While we can catch only partial glimpses of the sublime and the interesting, excellence and cuteness tend to spell out "the whole thing." This is one reason why the cute is so popular in times of postmodern fragmentation. The cute and the excellent are available, their forms are defined, and they deliver the totality of their content. But they can do so only because they have so little content. The sublime and the interesting are evasive, fleeting, formless, and constantly escaping. They do not deliver, instead they withhold. For Lyotard the sublime is an "unmeasurable presence" and the same is true for Schlegel's interesting. We can thus add some features to the square (Graph 14).

The cute object represents a totality that can be—literally—embraced as a whole whereas the sublime and the interesting are partial. This does not mean

Deculturation   Culture

CUTE   **SUBLIME**

erotic   erotic

available   fleeting
defined   formless
delivers   withholds

nonerotic   nonerotic

EXCELLENT   **INTERESTING**

Deculturation   Culture

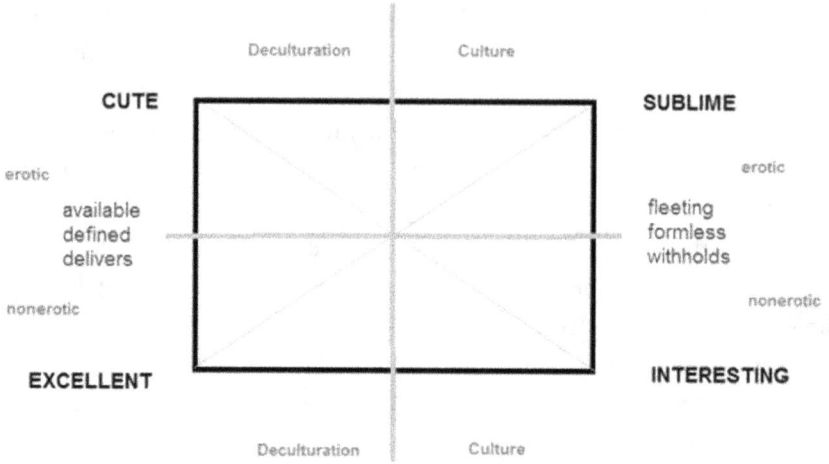

Graph 14 Availabe and defined; fleeting and formless.

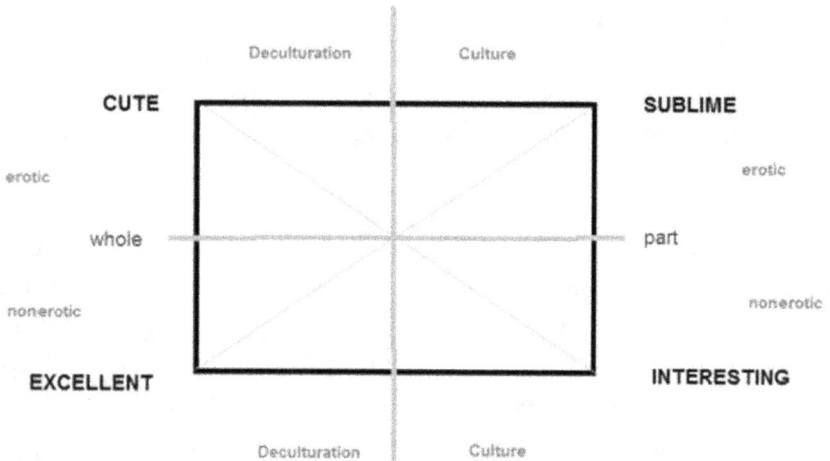

Deculturation   Culture

CUTE   **SUBLIME**

erotic   erotic

whole   part

nonerotic   nonerotic

EXCELLENT   **INTERESTING**

Deculturation   Culture

Graph 15 The whole and the part.

that the cute and excellence have access to absolute truths, but the perceptions of the cute and the excellence depend on a sense of purity provided by a rhetoric of wholeness. Schlegel saw the interesting as interspersed with good and bad. It is the mixture that makes things interesting. There is no such relativism in the excellent (Graph 15).

The purity input is particularly obvious in cuteness, which is supposed to be pure and innocent. Some terms can be added to the square (Graph 16):

purity, innocence   Deculturation   Culture

CUTE   **SUBLIME**

erotic   erotic

nonerotic   nonerotic

EXCELLENT   **INTERESTING**

Deculturation   Culture   diversity, mixture

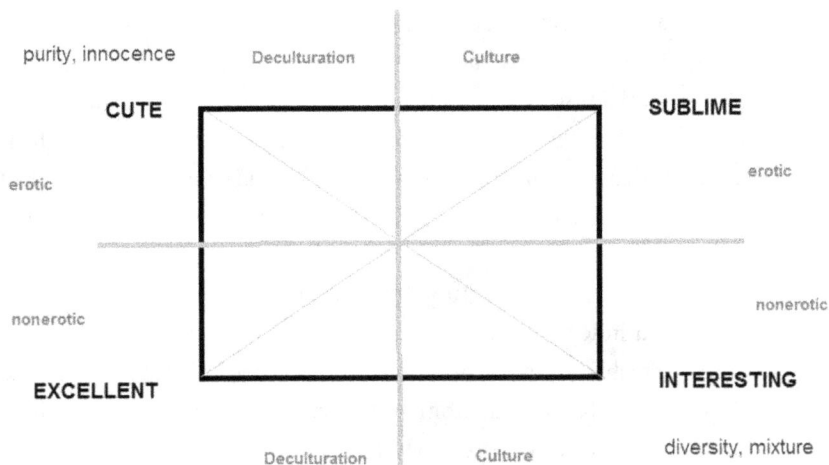

Graph 16 Purity and diversity.

The excellence, the sublime, and the beautiful

Both the sublime and the interesting act within the realm of culture and through culture. In the experience of the sublime, the "inter" (between) represents an erotically charged zone drawing us toward an unknown end. The experience of the interesting is not erotically charged but still—if we follow the traditional sense of the word "interesting"—we want to obtain knowledge and are not satisfied with the "merely interesting." Neither the sublime nor the interesting can exist without culture whereas the cute and the excellent thrive in a zone of deculturation.

It has been said above that the square is dynamic. The four terms are not mere dichotomies, but elements that can move from one place to the other. The interesting can degenerate toward the excellent and the sublime can be submitted to deculturation. An evolution visible since the Enlightenment has pushed the sublime down the slope on the square's diagonal toward the excellent. When the sublime is deprived of its cultural and its "erotic" aspects it becomes excellent. When it remains cultural but abandons its eroticism, it descends on the right vertical and becomes interesting.

The sublime is cultural, but it has a noncultural component, which makes it inclined to move toward the field of kitsch and deculturation. Kant has already noted that the sublime does not operate in the same cultural spheres as the beautiful. In *Observations* Kant gives the example of the "Witz" (wit, spirit, esprit, but also joke) that he believes to be beautiful, while understanding (*Verstand*) is sublime (1965: 18/211). In this early piece on the sublime, Kant presents wit and jokes as dependent on cultural situations. Almost thirty years later, in the *Critique of Judgment* (1793), Kant presents the sublime even more radically as not merely dependent on understanding but as "an indeterminate concept of reason" (*Vernunft*) (1911: 51/German: 165). The sublime is universally valid and independent of culture.

While understanding (which supports the sublime) is supposed to be generally valid and independent of culture, wit and jokes, just like beauty, are often incomprehensible when exported outside their original cultural spheres. Wit and beauty are relative and submitted to cultural diversity. The sublime transgresses cultural borders more easily because it is more abstract. Beauty appears in the cultural light of real life while the sublime takes place in the night of abstract concepts. This is what Kant means when writing that "the night is *sublime,* the day is *beautiful*" (1965: 16/208). The sublime is absolute, and beauty is relative. Of course, the absolute truth of the sublime will never be attained because it is always incomplete, while beauty and kitsch can be experienced as fulfillments. In the aesthetic experiences of cuteness, kitsch, and excellence, things are spelled out, they fulfill, and are made available, which is the case neither for the sublime nor for the interesting.

Often, when Kant speaks of the sublime one has the impression that he uses this concept to combat the vulgar taste of kitsch: "The sublime must be simple, the beautiful can be decorated and ornamented" (1965: 17/210). Ngai's categorical opposition of the cute and sublime is grounded in this pattern that emerged with Kant at the time of Enlightenment. The cute arises next to kitsch and is therefore incompatible with the sublime. The colossus is kitsch because it is inappropriate or even obscene while the sublime object, though it might be as large as the colossus, escapes kitsch because it is less concrete. The column will never be kitsch even when it is very tall. The column is not massive and therefore more abstract. On the first pages of *Observations*, Kant presents beauty in an almost "folksy" fashion and contrasts it with the sublime. In a lighthearted manner (which is highly unusual for the Königsberg philosopher) Kant states that "brownish color and black eyes are more closely related to the sublime, blue eyes and blonde color to the beautiful" (1965: 20/213).

The aesthetics of the sublime is part of a larger Enlightenment project, which contradicts exuberance and vulgarity by putting forward the sober and intellectual capacity of the *Verstand* (understanding) as universally valid. Many abstract Enlightenment ideas, especially those of absolute totality and of absolute freedom, are attached to the sublime. The sublime does not take place in the concrete world of beauty but in the realm of ideas and reason. It is not submitted to the contingencies of culture, which is why it will be illustrated predominantly via experiences with nature. All this could make us think that the sublime is absolute and that it solves all question of relativism in art and ethics. The problem is that the sublime is an unmeasurable presence that "exceeds what imaginative thought can grasp at once in a form" (Lyotard 1991: 53). By making the sublime graspable in the form of a positive content, the universal and *Verstand*-based quality of the sublime can be turned into the excellent. Now it can be empirically measured.

The sublime is a cultural notion, but since its inception it carried in itself a tendency toward the noncultural. Derrida notes that for Kant there is "no 'suitable' example of the sublime in the products of human art" (Derrida 1987: 122). Examples of the sublime are generally not taken from art or even from culture but from nature. In the Second Book of the *Critique of Judgment*, Kant explains that the sublime manifests itself in "rude nature [roher Natur] merely as involving magnitude (and only in this so far as it does not convey any charm or any emotion arising from actual danger)" (1911: 57/175). For beauty, things work the other way. Even when beauty appears *in nature*, it should be a "cultured" nature: "Lofty oaks and lonely shadows in sacred groves are *sublime*, flowerbeds, low hedges, and trees trimmed into figures are *beautiful*" (1965: 16/208). I am not saying that for Kant beauty is relative. Like the sublime, beauty is independent of judgments of the senses and aims to have universal validity. Like the sublime, beauty is "for itself," too. However, the "for itself" character is formulated in a much stronger fashion with regard to the sublime, which makes it look similar to the excellent from the beginning. Though the sublime is cultural, it goes beyond the merely cultural because it aims *directly* at the infinite and the abstract. Compared with beauty, the sublime comes much closer to religious sentiments considered as absolutely valid. Of course, the absolute will never be reached because the sublime projects infinity. Nature is not appreciated as nature but nature "is sublime in such of its phenomena whose intuition conveys the idea of their infinity" (1911: 58/177, transl. modified). The aesthetic judgments spelling out the sublime are never relativistic judgments. They are not judgments of taste that we use for questions of beauty.

Through the sublime, Kant moves his aesthetics from the concrete to the abstract: "A judgement of this kind is an aesthetic judgement upon the finality of the object, which does not depend upon any present concept of the object, and does not provide one" (1911: 17/100). Beauty is concrete while the sublime can be attached to formless (formlose) phenomena: "The beautiful in nature is a question of the form of object, and this consists in limitation, whereas the sublime is to be found in an object even devoid of form" (1911: 51/165). The sublime transcends all forms, which concerns not only aesthetics but also ethics: "True virtue can only be grafted upon principles, and it will become the more sublime and noble the more general they are" (1965: 24/217).

The aesthetic judgment is not limited to a judgment of taste, but it springs "from a higher intellectual feeling [Geistesgefühl]" (1911: 18/102). This is how it can refer to the sublime. Through his discourse on the sublime, Kant shifts aesthetics from quality to quantity. Beauty is a "presentation of an indeterminate concept of understanding" (*Verstand*) while the sublime is "an indeterminate concept of reason" (*Vernunft*) (1911: 51/165). Consequently, "delight is in the former case coupled with the representation of quality, but in this case [in the case of the sublime] with that of quantity" (1911: 51/165). The sublime is not the "relatively great" that we encounter in concrete cultural contexts in the form of the monstrous (*Ungeheuerliche*) or the colossal (1911: 57/175). Sublime objects are "absolutely" (*schlechthin*) great so that "in comparison with this all else (in the way of magnitudes of the same order) is small" (1911: 58/169).

Though Kant determines both the beauty and the sublime through self-sufficiency (by disconnecting beauty from the good),[1] one main difference between the beautiful and the sublime remains constant. The perception of beauty serves "the furtherance of life and is thus compatible with charms and a playful imagination" whereas the feeling of the sublime "arises indirectly, being brought about by the feeling of a momentary." The sublime is "dead earnest" and contains no play (1911: 51/165). It escapes cultural relativism or culture simply because it is the sublime "schlechthin": "A pure judgement upon the sublime must, however, have no end belonging to the object as its determining ground, if it is to be aesthetic and not to be tainted with any judgement of understanding or reason" (1911: 57/175). In other words, the sublime is objective just because it is purely subjective. We find the sublime in ourselves; but there, in ourselves, we do not find it in the form of cultural prejudices (subjectivity) but in the form of a certitude: "For the beautiful in nature we must seek a ground external to ourselves, but for the sublime one merely in ourselves and the attitude of mind [Denkungsart] that introduces sublimity into the representation of nature" (1911: 52/167). This is indeed pure Kantianism. Beauty is associated with form and quality, while the sublime is associated with formlessness and quantity. The sublime is not noumenal but perceptual. The finality of form within beauty isolates the object from its broader context. As a result, the concept of the sublime "gives, on the whole, no indication of anything final in nature itself" (1911: 51/165).

Conclusion: A religion of excellence

Jean-François Lyotard has delivered a critique of the transcendental aspects of reason and of transcendence within the romantic sublime (together with the romantic absolute) and it can be transferred without problems to excellence. Lyotard attempts to disconnect the sublime from transcendental speculation and to link this kind of aesthetic experience to phenomenal perception to sense perception. Lyotard finds that the sublime "places itself out of the reach of all presentation: the imagination founders, inanimate. All of its forms are inane before the absolute. The 'object' that occasions sublime feeling disappears" (Lyotard 1991: 76). Other authors find that the sublime becomes superficial for similar reasons. This is interesting because it signifies that the sublime represents one more example of how a notion that was supposed to combat kitsch can become kitsch in its own right. Roland Hepburn finds that a theoretical overemphasis on transcendence has led many aestheticians to focus solely on "the immediately given perceptually qualities, the sensuous surface" (Hepburn 1993: 72).

The above assumption can be confirmed: there are resemblances between the cute and the sublime. Both qualities have similar functions. It has been said that the cute offers psychological comfort in a world dominated by rational excellence; the same is true for the sublime. The sublime can offer relief in a world marked by secularization and materialism that is devoid of meaning. Bettina Reiber (2009) argues that the sublime, as an awareness of human reason's extraordinary mode of transcendence toward the world, offers relief in a postmodern world suffering from the loss of meaning. The sublime is thus religion in disguise. Crowther (1989) proposes that the sublime, through its quasi-religious character, "leads to metaphysical insights" (174). However, contrary to kitsch and cuteness, the sublime offers a relief *in the form of culture*. The sublime can have functions similar to those of the cute, but it will assume those functions differently.

Reiber's suggestions that the sublime offers relief are surprising given that for Edmund Burke the sublime was mainly a psychological condition of terror. The sublime cannot be *only* a pseudo-religious refuge bringing relief from modern rationalism. The Burkean sublime tends to threaten toward annihilation. For Burke, the source of the sublime is "whatever is in any sort terrible, or is conversant about terrible objects, or operates in a manner analogous to terror" (Burke 1998: 58). This can be related to excellence. Broch, in his essay on kitsch, offers an original interpretation of the romantic ambitions to create the sublime: it is a search for excellence. According to Broch, romantic musicians were "incapable of producing average values" but romantic musicians *had to be* excellent, because otherwise their music would tip over into kitsch: "Every slip from the lofty level of genius was immediately transformed into a disastrous fall from the cosmic heights to kitsch" (Broch: 52). This was different from the baroque period, where even minor musicians would never come close to kitsch. It is easy to kitschify Berlioz but almost impossible to kitschify Bach. In the context of the Reformation, which produced a mixture of theological-sacred and rational-secular values, religion, politics, and aesthetics became more "democratic." Now it was no longer just the church, but every individual that was responsible for the right ethics, the right aesthetics, etc. These were the first steps toward a liberal culture whose development would later be dramatically accelerated by Enlightenment thought. What happened next has been described by Scruton in the passage that has already been quoted above: "Under the jurisdiction of religion, our deeper feelings are sacralized" but "the loss of religious certainty facilitated the birth of kitsch" (Scruton 1999). Broch writes in a similar vein:

> This brought the act of revelation into every single human mind. . . . The mind settled the account and became presumptuous and boastful. It became presumptuous because it had been assigned this cosmic and divine task, boastful because it was well aware that it had been given too much credit, that it had been loaded with a responsibility that exceeded its resources. This is the origin of Romanticism. (Broch: 56)

The French Revolution was followed by terror and uncertainty, and many would have liked to turn back to religion. But religion could no longer be experienced in the old way. As it had become "democratic," it was no longer prepared to deliver absolute certainty. As a result, absolute values would arise *in art*. And they had to rise quickly and also be easy enough to grasp, which led to the emergence of kitsch. Kitsch is the result of a desire for forced loftiness and forced sublimity. Calvinist-Puritan movements recognized the danger and attempted to contain kitsch through asceticism. Lutheranism tried the same and one of the outcomes is Bach. Sometimes the fundamentalist, decultured asceticism of Protestants became kitsch in its own right. Alternatively, absolute values would arise in the economy, which characterizes the birth of liberalism.

Fast forward to the twentieth century: with the help of liberalism, a range of pseudo-religious values could penetrate all areas of the industrialized civilization. At the end of the millennium, the phenomenon would be called postmodernism. David E. Nye (1994) precisely describes this process when tracing, in his *American Technological Sublime*, the progression of culture from the romantic natural sublime to the postmodern sublime.

The most recent manifestations of pseudo-religious culture revolve around kitsch and excellence. It has become clear in this chapter that the sublime played an intermediary role in their developments. Though the sublime does not share with excellence the state of deculturation, from the beginning the sublime contained the strange mixture of the threatening and the promising that we also encounter in the notion of excellence. This shows that excellence has the same Judeo-Christian connotations that Broch detects in kitsch. (It is not surprising that the Japanese have a different attitude toward kitsch as well as toward *kawaii*, which is their version of the cute). The sublime used to communicate its values in a romantically mystifying manner; however, vastness, magnitude, infinity, obscurity, darkness, and solitude need culture while excellence is simply communicated as excellence. Excellence does not need culture but, on the contrary, deculturation fosters the spread of excellence.

In a chapter entitled "Whatever Happened to the Poor Old Holy Ghost," Karl Pawek writes in Dorfles's volume on kitsch that with the beginning of Enlightenment "the psychic and moral Christian event [had been exchanged] for the objective, ontological event" (Pawek: 148). What is lost is culture. In this sense, Enlightenment enabled the propagation of the nonculture called excellence. Pawek believes that Enlightenment "presupposed a loss of weight in the theological object, the substitution of something sweet and nice for something extremely powerful" (148). Pawek's article is about kitsch and he suggests that those theological transformations produced the initial forms of kitsch in European culture. Those thoughts parallel Scruton's who holds that "the loss of religious certainty facilitated the birth of kitsch." The present chapter has shown that at a later stage, the same process created the culture of excellence. Excellence remains strongly related to kitsch, be it only for the reasons quoted by Pawek and Scruton. It is therefore utterly strange that, at the same time, kitsch and cuteness can be conceived as counterreactions to the harsh culture of excellence. However, looking closer, this is no surprise: what both kitsch and cuteness share with excellence is their state of deculturation.

The perception and appreciation of beauty depends on acts of acculturation whereas the sublime is abstract and functional in any context. The sublime is a religiously tainted cultural concept, but in modern Western culture and under the influence of deculturation, it moves toward excellence. The sublime is opposed to the excellent, but it maintains an intrinsic connection with the excellent simply because the sublime is not merely beautiful. This is how the sublime could "degenerate" into excellence. It could also be de-eroticized because excellence requires gender-neutral standards.

The conclusion is that decultured modernity begins in the eighteenth century with the aesthetics of the sublime; and that it evolves up to the present age in which we can admire cities like Dubai. Dubai never aimed to be beautiful but only sublime. Slim (not colossal) skyscrapers stand where only a decade ago there was a flat desert. The contrast between what was and what is makes Dubai's grandeur ungraspable and overwhelming. Dubai is the world's most sublime city; and it is also the world's most excellent city.

Note

1   "The beautiful and the sublime agree on the point of pleasing on their own account [für sich selbst]. Further they agree in not presupposing either a judgement of sense or one logically determinant, but one of reflection [Reflexionsurteil]. Hence it follows that the delight does not depend upon a sensation, as with the agreeable, nor upon a definite concept, as does the delight in the good" (1911: 51/ German: 164).

6

Can Liberalism Be Saved?

From liberalism to "victimism"

The "really existing liberalism," as Jean-Claude Michéa has called it, is very different from what the inventors of neoliberalism intended. Lasch holds that liberalism "has carried the logic of individualism to the extreme of a war of all against all [and] the pursuit of happiness to the dead end of a narcissistic preoccupation with the self" (Lasch: xv). Since socialism preaches the love of the other, were the enemies of socialism (that's what Milton Friedman and Friedrich Hayek, the founders of neoliberalism, were) not bound to end up with self-love? There is a logical pattern leading from liberalism to narcissism, but this logic is tortuous. Initially, liberalism was against aristocrats and all those who thought they were born to rule; liberalism wanted to liberate the ignorant masses and fought for equality before the law. The seventeenth-century philosopher John Locke, who played a crucial role in the establishment of liberalism as a philosophical tradition, opposed absolutism and fought for a representative democracy and the rule of law. Locke and before him John Milton criticized the aristocratic and hierarchical order of their societies. Their arguments of moral equality were mainly directed against slavery. Liberalism introduced new ideas of moral freedom linked to the Christian idea of conscience. It wanted to create free individuals guided by conscience working for the common good.

Contemporary liberalism, on the one hand, often stands for an individualism guided by self-interest or group interest and politically mandated victimhood and, on the other, for a misguided compassion. This was intended neither by the founders of liberalism nor by the founders of neoliberalism like Friedman and Hayek. Still, Winston Churchill and Ronald Reagan understood liberalism as a majoritarian democracy guaranteeing free speech, free association, and free media. Today it stands for the weakening of traditions, the overproduction of legislation, the cult of mediocrity, and the idea that minority rights should penetrate every aspect of life.

The path leading from earlier liberalism to the present narcissistic form of individualism leads through deculturation. Deculturation enabled relativism, which became the basis of victim-oriented liberalism. This development has a long history, but its last push came with the Cold War as has been explained in Chapter 3. The relativism that came with the disappearance of patriotism and religion as well as the skepticism toward progress led to a disinterest in something else that could have provided a basis for political culture: history. History or historical culture ceased being the foundation of ethics and politics. This was not the initial idea of liberalism either. According to Lasch, initially, liberalism had a strong interest in the study of history.

The increasingly relativist globalizing world of the 1970s in which even the dollar began to float became the new face of liberalism. Leftist intellectuals did little to contain it. On the contrary, academic disciplines exalted the new "anti-foundational thinking" often by misunderstanding the subtle character of hermeneutics or deconstructionist theories. Identity politics, another leftist pet topic, stopped searching for identities in the rich fabric of culture and historically constituted communities but referred instead to statistics. As a result, group identities became more important than cultural identities. Identity became politicized. A strongly claimed Marxist heritage did not contradict this way of thinking and instead consolidated it. Science tried to amend this relativism, but the new methods, impressive through their use of technicalities, remained equally unable to grasp cultural realities. Algorithms and psychoanalytically informed clinical ideas became the new sources of truth about society, ethics, and identities. According to Lea, "Political struggle had been turned into a branch of a burgeoning therapy industry" (Lea: 13). Nothing could stop the narcissistic situation of a war of all against all.

Though many people seem to think so, the "war of all against all" was not the kind of liberalism that Friedman had in mind but rather what he wanted to avoid. Originally, neoliberalism was conceived as a reaction against the exaggerated individualism of liberal laissez-faire economics. In "Neoliberalism and its Prospects" Friedman describes the nineteenth-century model of liberalism, which held that the state could only do harm, as a "negative philosophy." This was also the opinion of Friedman's predecessors, the earlier economists in the Chicago school. For Friedman, laissez-faire "underestimated the danger that private individuals" represent. The novelty of neoliberalism was that it recognized the "important positive functions that must be performed by the state" (Friedman 1951: 91). Hayek, too, distinguished neoliberalism from a dogmatic laissez-faire attitude when writing: "The liberal argument does not advocate leaving things just as they are; it favors making the best possible use of the forces of competition as a means of coordinating human efforts" (Hayek 2003: 45).

Fast forward from the 1950s to the liberal culture of the twenty-first century. The following impressionist sketches of liberal culture presented by Michéa (2007: 142) are parodic but, sadly, they match reality almost perfectly. In France, the association of obese people requires the retreat of government campaigns propagating healthy diets because these campaigns would undermine their self-esteem. "Veggie Pride" accuses nonvegetarians of "specism" because eating meat leads to discrimination of animals. Humans and animals are equal and eating meat is fascist. In Germany, prostitution is seen as a trade like any other trade. Prostitutes can go to the unemployment office and in the future, the national education system will be responsible for the training of prostitutes, deliver diplomas, programs comprising theoretical and practical knowledge and, of course, tests and inspections.

This is neither laissez-faire individualism nor Friedmanian state-controlled neoliberalism but simply "victimism." The utopian project of self-determination and protection of the individual has been led astray. The state is asked to protect the weakest individual at any cost. "Liberty" is no longer based on Enlightenment premises, which sought to liberate the individual from arbitrary wills, superstitions, and ideology, and to equip the individual with a critical consciousness. Liberty is implemented through restrictions on speech, multicultural educational curricula, and affirmative action. Liberty has become an ideology. As a result, residents of former communist countries find the liberal "liberty" talk reminiscent of the newspeak common in socialism, as reports Ryszard Legutko: "There are no topics, no matter how trivial, that the liberal democrat could raise or discuss without mentioning freedom, discrimination, equality, human rights, emancipation, authoritarianism, and other related notions. No other language is used or even accepted" (Legutko: 43). The result is the contrary of liberty: a mentality discouraging dissent, discussion, and debate.

How could liberalism end up there? True, the corporate system had an important influence. Lasch describes neoliberalism as a new form of monarchism rejecting "priestly and monarchical hegemony only to replace it with the hegemony of the business corporation, the managerial and professional classes who operate the corporate system, and the corporate state" (Lasch 218). However, the reason is not that liberalism was overrun by a more powerful form of capitalism. Liberalism bears the germs of its own decline in itself.

The above tales of modern liberalism are thinkable only in a world that has lost all its cultural landmarks. The development from classical liberalism to present day "absurd liberalism" followed a consistent logic, and both the leftists and the initiators of neoliberalism are responsible. In Friedman's vision of neoliberalism, laissez-faire was substituted by "competitive order." The state would not be absent but would provide a framework seeing that the competitive order operates correctly. This is the gist of neoliberalism: cultural rules should be avoided and replaced with moralizing correctness. The introduction of moral correctness distinguishes neoliberalism from classical liberalism. The idea of correctness is appealing not only to conservatives: progressive liberals embrace it even more enthusiastically. Friedman was a cultural liberal who supported the legalization of drugs and prostitution and was in favor of gay rights (see Friedman and Szasz: 65). However, "correctness instead of rules and regulations" also appeals to people who do not sympathize with Friedman's economic ideas.

What is the problem with correctness? Contrary to goodness or virtue, correctness is an abstract and shapeless moral appeal unmediated by concrete cultural conditions. For centuries, morals have been regulated by cultures, and as a result, ethics could not become puritan. The new liberalism has changed this pattern. Correctness is puritanism in disguise. In the past, cultures could regulate "bad" elements such as "incorrect" jokes. Cultures could also regulate the relationships between men and women. The rules about how to behave were flexible. The result of this cultural flexibility was tolerance. When culture disappears, tolerance becomes dogmatic. It needs to be implemented via static standards of correctness. Legutko describes this situation and discovers amazing parallels between liberal democracy and communism: both succumb "to a totalitarian temptation—their angry rejection of even the slightest criticism, their inadvertent acceptance" (Legutko: 114). In a situation of deculturation, tolerance becomes totalitarian. Correctness is more static than laws and rules, because laws and rules are accommodated in cultural contexts and can even be bent through culture. Rules are not *necessarily* followed, and most people have developed a natural tolerance toward this fact. Bending correctness, on the other hand, is unacceptable. Rules are dynamic whereas correctness is static.

Correctness is not about rules, but it has the semblance of virtue: being politically incorrect means being bad.

The replacement of rules with correctness has disastrous consequences. By fighting against all sorts of discriminations, liberalism abandons moral values rooted in cultures and creates a rigid and suffocating moralism. Political correctness regulates certain behaviors but does not suggest a concrete vision of society in terms of culture. This is no surprise because the new liberalism has no means to establish values, educational selection, and moral pressure *culturally*. Instead, it tends to define morality through the feeling of guilt toward the others, a practice that will sooner or later lead to the culture of self-victimization. As has been explained in Chapter 5, paradoxically, liberal self-victimization intends to *escape* the very same culture that liberalism created: the culture of excellence. However, the culture of excellence is part of the package that the politically correct individual has embraced. The "objectivity" of big data, which is a result of excellence culture, merely fosters this self-victimization because, according to Philippe Vion-Dury, big data "discriminate less against minority groups" (Vion-Dury: 176). "Big Mother," a term coined by Michel Schneider (2002), does not punish citizens through imprisonment but rather by installing in them the feeling of guilt. This technique is particularly suitable in times of globalization and virtualization. The global world is so fluid and virtual that confinement to a limited physical space has become difficult. Humans are therefore conditioned by means of abstract imperative of consumerism, tolerance, and correctness. In the past, one castigated the body while today one conditions the mind. An apparently apolitical interiorization of self-control is spelled out in terms of correctness.

The trajectory of liberalism

How could liberalism end up there? "To be liberal" denotes an idea of modern freedom. Liberal positions build upon Enlightenment values and put forward the right to difference, freedom of religion and speech, democracy, international cooperation, and societal permissiveness. In the twentieth century, fascist regimes abolished those freedoms, and Marxism distanced itself from liberalism holding that liberalism merely serves to idealize bourgeois society. In the postwar Western world, being liberal or having the possibility to live in a liberal society has been cherished as a precious good by most people.

Fascism was anti-liberal. However, why did fascism arise in the first place? Why did a large part of the German and Italian populations support extremely anti-liberal policies? The causes cannot be reduced to a bad economy and brainwashing. The real reason is that fascism encountered liberal societies in a weakened state. At the end of the nineteenth century, the belief in liberal ideals had crumbled away in Europe. Nietzsche stated in 1888 that liberalism had become flat and shallow (Nietzsche 1997: 74). Rawls writes that "a cause of the fall of Weimar's constitutional regime was that none of the traditional elites of Germany supported its constitution or were willing to cooperate to make it work. They no longer believed a decent liberal parliamentary regime was possible" (Rawls 1993: lix). Those developments will be analyzed more closely in Chapter 8.

After centuries of wars and revolutions, liberal democracies became the norm in the Western world. The last building phase of liberalism took place after the Second World War when liberalism would be universalized. Western countries, Japan, and some other non-Western countries established social liberalism most efficiently by expanding the welfare state. Classical liberalism was tamed, which Friedman perceived as a shift toward socialism: "The triumph of Benthamite liberalism in nineteenth-century England was followed by a reaction toward increasing intervention by government in economic affairs. This tendency to collectivism was greatly accelerated, both in England and elsewhere, by the two World Wars" (Friedman 1982: 10). Friedman contrasts freedom with welfare: "Welfare rather than freedom became the dominant note in democratic countries" (11). However, the liberal welfare state on whose premises the "absurd liberalism" described above was destined to grow *is* a form of liberalism and perhaps even its most utopian materialization. A free, tolerant society determined by excellence culture develops an internal victim culture. Though Friedman was not aware of it, what he calls "socialism" had been part and parcel of his own liberal recipe.

What happened next was the democratization of liberalism. Legutko explains that though many people think that liberalism had been introduced into democracy, the reverse is true: by becoming democratic, liberalism became "a doctrine in which the primary agents were no longer individuals, but groups and the institutions of the democratic state. Instead of individuals striving for the enrichment of social capital with new ideas and aspirations, there emerged people voicing demands called rights" (Legutko: 21). This is the creation of victim culture through liberalism.

Neoliberalism

The aversion to liberalism is most understandable when liberalism imposes itself in the shape of neoliberalism. Though invented much earlier, the term has become extremely popular since the early 1990s. Of all the liberties (speech, press, religion, etc.) held up by liberalism, neoliberalism has singled out the liberty of the market, which it hyperbolizes. As mentioned above, this was not necessarily the concept of Friedman and Hayek, but that's what neoliberalism stands for today. Neoliberalism remains a form of liberalism because it shares with other liberalisms the idea of progress and the conviction that some kind of freedom needs to be universalized. George Soros, a liberal himself, criticized neoliberalism as "market fundamentalism" (Soros 1998).[1] Neoliberalism is often associated with terms like monetarism and neoconservatism though there is no direct link. Though Friedman's purpose was to contradict laissez-faire economics when designing the principles of neoliberalism, neoliberalism also came to be understood as an updated version of laissez-faire. The result is a further paradox: liberalist individualism can be understood as laissez-faire economics, which is a key component of American conservatism. This is paradoxical because conservatism rejects many typically liberal values. The old paradox of the individual and the general reoccurs: how can a universal economic rule be harmonized with individual freedom? Will the component that can most easily be "universalized" (the economic component) not work against liberties of individuals?

The link between economics and politics has always been present. Friedman believed that economic freedom is a necessary condition for political freedom. His argument was based on the observation that centralized controls of economic activities were always accompanied by political repression. Therefore, economic freedom is an essential part of general freedom. One cannot be free without being also economically free. This is not to say that economic freedom brings about political freedom automatically (as some supporters of liberalism argue) and even less to say that political freedom brings about economic freedom (as some critics of liberalism argue).

Neoliberalism as it is commonly understood today is a "universalized individualism" and therefore built on the same paradoxical grounds as any liberalism. Neoliberalism and progressive liberalism share many paradoxical features. Liberalism, which so much insists on individualism, tends to engender "big" structures such as *either* big governments *or* big businesses (depending on the sort of liberalism one adheres to). Strangely, the communitarians combating liberalism are often not opposed to neoliberalism.

In this new context, the confrontation of the individual and the general needs to be examined anew. Liberal freedom is desirable, but it always comes at a price: "free" thought cannot be determined by communitarian values because thinking freely (in a liberal way) means to think universally. In other words, the freedom not to think universally is not permitted in liberalism. Can this paradox be solved? Charles Taylor has put forward a proposal emerging from the philosophical tradition of hermeneutics, which tries to unite the individual and the particular through critical reflection. In an article called "Conditions of an Unforced Consensus on Human Rights," Taylor imagines a cross-cultural dialogue during which both sides insist neither on the universal validity nor on their right to maintain individual views, but constantly allow, through a critical communicative discourse, for the possibility that their own beliefs may be mistaken (Taylor 1999).

Contemporary right-wing parties in Western countries, who are the new enemies of liberalism, rediscover an old paradox that they use as a weapon against liberalism: liberalism installs a dictatorship of freedom. Universalistic positions of liberalism prevent people from choosing other—mostly communitarian—lifestyles. From a certain point of view this appears strange because the universal values of liberalism (now very much present in the form of social welfare) should be considered precious for any individual and not be lightheartedly discarded. At the same time, communitarian arguments have retained some of the rhetoric power that had propelled them to the foreground in preceding decades. Communitarians defend individual cultural values in concrete cultural contexts. Personalized human existence is impossible without those values. Communitarians are not against norms but hold that norms should be interpreted within the horizon of a community. That this is not merely chauvinistic becomes clear when considering corresponding arguments brought forward within the Western intellectual community in the 1980s. John Rawls (1971) had defended liberal democratic societies on the grounds of everything that has been said above about liberalism. As a counterreaction, Taylor (1985) pointed to the importance of culture as a collective good and argued that moral judgment will depend on the interpretive framework within which agents act and any abstraction from this context makes judgments invalid. In parallel, Alasdair MacIntyre (1981) rediscovered pre-Enlightenment virtues that the ancient Greeks had not defined as abstract norms but as concrete values. Those values were expressed in the philosophy of virtue ethics that universalizing Western Enlightenment philosophers had almost forgotten.

The paradox of liberalism

The democratic liberal model was universalized in the West, which is the reason why, at first sight, the process does not evoke the picture of a crisis but rather of a success. Still, a crisis was attached to liberalism since the beginning. The problem is not the confrontation of liberalism with anti-liberalism, but liberalism has been suffering from an internal contradiction. Liberalism has always been its own worst enemy. The idea of liberalism is based on two contradictions that move to the foreground during certain historical periods and recede to the background during other periods. These paradoxes explain the difficulties pertaining to the definition of liberalism or even to its association with a certain political spectrum. Today, liberalism can signify laissez-faire capitalism, or it can be identified with socialism because of its tendency to defend common people and to seek social justice. Friedman was against both laissez-faire and socialism.

New far-right thinkers have established links between cultural liberalism and economic neoliberalism, concluding that any sort of liberalism is intrinsically imperialistic. This is odd because liberalism was against collectivism. Collectivism was favored by the Church (which was against individualism) and by socialism beginning right after the Russian revolution because socialism disregarded individual ownership. Seeing parallels between leftist cultural liberalism (which leans toward socialism) and economic neoliberalism appears to be nonsensical. However, the defense of the individual, which is a strong feature of progressive liberalism, makes such comparisons possible. The above-described replacement of rules with correctness is one reason. The other reason is the paradox of "universal individualism" that will be analyzed below.

The French conservative journalist Alexandre Devecchio writes in a recent book on the new far-right that "[cultural] liberalism was the Trojan horse of the free circulation of capitals promoted by financial globalization through which the initial liberal naïve optimism could be logically extended by opening the borders" (68). Conservative French philosopher Bérénice Levet speaks of the "tacit pact between cultural leftism and economic liberalism" (Levet: 58). This is strange given that in 1982, all the world's progressive liberals tended to see Reagan's election as a disaster. It is also difficult to find a progressive liberal who likes Thatcher. And how can we reconcile those thoughts with Legutko's comparisons of liberalism with communism? Still the theory of "leftists working for neoliberal capitalism" persists.

As mentioned, there are two paradoxes. The first one concerns liberalism's relationship with the market economy. Liberalism began in capitalist market societies believing that the freedom of the market fosters the freedom of the individual. This conviction goes back to John Stuart Mill's mid-nineteenth-century liberalist philosophy. The problem is that the self-developmental dynamic supposed to foster the individual, which is believed to be implicit in economic liberalism, could not always be observed in the capitalist practice. Since Mill, "liberal" has been assumed to mean "capitalist." However, as Macpherson pointed out, in that case, "'liberal' can [also] mean freedom of the stronger to do down the weaker by following market rules" (Macpherson 1977: 1). Liberalism wanted freedom for all individuals and wanted to implement this freedom via a capitalist market economy—the oppression of the individual *through* capitalism represented a contradiction from the beginning. Long after Friedman, this contradiction would be solved by imposing standards of correctness. A more recent result is the liberalism of Silicon Valley, which fights against corporations and archaic traditions, though, at the same time, it installs an oppressive Big Mother culture of excellence. Both projects are inspired by the liberal imperatives of tolerance.

The paradox of "universal individualism"

Liberalism pretends to be universal though it is also claiming to foster individualism. Liberalism is often presented as the ideal form of individualism because it guarantees individual freedom. However, while liberalism indeed permits the existence of individual differences within its societies, it also strives toward universalism. Liberal values are rational and therefore bound to be universal and not just cultural or communitarian. The result is a paradox: though the liberal position encompasses the right to difference it has difficulties fostering differentiation in the form of individual cultures that disagree with liberalism.

Both assumptions, the one holding that economic freedom fosters individual wealth, and the assumption that the universalization of this philosophy of freedom can be harmonized with the wishes of every individual, are mistaken. They are the products of theoretical perspectives that neglect the practical realities of persons and cultures. As general ideologies, they are ethically valuable, albeit only because they are based on good intentions. But their individual application poses problems.

Liberalism became a political movement during the age of Enlightenment, and the contradiction between the individual and the universal arose right at the beginning. French Enlightenment philosopher Montesquieu attempted to unite universal and communitarian values by insisting in his *Esprit des lois* (1748) that political institutions should not only preserve civil liberties and the law but also reflect the social and geographical aspects of each community. His intentions were laudable, but he was merely pointing to a problem instead of solving it. Liberalism is universalist because its basis is rationalism. The principles of liberalism are universal laws that are not supposed to be corrupted by particular contingencies such as cultural affinities. As a result, for the liberal, the freest individual is culturally neutral and only determined by an abstract form of rationality. Any individual in disagreement with this universalism will experience liberalism as a form of totalitarianism.

Several philosophers attempted to tackle those internal contradictions associated with liberalism and, by extension, to the heritage of Enlightenment. Adorno and Horkheimer critiqued Enlightenment culture (without drawing the link with liberalism) when writing in their *Dialectic of Enlightenment* (1944) that Enlightenment (the authors do not speak of a certain historical period but present Enlightenment as a general Western cultural phenomenon) is always striving toward totality. Western society is determined by this "totalitarian" ambition, which is, paradoxically, based on the project of overcoming all totalitarianisms. Those radical leftist thinkers conclude that rationalism is totalitarian.

Seen through this perspective, communitarianism becomes the opposite of liberalism. Communitarianism splits up totalities. Though the progressive liberal strives to be multicultural, a certain totalitarianism remains hidden in this position. Slavoj Žižek summarizes this contradiction when pointing out that the multiculturalist respects the other's identity but conceives of the other as "self-enclosed 'authentic' community towards which he maintains distance rendered possible by his privileged universal position. . . . The multicultural respect of the Other's specificity is the very form of asserting one's own superiority" (Žižek 2007: 171). The root of the problem is, once again, deculturation. Žižek holds that the multiculturalist occupies a "privileged empty point of universality from which one is able to appreciate (and depreciate) properly other particular cultures" (ibid.). In the present book I identify this multicultural liberal point of view as culturally empty or as decultured. The problem is not the lack of diversity in the sense of ethnic mixtures (an idée fixe of liberal democracies) but rather the lack of a cultural pluralism able to accept those ideas *that are not purely egalitarian*. Legutko, as the defender of conservative culture that he is, makes this clear by citing an extreme case. He describes the refusal of democracy's other in democratic egalitarianism as a refusal of the aristocratic element: "Divergent elements such as the democratic and the aristocratic, where one would offset the weaknesses of the other, were not incorporated into one system. Liberalism did not diversify democracy because it was a different type of liberalism than the one the American Founding Fathers, Tocqueville, and Ortega hoped for: not aristocratic, but egalitarian" (Legutko: 61). Liberalism was against aristocrats in the first place, and its democratization could only reinforce this tendency.

Not only aristocratism but also communitarianism is opposed to Enlightenment-based universalism because communitarianism introduces elements of cultural, racial, and geographical relativism into discussions revolving around values and identities. Legutko explains that the exclusion of such elements was also the aim of communist regimes. Society needed to be harmonized with a unique political system and we find the same aspirations in liberalism: "Liberal democrats were guided by a similar assumption as the communists before them: both disliked communities for their alleged anachronism and, for that reason, thought them, because deep-rooted, to be the major obstacles to progress. Both believed that one cannot modernize society without modernizing communities, including rural areas, families, churches, and schools" (Legutko: 77).

Communitarianism does not negate the existence of values as such but criticizes the liberal universalist attitude toward values. It does so first, because it contests the idea that any values can have universal significance; second, because it suspects liberal values to be merely particular and not absolute at all. Liberal beliefs can be founded on randomly established standards, too. They are the *cultural* standards of Western Enlightenment. Communitarians ask liberals to be more tolerant toward nonuniversal values. Often this request is misunderstood. Liberalism, which is inspired by Enlightenment, is *the* philosophy of tolerance, and accusing liberals of being intolerant is simply absurd. Furthermore, the critique of absolute values represents the core of any Enlightenment philosophy. Liberalism emerged explicitly as a fight against absolutism, and tolerance toward other opinions has been one of its main principles. Because liberal thought is rooted in ratio-universalism fighting absolutism, the tolerance principle has been made universal, too. The result of this paradoxical constellation involving rationalism and universalism is that tolerance becomes dogmatic. Dogmatic tolerance occurs when tolerance lacks the particular self-reflectivity that should be part of any free and enlightened way of thinking. When tolerance is preached for its own sake it becomes self-righteous. Openness and tolerance for its own sake will be advertised as cultural values, but those are pseudo-values.

A dogmatic kind of openness becomes particularly obvious in the realm of aesthetics. Bourdieu (1984) explains that in art and fashion, "being distinct" is only possible by constantly going for the newest of the new because old things are "indistinct" and commonplace. The result is a cultural omnivorousness and openness to everything. Relativism is a side effect because, in the frantic search for the new, high and low art can no longer be distinguished. The anxiety-ridden social climber or even the professional artist must seek newness at any cost. In liberal, "open" societies, distinction is everything. The striving for excellence is the next step.

The liberal attitude toward culture is characterized by a complex interlinking of openness and closedness. On the one hand, any dogmatism is based on prejudices. Legutko describes the "democratic man" as a narcissist: "a rather uninspired being, not much interested in the world around him, closed within his own prejudices, and amenable to impulses of mimicry" (Legutko: 6). On the other hand, the democratic liberal can appear as narcissistic for exactly the opposite reason, which is the analysis of Christopher Lasch. The self-centered individual frantically searching for the newest of the new is driven by narcissism: the "constant experimentation in the arts has created so much confusion about standards that the only surviving measure of excellence is novelty and shock value" (Lasch: 106).

A typical philosopher who saw modern Western liberal democracies as "the best of all political worlds of whose existence we have any historical knowledge" is Karl Popper (1999: 90). Popper fought "closed" totalitarian political thought by developing the model of an "open society," which is tolerant and always open to change and criticism. According to Popper, the "closed" model had been invented by Plato. Athens of the fifth century BC was democratic and supported as such by Socrates. Reactionary forces combated this open state and reinforced class hierarchy, conformity, authority, and tradition. Sparta had a lot of influence as it focused on internal stability and military prowess. In the end, under Plato's influence, a form of "holism" defeated openness, individualism, freedom, and personal responsibility. Plato privileged the structures of the Greek polis but neglected the rights of individuals. For Plato "only a stable whole, the permanent collective, has reality, not the passing individuals" (Popper 1966: 80). The result is a totalitarian system as opposed to a liberal one. Popper uses not only the word "holist" but also "organic" in the sense of "closed" as an antonym of open and liberal.

At the same time, by producing this analysis, Popper acknowledges that the crisis of liberalism is as old as Athens' open society. Popper sees that citizens can easily feel isolated and anxious in those "open societies." There is a human need for regularity and communality. However, for Popper, freedom, social progress, growing knowledge, and enhanced international cooperation are more valuable than regularity, *Heimat*, traditions, neighborhood, collegiality, and a shared common life. Sacrificing a part of the latter communitarian values is "the price we have to pay for being human" (Popper 1966: 176).

Popper's model of the "open society" has been accepted as a model for liberal thought. George Soros's Open Society Foundations and the Open Society Institute operating in Eastern Europe, which have been named with reference to its founder's teacher Karl Popper, are supposed to foster liberalism in former socialist countries. The Soros Foundations played an important role in the 1990s when Central Europe was moving toward democracy. Resistance arose only twenty years later. In Hungary, where Soros is based, the authoritarian government of Viktor Orbán attacked the Soros foundation precisely for its openness. "Openness" does not sit well with post-socialist Hungarian and Central European populations in general, especially since Europe is threatened by mass immigration from the south and is *closing* its borders. "Open society" is misinterpreted as "open country" ready to accept immigrants. However, there is more to the Central European skepticism toward liberal forms of government than a fear of foreigners. Here populations refuse a certain concept of liberalism. To Central Europeans, liberal policies striving to change the world or to "make humanity happy," as the Polish-German journalist Adam Soboczynski wrote about the East European situation (Soboczynski 2016: 39), smack of socialist "positive thinking" talk that has lost contact with reality. It smacks of totalitarianism evoking memories of communism. Communists neglected a shared common life and concentrated on "big goals" like freedom and progress. The biggest goal (the universalization of communism) could never be achieved: in the last years of communism resources were barely sufficient to feed the population. Still, the universalist propaganda continued, which is why in Eastern Europe, liberal openness talk is quickly identified with socialist internationalism. "Happiness for all" projects are likely to be ridiculed because in the past those ambitions were so strongly out of touch with reality. When Popper says that communal life needs to be sacrificed or reduced to tackle big goals and that this is "the price we have to pay for being human" (Popper 1969: 176), many Central Europeans will find this implausible. In times of crisis, the community was almost the only remaining efficient institution. During the communist decades, the communitarian micro-economy was functioning and keeping citizens alive.

Popper's liberalism as well as the neoliberal world "as we know it" resemble that of socialism in at least one respect: in both cases, technocrats created an alternative reality determined by excellence talk. This excellence talk appeared in socialism in the form discourses insisting on the quick generalization of communism on a global basis. Liberals hated socialism but, in the end, they created a very similar phenomenon. The problem is deculturation, though the deculturing program was introduced at different stages. Communists ignored culture and wanted to refer to a pristine state of civilization that preceded cultural pollution. Liberals did know culture but judged it detrimental to their project. In both cases, culture had to be abolished. Legutko summarizes: "The vulgarity of the communist system was precultural while that of liberal democracy is postcultural'" (34).

A brief look at another critic of socialism clarifies this parallelism. This critic is Georges Sorel. Sorel did not opt for liberalism but criticized the formal character of socialism. In his *Reflections of Violence* (1908) Sorel describes that socialist empty talk can be very persistent, even when the facts have time and again been contradicted by history: "They have constructed magnificent clear-cut and symmetrical formulas; but they could not make them fit the facts; rather than abandon their theories, they have preferred to declare that the most important facts were simple anomalies which science must ignore if it is to obtain a real understanding of the whole!" (Sorel 2003: 42/Engl.: 42). Sorel amalgamates his critique of socialism with a critique of Enlightenment thought that led to liberalism, finding in both socialism and liberalism a mismatch between the theorized reality and the real reality. For example, Republicans after the French Revolution did not want to see the reality of class struggle but judged

> all things from the abstract point of view of the Déclaration des droits de l'homme, they said that the legislation of 1789 had been created in order to abolish all distinction of class in law: it was for this reason that they were opposed to proposals for social legislation which, almost always, reintroduced the idea of class and distinguished certain groups of citizens as being unfitted for the use of liberty. (46/51)

Both socialists and liberals insist on absolute truths disconnected from cultural realities. The result is a mismatch between the theorized reality and the real reality, a mismatch that thinkers like Sorel and Nietzsche pointed out very early.

Popper was not naive but understood that open societies need to be kept under constant rational scrutiny so that individual members will be served and not overlooked. No big goal should be pursued for its own sake. Some critics (the abovementioned Eastern Europeans, for example) find that big goals have been pursued for their own sake, and the result is a crisis of liberalism. The phenomenon is not limited to Eastern Europe. Populist movements all over the world are reacting to a crisis linked to the centuries-old paradoxical relationships between the universal freedom and the individual good. Radical Islam is part of this picture as it claims to combat the concept of the deracinated, neutral human extant in liberal societies. True, Islamism adds anti-colonial and religious dimensions to this anti-liberalism, but in the end, the anti-liberal combat follows the same rules. Adorno and Horkheimer's finding that rationalism can be totalitarian has consequences in realms where they had not been expected.

"Enlightenment fundamentalism"

How dramatic the situation is becomes clear when considering that some have decided to call the totalitarian rationalism of Enlightenment another kind of "fundamentalism." This is shocking in the light of the fact that the critique of absolute values represents the core of any Enlightenment philosophy. The term "Enlightenment fundamentalism" did indeed appear in academic discussions and attracted some attention. It occurred in the debate revolving around the work of the radical critic of Islam, Ayaan Hirsi Ali. The British historian Timothy Garton Ash called Hirsi Ali an "Enlightenment Fundamentalist." Though Garton Ash relativized his statement later, it is interesting to note that such a concept could emerge in the first place, especially since it echoes the idea of "fundamentalist secularism" regularly appearing on Islamist websites. "Enlightenment Fundamentalism" overlaps with what the religious Islam specialist Ziauddin Sardar has called the philosophy of the "militant, dogmatic secularist" (Sardar 2003: 231) who has, as adds Sardar, the imperialistic tendencies of "dehumanization, domination and meaninglessness" (165). Has Enlightenment created a new totalitarian "myth of Enlightenment"? If yes, this would confirm Adorno and Horkheimer's thesis that Enlightenment never provided a myth-free view of the world because it decided to ignore its own mythical basis (see *Dialectic of Enlightenment*, Excursus I).

The above debate, which involved Garton Ash, Hirsi Ali, and Ian Buruma, has been documented by Paul Berman in his *The Flight of the Intellectuals*

(New York: Scribe, 2010), and I agree with his conclusions. However, some ideas need to be developed further to explain what is really at stake when (non-Western) religious people meet Western "modernists" and feel that the latter are too stuck on their Enlightenment values. First, it is obvious that the word "Enlightenment" has been profoundly misunderstood. The Enlightenment that many religious fundamentalists (but also Garton Ash) put forward is a fantasy mix of positivism, scientism, and skepticism that did not exist at the time of Enlightenment. Enlightenment thought was not as radically anti-religious as is often supposed today. Until the end of the eighteenth century (thus roughly until the end of Enlightenment), practically all great scientists were preoccupied with religious problems, seeing God as "the grand clockmaker." Further, Enlightenment did not base all philosophical considerations on science and reason. Reason in the history of Western thought—and especially in the Enlightenment period— was rarely seen as a provider of absolute truths. Enlightenment philosophers were aware that reason, exactly like human institutions, is constructed according to random situations. In other words, reason was not the faithful reflection of abstract truths, but rather the rationalization of certain social customs that can be *more or less* reasonable and must be criticized accordingly. Scientific truths depended on place and time. This means that when Enlightenment developed its generalized critical spirit influenced by reason, it took care to also criticize itself and its own reason. Caricatured presentations of "Western reasonableness" as a fanatic adherence to reason overlook this fact and invent a purist version of Enlightenment.

A certain constructive relativism that has become part and parcel of modern Western culture descends from this Enlightenment capacity to imbue one's life with critical discourse. This includes self-criticism, which is why, normally, Enlightenment thought *cannot* end up as an "Enlightenment fundamentalism." The exaggerated belief in relativism—famously described by Allan Bloom in his *The Closing of the American Mind*—is a completely different matter. It exists and it could be called "relativism fundamentalism." This relativism has penetrated liberalism.

Enlightenment and liberalism must be criticized at the moment they lack self-reflexivity and self-criticism. Normally, given the "critique of reason" inherent in later Enlightenment thought, any linking of Enlightenment to fundamentalism is unjustified. Even Adorno and Horkheimer did not go that far. The term "fundamentalist *liberalism*," on the other hand, can make sense in some cases. The argument is twisted as it reiterates one of the above-described paradoxes. Since Enlightenment was fighting against absolutism, it turned toward "relativism," and it is this relativism that conservatives like Bloom criticize. More precisely, what Bloom criticizes in the enlightened culture of reason is not really the relativism but the "absolutism" with which relativism is enforced. This gets us to the heart of the liberal paradox because it shows that liberalism is an absolutist relativism engineered by a relativist individualist striving to be universal.

Bloom drafts some pertinent pages against the Western infatuation with "all things being relative" in which he perceives the emergence of a new "absolutism" (Bloom 1987: 25). Bloom attacks a liberalism suffering from its own inherent paradox of declaring tolerance to be a universalist and absolute principle. The modern Westerner is relativist and distrusts anybody who believes in something. For the liberal, the believer is dangerous because she is likely to turn into a fanatic at any moment. Instead one prefers to say that everything is relative: "History teaches that all the world was mad" and therefore "we should be tolerant. Finally, you should never think you are right" (25). Truth with a capital 'T' is seen as totalitarian. According to Bloom, this is the typical Western attitude, which he calls the "anything goes relativism" practiced by what he dubs the "Nietzscheanized Left" (217). Nietzsche, who declared that "God is dead," is seen as the founder of a naive and exaggerated kind of relativism. This relativism becomes a new absolutism because fanatic relativism is nothing other than "relativist fundamentalism."

Conservative Christians attack liberalism from the same angle. In conservative intellectual circles, the enemy tends to be configured as a mixture of relativism and liberalist totalitarianism. Former pope Benedict insists that the "dictatorship of relativism" represents the core challenge of the church (Ratzinger 2005 and 2010: 51). In a mass held in 2005, Benedict traces the root of the relativism problem to Kant's "self-limitation of reason." What he means is that reason has limited and reduced our thinking to the "reasonable" insight that everything is relative—except reason itself, which is universal. This leads to the creation of the paradoxical concept of a universal reason spelling out the right to individualism. The result can only be absolute relativism.

Of course, this is not what universalist rationalism initially desired. However, according to Benedict, once relativism reigns, values must become purely individual, even if the relativism is based on universalism: "The dictatorship of relativism does not recognize anything as definitive and [its] ultimate standard consists solely of one's own ego and desires" (Ratzinger 2005b). When reason is reduced to nothing else except reason, the result is relativism. This relativism is not socially constructive (as it initially was supposed to be) but it fosters narcissism. Like with many paradoxes that cannot be solved, the final result is hypocrisy. Though the liberal mind hypocritically claims to help the other through a strict adherence to reasonable established universal values, in reality, its basis are "one's own ego and desires."

The gist of Ratzinger's argument is that absolute relativism is the product of reason. In his speech in Cologne (2005) he announces that "absolutizing what is not absolute but relative is called totalitarianism" (Ratzinger 2005). The former pope wants to establish values based on a realm "outside reason." One can of course argue that this relativism is rather due to a lack of reason (or how else could we define "one's own ego and desires"?). Once we have recognized that relativism consists solely of our own desires, why would we still defend it in terms of reason? However, that's precisely what Benedict believes is happening in liberalism. Liberalism insists on universal structures and defends those structures on the basis of reason, but by doing so it opens the door to uncontrolled individualism.

Pope Benedict's argument is easier to follow if we reframe it more consistently as a critique of liberalism. The shortcut from science to relativism is based on the paradoxical constellation of "absolute relativism" propagated by liberalist culture. Benedict is against the power of science in the social realm. He is against a culture of excellence because excellence of science is based on the narcissistic form of reason that has been described above. This becomes clear in his book *Truth and Tolerance: Christian Belief and World Religions*. Here Benedict seems to join Islamist thinkers like Sardar but also, to some extent, Adorno and Horkheimer when insisting that the malaise of modernity is due to the absolutism of relativism. In *Truth and Tolerance*, he names this paradoxical phenomenon an "amputated reason" (2003: 198). How can this "amputated reason" be defined more closely? Is it a reason that limits itself until it becomes blinded and is no longer able to see all aspects of the world in their concrete varieties? Does this limited concept of reason only see what it wants to see? Is it a sort of positive thinking ideology? In the context of a more general crisis of liberalism, Benedict's "amputated reason" can be characterized as an abstract form of reason or as a quantified form of reason that is no longer able to handle concrete cultural and social values but is hypnotized by decultured ideas of excellence.

The point of any relativism is to reveal absolute beliefs as relative because they are founded on merely communitarian standards and not on universal values. This relativism does not negate the existence of values as such, but it criticizes an attitude proclaiming random and particular values as absolute. However, sometimes this relativism becomes a universal value in its own right, and then it represents a new absolutism. I fully agree with Ratzinger until here. However, depicting "Western relativism" in such a restricted way is misleading and does not do justice to the real sense of relativism present today in the "Western mind." A more appropriate evaluation of modern "Nietzscheanism" will follow in Chapter 7.

The French intellectual right

Benedict does not believe in the Kantian or Popperian self-control of reason but wants to establish values based on religion. The very conservative spectrum of anti-liberal thinkers has rarely been considered in academic writings, but a brief analysis of some of their ideas can be instructive in the present context. French far-right thinker Guillaume Faye describes liberalism as "emerging from laicized evangelism, from Anglo-Saxon mercantilism, and from individualist Enlightenment philosophy. Modernity managed to establish its planetary project based in economic individualism, the allegory of progress, the cult of quantitative development, abstract human-rightism, etc." (Faye 1998). Faye criticizes four elements that represent the basis of liberalism: mercantilism, Enlightenment individualism, quantification, and an abstract form of reason. Like Benedict, Faye sees relativism as the core problem in the modern world. Faye explains the link between absolutism and relativism thus: because liberalism believes in absolute principles, it has an aversion toward selection. Selection is too arbitrary and too relativist for a liberal absolutist. However, *just because* selection is refused, the liberal ends up as a relativist:

> This hatred of selection rests on an anthropological prejudice: that all humans are "equally gifted." . . . One cannot accept that humans are unequally equipped in terms of mental and creative capacities as well as of character strength. This is a refusal of life well noted by Nietzsche. All hierarchies are condemned. And instead of justly organizing hierarchy and natural inequalities, one wants to impose egalitarian principles. (Faye 1998: 4)

Contemporary liberalism conceives of life as an abstract quality empty of culture. In France, more and more intellectuals are denouncing a "crisis of liberalism" and are aligning themselves totally or partially with far-right viewpoints. Among them are Alain Finkielkraut, Eric Zemmour, Michel Houellebecq, Elisabeth Levy, Jean-Claude Michéa, Michel Onfray, Jean-Pierre Le Goff, and Pascal Bruckner. Many had leftist backgrounds beforehand and most of them refuse to be absorbed by the populist dynamic of the Front National, but all find their place in a right-wing landscape increasingly advertising itself as young and dynamic. Recent books by the already-mentioned Alexandre Devecchio (2016) and Bérénice Levet (2017) insist that the new generation of far-right voters is no longer necessarily a community of reactionaries harking back to the past; rather, these voters are trying to create a future not based on empty terms like excellence but on concrete values derived from cultures. So far so good. But one can also point out that they have this in common with Islamists. Both Western populism and radical Islam are counterreactions to the culture of nihilism and emptiness that young people experience today in school, family, and professional life. Sympathizers of the new far-right and young Muslims extremists are reacting to the same existential crisis current in Western postindustrial societies. The declared enemy of *both* the young far-right voters *and* the Islamists is the liberal. The term "bobo" ("bourgeois-bohemian")[2] highlights the hypocritical character of tolerance-inspired leftists who have lost contact with the real life of common people. The typical bobo is the cosmopolitan liberal normally born between 1946 and 1964 (but who can also be younger), who benefited from a booming postwar economy but left the next generation a cultural desert in which all values have been deconstructed: "All are opposed to the 'bobo youth' seen as privileged, more and more uprooted, minoritarian and whose carefree lightness ignored the tragedy of the epoch, but with whom history will catch up sooner or later" (Devecchio: 274). According to those writers, liberalism has created a multicultural France of a fake tolerance culture fueled by repentance, victimization, and the nihilistic lack of enthusiasm for the future. The generation of "liberal progressives" (as Levet calls the bobos) is immature and unable to face important social problems. Bobos abandon questions of identity in favor of an empty talk about laicism. They are the gravediggers of their own culture and the young "Arab" population, which is overwhelmed by the alternative truths of conspiracy theories, antisemitism, and communitarianism, has no difficulties swiping away the body of this dying France.

Anti-racism inspired enthusiasm among the young in the 1980s. In France, the famous Mitterandian NGO movement SOS Racisme had some real vigor that could still be felt during the elections in 2007 (Nicolas Sarkozy against Segolène Royal). Today twenty-six-year-old Marion Maréchal-Le Pen, representative of the Christian right in France, is, according to Devecchio, the new Cohn-Bendit. Comedians like the half-Cameroonian Dieudonné changed from anti-racism to a strongly identitarian and anti-Semitic program. Dieudonné has the status of a rock star and among his fans are many young leftists, as *Le Monde* pointed out in 2014 (Seelow 2014). Like many of the abovementioned authors, Levet criticizes the nihilist and relativist culture brought about by the "liberalist" politics of the 1970s. Her critique of the culture of relativism coincides very much with Bloom's critique of the relativist "leftist Nietzschean" (2008), which might be a good English translation of the French "bobo." Apart from that, Levet reinvents many points that international critics of neoliberal education have been working on for years beginning with Bill Readings. But unlike Readings, who focuses on corporate capitalism, Levet is obsessed with progressive liberals. The findings are similar. Progressive liberals have created a "culture of novelties, of movement, of the flight forward" (28). A fake idea of progress brought about a total rupture of education with the country's cultural legacy. The liberal attitude that is permeating education leaves no place for great ideas, great works, historical events, or inspiring people. This "progressivism" is nihilist because it misunderstands the idea of progress. The left has been unable to provide an all-encompassing, cultural vision of modernity, which is the reason for the decimation of the French left in the 2017 elections. According to Levet, the only remaining ideal is an abstract notion of progress (a sort of excellence), always going for the newest of the new. Levet suggests establishing a more concrete reality based on history that contains values with which young people can identify.

Second, Levet points out that liberal culture misunderstands the notion of freedom. The individual is merely free in the sense of being cultureless. Citizens, students, parents, and politicians have become users (47) and as users, they are free to use whatever device they want. However, this freedom is based on cultural emptiness because it cancels the real freedom of persons able to represent and identify with a particular part of human civilization and make choices within a concrete cultural sphere. Users are "merely unbound but not free" ("Deliés mais non libres," 24).

Deculturation is accelerated by the atomization of society (today called multiculturalism) fostered by well-meaning and rational liberals. It has led to "cultural insecurity," a term coined by French geographer Christophe Guilluy. Right-wing criticism of liberalism reacts against a nihilist culture of relativism that lacks authenticity, action, and vigor. It is opposed to a globalized, uprooted, identity-less Western culture determined by anomie, the absurdities of an exaggerated anti-authoritarianism, the obsession with political correctness, and bureaucracy. The question is: why does it take far-right people to criticize all this? The reason is that roots, identity, and history have never been pet topics of leftists as they prefer to talk about openness, human rights, and tolerance. In the eyes of right-wing critics, leftist politics has led to the deconstruction of the country's cultural foundation, which becomes particularly dramatic when countries are under pressure because of immigration. Forty years of liberal culture, liberal education, and liberal politics brought about a spiritual, intellectual, and linguistic poverty that has consistently been disguised as a "progressive culture."

Levet wants to smash the progressive idols. But what are the alternatives? Levet writes: "We want faith in the instruction of the Enlightenment, the human sciences, and culture as the shaping powers of the human spirit that will happen through the contact with classical works" (28). Further down she writes that she wants to create "spirits able to make efforts, who have interiorized a cultural world, a language, a heritage . . . who can stem against the logic of consumer society" (56). To "the junk spirituality [of Islamists] we oppose a real spiritual life that was born in Greece: the passion to question, a critical spirit" (63). Is this not what anybody—including bobos—*should* want? This "conservatism" is not antithetical to leftist agendas as it does not call for conformity, totalitarianism, and the suppression of critical thinking. According to Levet, the new conservatives want to "attach their existence to something that is older [and bigger] than themselves" (43). What will *that* be? The Pope, Jeanne d'Arc, or Putin? Many options are not desirable. Another conservative, Ryszard Legutko, puts forward "the Church and religion, the nation, classical metaphysics, moral conservatism, and the family" (Legutko: 107). Levet is obsessed with the teaching of the classics. A lot of "learning by heart" will be used in the "reculturation" project because this will establish an intimate link with culture and language. But will reading Racine and Corneille turn young French people (including those of Arab origin) into responsible citizens? And maybe they do not want to read them because they live in a culture where those personalities are not valued. Is this again *only* the fault of liberals? Liberals did not invent iPhones and video games. Levet is convinced that liberals and not capitalism abolished the learning by heart method (56). However, if liberalism had never existed, would young people today stand in shopping malls reciting Racine? The crisis of education and Western civilization is due to the fact that there is no bigger objective, no aim that society as a whole is supposed to achieve. And it is too simple to say that liberals have simply deconstructed it away.

In spite of those fallacies, several interesting ideas can be extracted from this right-wing criticism, such as the necessity of assimilation, the hypocrisy of the liberal concept of living together, and the valid definition of civilization in terms of a Montesquieuian style to which all members should adapt (Levet develops this point with regard to the burkini affair). Still, it is questionable whether this rejuvenated right-wing movement will produce the right cultural policies. Where will this obsession with anti-liberalism, fueled by juvenile innocence and enthusiasm, lead? Can the whole world be divided into globalized, societal neo-bourgeois, on the one hand, and traditional, catholic petty bourgeois anti-liberals, on the other?

In the end, those anti-liberals are given to simplifications similar to those of liberals. Problems that right-wing philosophy cannot solve are put on the bill of progressive liberals. Not only liberals but also anti-liberals suffer from the fundamental paradox underlying liberalism's relationship with reason and Enlightenment. Levet writes that "we want faith in instruction in Enlightenment" (28). A hundred pages later she states that "the idea, transmitted from Enlightenment, that liberty needs to be grasped at any costs, focused only on rights and brought about a break with traditions" (155). Is Enlightenment what we want or is Enlightenment the origin of all liberal evils? Of course, it is both and leftist thought has gone to great lengths to "solve" this paradox, though in reality it cannot be solved.

Binary oppositions of young and enthusiastic conservatives to edgy, narcissistic bobos distract from the real problem. Why did progressive liberals develop their culture of openness and self-criticism in the first place? Because they felt strong and secure. The new right-wing movement, on the other hand, acts out of weakness and insecurity. Idealizations and diabolizations are lurking everywhere and they should be skeptically examined and not be reinforced in the hands of those intellectuals. Instead of obsessively fighting against liberalism, it is more constructive and more logically cogent to fight against what Gilles Lipovetsky has called "hedonist capitalism" because, in the end, that's what we all dislike. And the solution is certainly not a return to "authoritarian capitalism."

Liberalism and freedom

Liberals (both the progressive and the conservative type) venerate the decentralized and the global, which they sometimes refashion as the glocal. The decentralized and the global are expressions of freedom. The anti-liberal prefers centralized constellations and national items sustained by icons and symbols. The anti-liberal attitude can quickly develop toward vulgarity, authoritarianism, and kitsch. Liberals desire improvements in society but they require that those improvements should always benefit all people. That attitude can be kitsch, too.

When progress benefits all people in such a universal fashion, progress tends to be measured in quantitative terms and not in terms of quality. True, it becomes objective and measurable, but seen from an individual point of view, it becomes random and relativist. Both the liberal and the critic of liberalism have great difficulties dealing with these contradictions.

The other contradiction is the already-mentioned paradox of freedom in a liberal world. Freedom is important, but the liberal defines herself as free not because she is different (which would tend toward communitarianism) but rather because she is following the universal rule of freedom. At the same time, liberalism is a politics that solemnly declares that it will tolerate differences. The liberal is supposed to be tolerant enough to accept differences, but how can differences be reconciled with liberal universalism?

Once again communitarianism appears as the contrary of liberalism. Communitarianism is all about difference. The belief in progress characteristic of liberal universalism does not tolerate indigenous or communitarian movements. Liberalism preaches freedom and tolerance as parameters of progress, and since communitarianism contradicts the dynamics of this progress, communitarianism is the enemy. However, the liberal anti-communitarianist anger cannot be directed against "the other" because that would simply be intolerant.

The liberal cannot embrace culture because culture is never progressive. For the liberal, any culture is "backward" as it contradicts progressive developments of civilizations. Liberalism is not against this or that culture but against culture in general. However, at the same time, disrespecting other peoples' cultures would be intolerant. Therefore, the liberal makes a categorical decision: the culture of others needs to be protected and the protection of one's own culture should be considered egoistic and imperialist. Since one should be tolerant toward others, one also should be tolerant toward their cultures. Culture is not appreciated *as culture* but as a sign or a symbol of the (exotic) other that needs to be respected. In this sense, culture has not been entirely eclipsed for liberals, but it leads to a strange pattern. Because tolerance is the motto, the value of other cultures needs to be acknowledged while the culture of the majority should not receive much attention as this would denote intolerance toward minorities or, in extreme cases, their cultural oppression. Therefore, the progressive liberal excels in the protection of minorities. The main purpose of the liberal's culture agenda is not to protect culture but to relieve the liberal's bad conscience. Feeling guilty because of the preponderant universalism that liberalism is spreading, liberals decide to play down the cultural claims of their own majority and to foster the life of minorities.

The exaltation and unconditional embrace of the other has created in liberal societies an ethics of openness considered supreme. Openness toward other cultures and other social classes is also a paradigm typical for postmodern cultures based on relativism. It developed in the Cold War period in Western countries at a time when enforced closedness was seen as a supreme evil. At that time, openness toward history, especially openness toward the communist other, was seen as a virtue. Hannah Arendt has described this very clearly: "The pathos and the élan of the New Left, their credibility, as it were, are closely connected with the weird suicidal development of modern weapons" (Arendt 1970: 13).

Postmodernity started in 1979 with the Iranian revolution, when the world realized that modernity and progress are no absolute values but that some prefer to go "backwards." Nobody embraced postmodern relativism more enthusiastically than Michel Foucault who, in one of the most relativist gestures ever made by a Western intellectual, supported Khomeini's revolution because its "political spirituality" would replace Western decadence (in Afary and Anderson 2005: 209). By celebrating the victory of non-Western spirituality, Foucault declared Western culture historical and outdated. By embracing the non-West, the liberal open mind concluded that Western man is pretentious, megalomaniac, and irresponsible. The gesture was motivated by the fear of enclosure but also by guilt. Embracing the other became pretext and motivation for a full-fledged ethics that would mark intellectual life in the 1980s and 1990s. Instead of courageously embracing *its own* future, the West would produce a postmodern culture determined by openness toward the *other*.

Why did this happen? Was the West really too scared of its own evil nature? Had the West lost all confidence in its own ethical potential? The situation is rather unique in the history of mankind. Despite its long cultural heritage, the West became afraid to impose its culture upon others. From now on, the West would provide technology and entertainment to the entire world but no spirituality or philosophical insights. Spirituality would be imported from the East. In a liberal fashion inspired by Fukuyama's "end of history" vision, the postmodern West began celebrating its own well-being enhanced through shopping malls, antidepressants, and rave parties. What is lost in this "best of all worlds" vision is a futurist belief in one's own future based on one's own values and one's own spirituality. That, however, would be considered narcissistic. The Cold War period produced a relativism whose most extreme manifestation is Foucault's uncritical embrace of the non-West. By trying to avoid the decadence of imperialism, this relativism becomes decadent in its own right. By trying to avoid narcissism, the West becomes narcissistic.

In the decades to come, the global situation has not much changed but many things have become crasser and more dramatic. Now a liberal post-Cold War generation clashes with those who are looking for values. The former practice yoga and the latter join the far right or sometimes ISIS. The latter are struggling to leave the rust belt while the former can imagine nothing better than living in a loft on the roof of a postindustrial ruin. According to Philippe Muray, postmodern culture prefers "lost spaces, demolishes non-stop, creates empty dead spaces and fallows" (Muray 2002: 84). Postmodern skepticism is the symptom of an ill-digested Enlightenment heritage and it culminates in the kind of infantile relativism described by Allan Bloom.

Deculturation creates freedom, but the liberal is free only because she has accepted her own cultural disembodiment. The politics of liberalism has created a decultured sphere of excellence sanitized in line with the model of neoliberal urban spaces. Those places are haunted by excellence, but still they do not manage to appear real. Excellence has rather become the manifestation of the loss of the real. Gilles Lipotevsky writes that today

> everywhere the real must lose its dimension of alterity or thickness of the world [épaisseur du monde]: restoration of ancient quarters, the protection of sites, the promotion of cities, artificial lightening, "landscape pans." . . . The real needs to be sanitized and ultimate resistances need to be suppressed to create a space without shadows that is open and personalized. The reality principle has been replaced with the transparency principle. The real has become a place of transit (Lipovetsky: 106, my translation).

The same can be said about any cultural experiences framed by liberalism. There is no cultural density that could be experienced (loved, hated, criticized) in the form of a concrete alterity. All that remains is transparency, which includes an abstract openness toward "the other" that needs to be embraced at any price.

Deculturation: The ideology of indifference

Liberalism is against culture. Culture is neither rational nor universal, but culture has a communitarian origin. Culture is about rules and traditions and not about freedom from rules and traditions. Liberals preach freedom for everybody and the logical consequence is that the liberal self (or what is today regarded as the civilized Western human) must be "liberated" from all cultural contingencies. Liberalism is not against this or that culture, but it is indifferent toward culture. The relativism declaring all cultures equal no matter if it's Shakespeare, graffiti, a pile of bricks, or folk music, is a manifestation of this indifference. Once again, this has to do with the internal paradox of liberalism. Liberalism *must* be against culture because this is the only way to control the clash between ambitious rational-universal values on the one side and tolerance toward irrational, cultural, and "exotic" communitarian values on the other. Consequently, the moral good or aesthetic beauty will no longer be established with reference to cultures but quantitatively, that is, culturally neutrally. The good is supposed to represent an absolute truth, which brings liberalism close to religious fundamentalism. In fundamentalism, the category of "good life" is derived—circularly and narcissistically—from one's own religious (and not cultural) prescriptions.

In a free society, culture (including our own culture) is not supposed to matter. In liberal societies, everything must be evaluated by means of a universalist pattern. Liberalism degenerated into a fundamentalist philosophy of quantification determined by circular reasoning. This explains why liberal people are less concerned with their own culture but tend to be subjugated by supranational integrations. What matters is not the community of a country but the "European Community" or the "World Community." Supranational integration denotes tolerance and openness toward other cultures. At the same time, supranational integration is a means to spread liberalism because liberalism is universal by nature. It has been said above that Central Europeans identify this supranational integrationism with socialist and totalitarian internationalism and an ideology that naively proclaims to "make the whole world happy." The root of the problem is the contradictory liberalist attitude toward cultures.

The spreading of liberalism has always been determined by this paradoxical pattern. When accepting immigrants and insisting that their cultures need to be respected under the large heading of supranational integration, liberals can indulge in the satisfaction that now their universalism accords perfectly well with the contrary of universalism: they are also fostering the autonomy of individuals. Everybody has the right to liberal freedoms, and the integration of "different" (mostly non-Western) people into the universalist-liberal system is seen as an act of tolerance. After all, individual autonomy is a liberal value.

Liberals rarely realize that they are squaring the circle. Since liberalism is against communitarian contingencies, strictly speaking, the integration of differences into the universal system should not be on the program. But because liberalism claims to know the common good of *all* people, it believes in its own capacity to harmoniously absorb those differences into its own universalism.

Confronted with the above paradox, liberals will usually provide the following answer: the "different" elements should not be violently integrated into liberalism's universalist sphere, but we should simply suppose that all the world's people strive to be free, deracinated, and neutral beings. Everybody wants his life to be determined by an abstract form of rationality. Many misunderstandings have resulted from this way of thinking—for example, certain illusions about the assimilation of those who are different. Many liberals are in disbelief when being confronted with the rejection of liberal universalism by those who tend toward communitarianism.

Communitarianism has a problem of another kind. Facing the dominance of liberal society, communitarianism goes for the other extreme, which represents the problematic element in the abovementioned far-right thought. Cultural identity, nativist and historicizing arguments, self-interest, authoritarianism, and an obsession with security (leading to a restriction of individual rights) will be proposed as a bulwark against liberalism. Communitarianism also represents another danger: it is easily tempted by violence because the minorities feel weak. Liberalism is powerful and therefore it needs no violence and is even strongly opposed to violence, as wrote Hannah Arendt: "Since violence is distinct from power, force, or strength liberals are against violence because they believe to be strong. Death penalty, an extreme act of state violence, is opposed by liberals" (Arendt 1970: 4).

Neoconservative and progressive liberalism share this paradoxical starting point, and both end up with similar solutions. Both propose a pseudo-rational and contradictory concept of freedom. Liberalism (no matter which kind) is based on a cultureless concept of freedom. It is a freedom based on narcissism, which is why both liberalisms tend toward the production of kitsch-like realities. Kitsch is present not only in neoliberalism with its bombastic aesthetics à la Dubai, an exaggerated belief in the individual, or the exaltation of social Darwinism. It is also present in progressive liberalism with its humanitarian appeals to pity. The culture of excellence, which is just another kind of kitsch culture, is the product of both the conservative neoliberalism and the "progressive" thinking common among leftist liberals. The cultureless notion of excellence, which creates kitsch and bullshit alike, is produced in the name of freedom. The result of this decultured freedom is a kitsch liberty. It unconditionally believes that the denial of all (cultural and social) obligations except that of tolerance signifies the supreme achievement of Enlightenment values.

My analysis might sound counterintuitive because it represents the liberal as a sort of radical. Is the modern and progressive liberal not the only person able to combat both the progressive and the archaic and retro-oriented radical? Is liberalism not the contrary of radicalism and therefore the ingredient that is most needed in the contemporary world? Michael Mazarr describes the "radical personality type" as a person submitted to dogmatism, . . . aggressiveness, intolerance, paranoia, a conspirational outlook, and a sense of conformity and obedience to community standards" (Mazarr 2007: 69). Mazarr also adds that the radical has "an inferiority complex leading to excessive feeling of superiority." Nothing can be more opposed to the liberal, who is tolerant, relativist, and polite. However, in reality, liberalism did not live up to its ideal. Liberal tolerance became dogmatic as liberalism required its own conformity standards. What is needed is a better, self-critical image of liberalism that avoids circular reasoning and narcissistic self-confirmation. Contemporary liberalism has become kitsch as it is only about tolerance and helping the weak refusing any critical input. Contemporary liberalism is a caricature of what "liberal" was once supposed to be.

Notes

1 Soros' book was written before Islamic fundamentalism and Christian fundamentalism became public key words.
2 The term was coined by David Brooks in his *Bobos in Paradise* (2000), where he describes a fusion of the countercultural and the white-collar-capitalist bourgeois.

7

Immigration and Relativism:
Toward a Better Liberalism?

So far, the image of liberalism painted in this book has been negative: a liberalism mined by relativism, institutionalized skepticism, and axiological neutrality. A philosophically bankrupt liberalism desperately backed up by the firm belief in the economy and in growth. Is it possible to design a positive form of liberalism containing a reasonable dose of tolerance without emptying itself into relativism? A liberalism not based on a concept of excellence issuing abstract beliefs resembling absolute truths of fundamentalists but a liberalism managing to define freedom in a philosophically sound and sophisticated fashion? An enlightened liberalism that has kept its cultural roots?

The subject of this chapter is immigration because immigration politics can be an indicator of how different liberalisms behave in difficult situations. For Giorgio Agamben, the refugee is the real challenger of the nation-state, which is a typical leftist point of view. While conservatives tend to be nationalists, a leftist tends to advertise her solidarity with the refugee. In "Beyond Human Rights," Giorgio Agamben describes the refugee as a "liminal figure" who reveals sovereignty as an illusion: "If we want to be equal to the absolutely new tasks ahead, we will have to abandon decidedly, without reservation, the fundamental concepts through which we have so far represented the subjects of the political (Man, the Citizen and its rights, but also the sovereign people, the worker, and so forth) and build our political philosophy anew starting from the one and only figure of the refugee" (Agamben 2000: 16). The progressive liberal accepts the other. However, as more and more immigrants from non-Western cultures gain liberal territories, liberal ideas are under pressure.

Non-liberals tend to deal with the "clash" topic in a vulgar and simplifying fashion and summarize it as a culture clash. However, few people have seriously evaluated the differences of cultures from which could or could not emerge clashes between cultures. In general, the liberal mind avoids those discussion and points to assimilation (that is, the erasing of cultural differences) as a solution. In other words, the liberal prefers the approach of deculturation. When everybody is decultured there will be no culture clash.

Samuel Huntington explains in his *The Clash of Civilizations* (1996) that all troubles arising in globalized society relate to insurmountable cultural differences between civilizational blocks. In a post-Cold War world, cultural identities and not ideologies are the primary source of conflicts. In the aftermath of 9/11, Huntington's thesis could be used to analyze differences between Islam and the West. Huntington's idea could even be misused to stir up hatred against Muslims. Today we know that much of what Huntington predicted was false. Civil wars in Africa and the Middle East have made more victims than East-West confrontations. Clashes do not take place between East and West but rather between the local and the global. And even if one sees the global as unequivocally Western, there is still a difference between fighting another culture only because it is different, and fighting a unifying, global force in the name of local identities. Still Huntington's concept hovers like a chimera over discussions between the so-called West and the Muslim world.

Will the recent massive flow of immigrants into Europe lead to culture clashes because the values and mindsets of those immigrants are incompatible with those of Europeans? Huntington traced mindsets to solid religious sources, which is a simplification. It is more useful to search for a concept of liberal relativism permeating Western culture and to analyze whether similar conceptions exist in the cultures of non-Western immigrants. The clash—if there is one—will not take place, as Huntington believed, between Christians and Muslims but rather between cultures marked by liberal secularism and cultures not marked by this tradition. That's why I want to submit here the "liberal mind" to a particular scrutiny. Originally, liberalism was supposed to relieve the world of religious clashes. Enlightenment wanted to ideologically pacify humanity. Locke, in his *Letter Concerning Toleration* (1689), argues that much civil unrest is borne of the state trying to prevent the practice of different religions. Liberalism was the solution. Governments should not make any decisions about religion and the result was the separation of church and state. Rawls claims that all liberalism attempts to answer one question: "How is it possible that there may exist over time a stable and just society of free and equal citizens profoundly divided by reasonable religious, philosophical, and moral doctrines?" (Rawls 1993: xxvii). Much of contemporary liberalism has moved away from such simple solutions. The acceptance of the other's culture and religion in all domains of life, which is at the top of the liberal agenda, complicates life instead of simplifying it. Can liberalism be saved?

Religion and relativism

Huntington talks about religions but forgets that secularism is a cultural factor at least as important as religion. Migrant waves from the Middle East and Africa reach Europe in the first place. In the Western world, but especially in Europe, the firm belief in God or literal interpretations of scriptures is met with incomprehension by most people. Most Europeans have a secular attitude that remains indifferent toward absolute values proclaimed by religion. This attitude is related to the "relativism" that has been the topic of the preceding chapters. The European indifference toward absolute values does not only concern religion. Liberal Europeans, probably more than any other people in the world, have ceased considering their national ideals as absolutes: the creation of the European Community can be seen as a result and as a catalyzer of this "relativist" mindset. The Brexit and nationalist movements are throwbacks but, as of now, the European Community is still standing based on its original ideals.

Upon immigrating to Germany, the Egyptian writer Hamed Abdel-Samad found his German friend's jokes about his own Christian religion confusing and insulting. Why was he making fun of his own religion? Only much later Abdel-Samad understood that his friend had "laughed at his own faith not because he failed to value it but because he was undogmatic, free of compulsion and able to hold his beliefs at arm's length, making room for satire and self-criticism." His friend was liberal and Abdel-Samad cogently concludes that "this is one of the possibilities of a culture of freedom" (Abdel-Samad: 200).

In Europe, a tradition of satires directed against religion goes as far back as Erasmus of Rotterdam's *The Praise of Folly* (1511). For centuries, a satirical humanist critique of the church attempted to emancipate human thought from divine rule. Voltaire and Swift but also Monty Python and Bill Maher use humor in this "relativizing" fashion. Muslim culture does not seem to have an equivalent. Any attempt to see religious truth from a relativist perspective tends to be seen as decadent. Bassam Tibi, one of the most liberal intellectual reformers of Islam living in Germany, contrasts his own version of Islam with the "value-relativism of today's Europeans" (Tibi 2007). Tibi quotes the moderate Islamist Hasan Hanafi (without fully agreeing with him), who holds that Europe is stuck in the "moral crisis of relativism" and that only Islam can solve this problem. The relativism approach most often occurs when religious people criticize a West that has lost all its values. Often Western relativism is referred to as "postmodernism" because the "postmodern" summarizes the absurdity of a liberal "anything goes" attitude, putting values upside down and seeing good and bad as equal. A whole range of Western thinkers (Nietzsche usually leading the list) will be rejected as "postmodern" because those thinkers suggest nuanced, relativist approaches toward society. Akbar S. Ahmed, author of *Postmodernism and Islam*, points out that the discussion of postmodernism has "not reached the main body of the Muslim world. Muslim societies, still mainly rural and tribal, were struggling to come to terms with nation-states. . . . Indeed, the struggle in the Muslim world was still very much with the main issues of modernity . . . [which is] progress" (Ahmed 2003: xii). Ahmed does not mention religion. Instead he puts forward an unmitigatedly positive attitude toward modernity and progress that prevents Muslims from joining the Western postmodern fold of humanity. This is no clash of Christians with Muslims and not even a clash between atheists and believers. It is rather a clash between those who desperately want to be progressive and enlightened, and those who have moved toward a more complex, relativist, and tortuous form of Enlightenment constantly questioning its own foundations. Ahmed recognizes that postmodernism is the manifestation of a crisis that has been part of modern culture from the beginning, which is the crisis of relativism. He sees that relativism submits even reality, which is one of the most basic human "values," to skepticism and the Muslim world cannot follow this step. Ahmed quotes thinkers like Frank Kermode and Alison Lee who show that the postmodern Western worldview for which "the continuities with the past involve irony and wit" and whose "response to reality is to treat it as unreal," leads to a "reassessment of the concept of realism" because "realism has not disappeared, but it is being challenged" (Ahmed: 18).

Can refugees be Nietzscheans?

Bloom criticizes the Western infatuation with "all things being relative" which he calls the "anything goes relativism" practiced by a "Nietzscheanized Left" (Bloom: 217). Bloom's critique of Western relativism partly overlaps with that of Islamists who see Nietzsche, since he declared that "God is dead," as the founder of an exaggerated kind of relativism. Relativism is said to become a new absolutism. Can liberal relativism be defined in a positive fashion? Is there a constructive way to understand the nature of this Western phenomenon? Western relativism is indeed closely linked to Nietzsche but also to the abovementioned satirical tradition, and it is important to explain the meaning of this Western particularity at the moment it enters into contact with the mindset of non-Western believers.

"What honest alternative is there in an absurd world?" asks Karsten Harries (83). Neither Islam nor nationalism is the answer. Nor is it techno-liberalism à la Silicon Valley. Postmodernism is no answer either as it ends up in the lightness of an unbearable relativism. Still, I believe that there is a positive understanding of the postmodern condition and of liberalism as an undogmatic mindset, free of compulsion, and open to satire and self-criticism. Abdel-Samad describes his impression of "Western" culture precisely like that, which is not so different from what was suggested by liberals from Locke to Rawls: stepping back from the absolute nature of one's own beliefs and to see one's own beliefs as less comprehensive. This is no naive relativism but a constructive use of the Western Enlightenment potential. I want to analyze this attitude by concentrating on Nietzsche.

Nietzsche's "tragic relativism"

Liberalism is deconstructive by nature, but it is not necessarily relativist. The weak nihilism that we find in some forms of liberalism comes neither from Adam Smith nor from Friedman but from Nietzsche and a tradition of European humanism opposing the positivisms of both empiricism and rationalism. If liberalism accepts this culture as its foundation it can be saved. But if it embraces neo-positivist culture of measurement and deculturation it is doomed. Gianni Vattimo has stated how the postmodern condition can be invested with meaning, holding that "in place of the nostalgic effort, characteristic of reactive nihilism [and] to go back to 'values', [the task of philosophy] is a question of actively continuing the 'active nihilistic' work of the destruction of absolutes" (Vattimo 2007: 37). Nietzsche's philosophy is the principle component of this "weak nihilist" package, but, as the quotation from Vattimo shows, it can easily be misinterpreted. Bloom attributes a particular kind of Western relativism to Nietzsche, or rather to a superficial interpretation of Nietzsche, extracting from the German philosopher's thoughts the potential of relativist "conflict-resolution, bargaining, [and] harmony" (Bloom: 228) and nothing else. This is according to Bloom the mindset of the "Nietzscheanized Left." However, while Nietzsche remains indeed important in any discussion of Western relativism, not every Western relativist will summarize Nietzsche's relativism as the simpleminded belief that everything is equal and that tolerance must be practiced for its own sake. This is rather the kitsch version of Nietzsche's thought and it is also a kitsch version of liberalism. Nietzsche has been hijacked to create a world in which everybody is tolerant and everything is good; the real Nietzsche, however, is the anti-kitsch philosopher par excellence. Nietzsche's concept of the bittersweet tragic is diametrically opposed to kitsch. The tragic, which will be the subject of the remainder of this chapter, is linked to a certain form of irony and ambiguity that constitutes the real foundation of European liberalism.

The Nietzschean input in contemporary Western culture is complex. In the first place, the special brand of relativism issued by Nietzsche is supposed to restore a tragic sense of life that has been lost in Christianity. Western culture is influenced by those ideas much more than by simplistic nineteenth-century positivist attitudes or the equally simpleminded reversal of those attitudes. The more substantial part of Western relativism is determined by a complex, self-critical, and ironical form of relativism that I want to call "tragic relativism." And any revigorated, non-crisis-ridden liberalism should revert to this original form of Nietzschean relativism instead of remaining stuck in a kitsch-like humanism reiterating bland "love-not-hate" statements. For Nietzsche, the tragic is not simply sadness; it also contains joy and beauty. To achieve a state of mind able to experience tragic events in a moderately relativist fashion, it is important to master the technique of irony. This is not the postmodern radical irony that has lost contact with truth and is just "playing around" because it believes that "anything goes." There is a profounder form of irony that is linked to Nietzsche's idea of the tragic, and this irony is important for an understanding of the Western cultural situation and its relationship with the believers. It is an irony that has interiorized the most tragic experiences of the past.

This tragic irony is the exact contrary of the decultured ironies of postmodernist "play." The latter tend to end up as kitsch or produce the "the worldview of kitsch [holding] that everything is wonderful," according to Steinvorth (211). Tragic irony is different as it implies the "worldview that the virtuous is bound to suffer." Steinvorth's formulation can be complemented with an observation by Kundera for whom kitsch is either shitless or tends to indulge in shit in a fit of pity. Nietzsche's tragic irony rejects both options. Steinvorth writes: "We indulge in the misery of the tragic hero, but not in a sentiment about our pity. . . . That virtue entails misery is a reason for unending complaint, but its presentation in public satisfies us as a public recognition of true virtue, including our virtue" (211).

If Western relativism is based on this Nietzschean concept of irony, it cannot be mocked as a superficial adventure of liberation (from religion, nationalism, the family, and culture). On the contrary, it is a cultural phenomenon that has been shaped over a long period of time by a long series of tragic events. Tragic relativism does not refuse cultures and religions but is imbued with those cultures and religions. However, it deals ironically with them. Why is this irony needed? The purpose of this relativism is not to make fun of cultures and religions but to bear them. The concept of tragic irony does not lead to deculturation but to the contrary. As opposed to the liberal postmodern spirit that attains a relativist attitude through a process of deculturation, tragic irony is mainly fueled by a process of culturation. Tragic irony is culture.

At the same time, tragic irony is fueled by the awareness of loss. The disastrous experiences of two world wars, generalized insights into the evils of colonialism, the disappointment with communist utopias, plus a disillusionment with scientific progress in some fields, have created a consciousness that treats any overly optimistic belief in absolute truths and ideal solutions with irony. This more sophisticated form of relativism is a cultural phenomenon that has been cultivated by a large variety of thinkers who were skeptical of the "best of all worlds" utopias. Isiah Berlin points to Montaigne, Machiavelli, Leibniz, and Rousseau, "who thought that no gain could be made without a corresponding loss." Berlin continues explaining that "something of this, too, seemed to lie at the heart of the tragedies of Sophocles, Euripides, Shakespeare" (Berlin 288). Though the central stream of the Western tradition preaches the "feasibility" of everything, a current of fundamental doubt expressed in the recognition that "all gains entail some loss" existed, too. "For what is here entailed is that the highest ends for which men have rightly striven and sometimes died are strictly incompatible with one another" (294).

This is a good characterization of the "Western mind" that many non-Westerners (as described above by Ahmed) have difficulties in grasping. Instead, they attack a caricatural form of postmodern relativism fed by superficiality and narcissism. But this is the contrary of what tragic nihilism wants. Lipovetsky writes that "contemporary narcissism unfolds in the astonishing absence of tragic nihilism" (Lipovetsky: 74). This postmodern mind is the contrary of the Nietzschean mind as it refuses loss and prefers to preserve and to recycle (73). Postmodernism adheres to the nihilism of cowards who don't want to face the tragic play of the world. It is precisely the nihilism that Nietzsche would have refused.

The Italian Marxist theorist Franco Berardi writes that the hippies of 1968 had to decide whether their desired utopia should be dogmatic or "ironic."

He adds that today we know that the former has led to terror and the latter to progress (Berardi: 16). In the 1960s, a certain "ironic" mentality began moving to the foreground in Western leftist culture and it was saying: nothing is what is appears to be, don't take anything for granted, especially not in capitalism. Absolute necessities do not exist. There is always a gap between the signified and the signifier. This awareness was determined by ironic relativism. The "Nietzscheanized Left" has distorted and simplified this concept.

Tragic irony is thus different from the postmodern irony playing with its own emptiness. It is not an arrogant form of irony negating all values. The latter should better be called cynicism. The ironical relativism current in the West uses some Enlightenment paradigms, but it mainly evolves out of the tragic insight that absolute truths are lost and cannot be retrieved. However, this does not mean that truth does not exist at all. A relativism based on Nietzsche's tragic nihilism is no straightforward pessimism. It is rather a nihilism with ironical connotations culminating in the conclusion that all worldly matters are "tragically relative." The irony implied is not superficial but serious and says a lot about the mode of existence of many contemporary Western minds.

Tragic irony also prevents fanatic relativism. The latter remains the kitsch version of Enlightenment culture. It could also be called Enlightenment corrupted by the "pride of the metaphysician." According to Steinvorth, the metaphysician insists "that the suffering of the virtuous is absurd and that there must be sense in the absurdity. This insistence turns into kitsch when the suffering is hushed up" (Steinvorth: 213–14). Tragic irony attempts to deconstruct precisely this metaphysical way of thinking.

Though the tragic-ironical way of thinking is woven like a red thread into Nietzsche's philosophy, the connection between the irony and the tragic is not a modern invention but the two have been linked since antiquity. In Greek tragedies, heroes do everything to prevent disasters but *by doing so* they produce the real disaster. This is tragic irony. The most famous example is King Oedipus who undertakes immense efforts to find his father's murderer and discovers in the end that he himself is guilty of the crime. I say "guilty" because in tragic irony there is no absolute innocence. Guilt is always shared. The connections by which the tragic situation has been produced could not have been prevented—they were given. Still, everybody is guilty. That's the meaning of tragic irony. In it we might even find a grain of humor because humor can help us to bear this tragic irony. Tragic irony might also inspire us to write a satire.

A large part of human history can be perceived through the model of this tragic irony. A recent example is colonialism. Colonies were trying to become free and self-determined, but *by doing so* many of them made themselves more dependent than ever within a globalized capitalist economic system. Of course, one can use Marxism and other theories to explain such developments, but the ironist is tired of such explanations because all of them remain based on a grand narrative built around an absolute truth. The ironist does not believe in such truths. Instead she prefers to refer to such events as tragic.

This is Nietzsche's approach: he does not believe in dialectical and Platonic explanations but decides to replace the dialectic with the tragic. Nietzsche formulates his tragic position like this: "Saying Yes to life even in its strangest and hardest problems, the will to life rejoicing over its own inexhaustibility even in the very sacrifice of its highest types—that is what I called Dionysian, that is what I guessed to be the bridge to the psychology of the tragic poet" (Nietzsche 1997: 80). This is no superficial relativism suggesting that good and bad are simply the same. Seeing life as tragic sparks a dynamic gaiety through which one attempts to unify—and not to erase—opposite extremes. This Nietzschean thought can be the basis of a constructive form of liberalism.

Tragic versus dramatic

Have Islamic leaders or Western and Muslim intellectuals who analyze the difference between a fundamentalist and a nonfundamentalist mindset ever bothered to understand this complex concept of Western relativism? Future clashes between cultural groups might be due to its misconceptions. A priori, nothing can be more opposed to this ironic spirit than a fanatic religious attitude. Neither religious people nor nationalists have the above-described Nietzschean irony of the tragic. Fundamentalists, of course, are worse as they tend to see everything in terms of black and white, good and bad. Naturally, they are unable to understand the particular brand of relativism that flows out of this irony either.

What is the main difference between a fundamentalist and an ironist? Fundamentalists and nationalists do not like the tragic but love the dramatic. The dramatic is always dialectically calculated and tends to be pompous and full of pathos. Usually, the dramatic is dependent on a grand narrative about good and bad. Nietzsche's relativism, on the other hand, is representative of a mindset that has interiorized the tragic sense of the world. It refuses to make statements about absolute truths in the sense of *we are innocent, they are guilty*. The result is not a simplistic drama with good guys and bad guys but rather an ironical tragedy.

The logic of fundamentalists and nationalists is based on a grand narrative developing straightforward 'true' and 'false' schemes. It is a drama and like all dramas it has a typical ending: instead of attempting to gain a Dionysian insight into life's tragic reality and to live their lives accordingly, the dramatist prefers a serene escape from reality. In the case of terrorism, the clearest manifestation of this attitude is suicide bombings.

It is important to note that the dialectical-dramatic attitude that opposes good to bad, life to death, belief to non-belief, and so on is not backward but modern. From a Nietzschean perspective, fundamentalists and terrorists are modern in the sense of Socrates and dialecticians, whom Nietzsche wanted to combat. Socratic thought is against contingency, ambiguity, variety, and . . . irony. Socrates, just like positivism, does not acknowledge the tragic sense of the world. It is therefore not the Western relativists who are naive positivist, but the positivists are the terrorists and fundamentalists because they declare a holy war against everything that is impure, nuanced, ironic, and tragic. Protestants who expulse the merchants from the Temple are similarly anti-tragic and resemble progressive liberals. They want to separate state and religion. However, as Olivier Roy correctly points out, this "has nothing to do with liberalism—quite the opposite—it is a form of fundamentalism (similar to that of Shia Islam)" (Roy 2013: 122). Nietzsche's alternative is tragic ironism. When an ironist talks about nationalism it might come out in the way described by Michael Mann: "French people often proclaim themselves as culturally superior, Americans assert they are the freest people on Earth, and the Japanese claim a unique racial homogeneity, these highly suspect beliefs comfort themselves, amuse foreigners, and rarely harm anyone else" (Mann: 2). In a word, they are ironic because they have interiorized the preceding tragedies of nationalisms that one does not want to reproduce.

The drama of conspiracies

The Nietzschean liberal position can best be opposed to the fundamentalist mindset. History is determined by tragic irony and Oedipus is guilty. The philosophy of tragic irony is opposed to a mindset of terrorists and fundamentalists who relish in conspiracy theories. For conspiracy theorists, nothing is tragic. The good is the good and the bad is the bad. If the bad ones win, then we have a drama. If "they" always win, then it's an eternal drama (which is the peak of kitsch). The drama of being the eternal loser will be explained with the help of a conspiracy theory, which is a further typical manifestation of kitsch. But the situation will never be recognized as tragic. We will punish "them" by blowing everything to pieces. Of course, "we" are never guilty of any crime because we are the good ones.

This fundamentalist kitsch conception of life differs very much from the Nietzschean idea that life is tragic. The tragic state of the world is not a plot invented by the Jews, the Americans, George Soros, or the freemasons, but it's just the way life is. We all have to assume our responsibility and only by doing so can we improve the situation. Even Oedipus is responsible for what he was doing. The purpose of conspiracy theories is to shift the responsibility to others, which is why they are kitsch. Steinvorth writes that kitsch "is an alternative to the tragic worldview and can connect to a metaphysics held by both the Enlightenment and Christianity. . . . In the end, this world is the best of all possible ones" (Steinvorth: 208). It is either the best or the worst and there is no mediating irony between them. This way of thinking is metaphysical and stretches through a part of the Western tradition until Nietzsche will ironize against it. For Steinvorth, "Aristotle, Augustine and modern Enlightenment agree that vice does not defeat virtue but virtue vice" (211). Tragic relativism attempts to deconstruct this metaphysical heritage. It also deconstructs its successor, which is modern technology that minimizes suffering in an attempt to create the best of all possible worlds.

Good space-bad space

The tragic as it appears in Greek plays depends on the assumption that the good and the bad can temporarily share the same space or that they can even overlap. The result is ironic relativism. Religious thinkers of the fundamentalist kind have been making big efforts to disentangle those two spaces. For them, no overlap is permitted. "Space" should here not be understood only metaphorically: the separation is also reflected in real-life space. Since this article is about possible culture clashes between "the West" and Islam, it is useful to address the space that is created through the veiling of women in Islamic culture. In the first place, it has to do with a refusal of irony. Islamists want peoples' entire life space to be "good" while the bad (or what is considered as bad) should simply appear out of sight. Islamists want to create, as Kundera would say, a "shitless" world. Islamists limit the good, the holy, and the sacred not just to religious precincts (to the mosque); they extend it over the entire life space. The implementation of religious dress for women emerges from the anti-tragic, non-ironic "good versus bad" mindset described above. Whereas in many religions veiling is only necessary in temples, Islamists aspire to extend the space of the sacred to everything. There is no irony allowed and, as a result, no sense of the tragic either. Eroticism, which is a source of many tragic encounters, must be banned from life space all together because it is seen as bad.

Ironists know that eroticism is a prime example of the play with the ambiguous whereas dramatists deny all ambiguity. For the fundamentalist kitsch dramatist, the world is in a perfect state when *only* the good exists and the bad has been entirely exterminated. The whole world will be construed in terms of simplicity, stability, understanding, and predictability. Of course, neither this nor the complete extinction of "the bad" and the "holyization" of everybody's life are possible. The fundamentalist concludes: as long as the "bad" subsists, the world must be seen as a drama.

The dramatic "all-or-nothing" attitude becomes obvious on many levels of Islamic thought and is not limited to the worst fanatics. It appears, for example, in the thought of the relatively liberal religious thinker Tariq Ramadan. Paul Berman in the abovementioned book has connected Ramadan to the discussion from which emerged the curious concept of "Enlightenment Fundamentalism" and draws an interesting link toward the tragic. Berman writes that in Ramadan's version of Islam

> the zone of the sacred contains only a single concept. The single concept is tawhid, or the oneness of God. Tawhid leaves no room for tension between the sacred and the non-sacred, such as you see in Western thought. Nor does tawhid allow for a Promethean spirit of rebellion. Nor does tawhid permit a sense of the tragic. A deep and tragic sense of doubt is not even a conceptual possibility. Tensions, rebellions, tragic doubts—these are Western concepts. There is no room for anything of the sort in the version of Muslim civilization that Ramadan draws from al-Ghazali and Ibn Taymiyya. (Berman: 16–17)

Tawhid (the oneness of God) is also one of the five key notions that the Islamic State (ISIS) focuses on in its periodical *Dabiq*.[1] For Salafists its affirmation is as important as eliminating idolatry (*shirk*), which also undermines the oneness of God. There is no doubt, no skepticism, and, as a consequence, no irony in radical Islamic thought. Tragic irony, in particular, is unthinkable because the zone of the sacred contains only one single concept and one single point of view from which the world can be interpreted. Tragic relativism mixes together the serious and the nonserious or the sacred and the nonsacred from which emerge satire, eroticism, and many humorous considerations of social and historical events.

It goes without saying that the Catholic Church is not much better. Roy analyzes a similar problem, stating that there is no room for nuance but "you're either one of us or you're not": "Religion is thought of in terms of 'full versus empty', of belonging, commitment and identity, and no longer of presence in the world. The 'world', i.e. the surrounding society, becomes suspect, threatening, contaminating, for it is hostile, materialistic and impure—in a word: pagan" (Roy 2013: 123).[2]

The shift from the tragic to the dramatic has still another dimension. Baudrillard perceives it as a shift from the universal to the global. Positivity, positive thinking, fundamentalism, political correctness, excellence, and so on—all those phenomena can be traced to a lack of tragic irony in a world that perceives itself as a monolithic global block:

> In the universal, there is still a natural reference to the world, to the body and to memory. A kind of dialectical tension and critical movement which found their form in historical and revolutionary violence. It is the expulsion of this critical negativity which opens on to another kind of violence, the violence of the global: the supremacy of the positivity alone and of technical efficiency, total organization. (Baudrillard 2012: 70)

The West with its distorted premises of liberalism does not fare much better than the fundamentalist. It is therefore no surprise that Legutko sees a sort of *tawhid* in the fundamentalist sense also in modern liberalism, though here it comes rather in the form of an ideology of fun. It is the mirror image of the religious tawhid: "In today's world entertainment is not just a pastime or a style, but a substance that permeates everything: schools and universities, upbringing of children, intellectual life, art, morality . . ." (Legutko: 40). Atheists are not tragic people either because they, too, refuse relativism. The ironic relativist will say the following to atheists: I *cannot* believe in God but still live in a culture that has been shaped by religious traditions. As a result, I can bring together in one cultural space the sacred and the nonsacred. This idea is opposed to religious as well as atheist absolutism, but it is also different from the naive relativism that declares everything to be equal.

Those who came off badly

Why do vast amounts of individuals fall on the side of conspiracy-theory-fundamentalism while others go for tragic ironism? The reason cannot be that the former have experienced more misfortunes than the others. Disasters of all kind have occurred almost everywhere. Belief—strong religious belief—explains a part of the difference. But then again, not all believers are on the conspiracy side. With Nietzsche I would answer that the main reason why some people or entire nations or regions fall on the side of conspiracy-theory-fundamentalism is that they feel inferior. This in itself is a tragic statement. Some people feel inferior, and Nietzsche even had a special term for them: they are those "who came off badly" ("die zu kurz gekommenen"), those who got the short end of the stick. In the modern world those people engage in self-victimization.

The concept of those "who came off badly" appears in the *Thus Spake Zarathustra* and you will not guess whom Nietzsche had in mind in the first place. Christians! Christianity is for Nietzsche the sum total of oppressive morals defended by those who got the short end of the stick. There is obviously more to Nietzsche than blunt relativism propagated by the "Nietzscheanized Left." While Bloom's Nietzschean relativists vibrate the untragic undertones of tolerant resignation incompatible with Nietzsche's Dionysianism, in reality Nietzsche is the philosopher of a Dionysian—that is tragic—affirmation of life. He is the philosopher of a world that has overcome the religious fictions maintained by puritans and all those who "came off badly." The latter are hostile to life and will do everything to submit the lives of others to their antilife standards. They indulge in ascetism. However, when they claim to have adopted those standards voluntarily, Nietzsche labels them as representatives of the "slave ethics" (*Sklavenmoral*). Nietzsche would have the same words for Islamic fundamentalists because they oppose abstract concepts to life and judge everything—including themselves—in terms of a "great idea." Conspiracy theories, self-victimization, and vengeance projects are the typical next step. According to Nietzsche, those who came off badly are constantly imagining how God will punish and torture those who are strong and revenge the weak. But why are they weak? Is it because of an international conspiracy? Nietzsche's depth psychological (*Tiefenpsychologie*) approach shows that they are weak because they have interiorized the ethics of slaves.

The mindset of tragic relativism is diametrically opposed to that of all people who continue thinking in clearly distinguished terms of good and bad.

Huntington's "culture clash"—if there is one—is more likely to happen between those who adhere to a dogmatic attitude that is incompatible with Nietzschean tragic ironism and so-called "relativists." The former are generally unable to instinctively grasp the attitude of tragic relativism. However, even many Muslim and Western intellectuals do not seem to have the slightest idea that the phenomenon of tragic relativism is so current and important.

Of course, there is also another mindset in the West. Some revert to simplified and binary modes of thinking as well as to conformism. Those patterns are reinforced as they are submitted to a subtle form of the tyranny of opinion. The "administrative fundamentalism" of excellence culture is just another kind of fundamentalism avoiding the tragic. The situation is scarily reminiscent of what happened in the 1920 in Germany. At that time, people would be attracted by the mystifying and irrational ideologies of the Nazis. The next chapter examines this historical parallel.

Notes

1 The other four are *manhaj* [methodology], *hijrah* [migration], *jihad* [combat], and *jama'ah* [organization] (see the first issue of *Dabiq* [2014]: 3).

2 Roy explains this problem in more detail: "The Second Vatican Council endorsed post hoc this 'embodiment of Christianity' in social activity. But the advent of Pope John Paul II in 1978 witnessed a return to the 'faith community' where the 'people of God' were paraded before the media. . . . By making the criteria of belonging more stringent, religions contribute to this growing dichotomy and to the erosion of a profane religious culture" (Roy 2013: 123).

8

Three Anti-Liberals: Burckhardt, Evola, and Meinecke

Liberalism was the norm around 1900 in Germany and Italy, and fascism destroyed it. Liberalism was a mixture of liberal and nationalist (as opposed to communitarian) sentiment. Liberalism was strong, but this strength made it look particularly bad in the eyes of is opponents. Liberalism's strength became its weakness. Liberalism appeared to be powerful, but a minority part of the population ceased recognizing its authority as they felt oppressed by the liberal majority.

The new form of resistance to liberalism took many liberalists by surprise. The new enemies of liberalism were no longer conservatism but revolutionary movements like fascism. According to German historian Friedrich Meinecke (1862–1954), fascism was the "deviation from the main line of a European development" (Meinecke 1963: 1). Fascism speaks about the *Volk* and the nation. In this sense, fascism imports culture (even though this culture is reduced to nationalism and has mainly a militant function) into a world of liberalism that was increasingly seen as decultured.

Fascism and contemporary populist movements as well as religious extremism have one thing in common: they react against liberalism and take advantage of a crisis linked to liberalism's paradoxical constellations that have been explained in Chapter 6. The liberalism they dismantle is sick. It has been shown above that since its inception, liberalism suffered from an intrinsic conceptual paradox concerning the universalization of liberty. Consequently, anti-liberal countermovements advertise one ideal: the freedom *not* to be submitted to the freedoms of liberalism. They see this as real freedom. Some require the freedom to be submitted to traditions, though liberals perceive the latter as unfree. However, to avoid the dictatorship of liberalism, one is ready to submit to the dictatorship of non-liberal governments. Very often communitarianism is nothing but a self-serving ploy invented by some leaders to justify their authoritarian rule. Anti-liberal communitarians do not realize that they are reproducing a paradoxical constellation similar to the one they are trying to avoid.

The irrational

Meinecke attributes the deeper roots of fascism to the disturbed state of "the psychological equilibrium between the rational and the irrational" (Meinecke 1963: 51). Meinecke was one of the most respected historians in postwar Germany and internationally. Though Zeev Sternhell calls Meinecke an "anti-Enlightenment thinker" (Sternhell 2010: 288), Meinecke's views can also appear as liberal. One of his most original ideas is that of a necessary equilibrium between rational and irrational elements in all societies. More precisely, he suggests that some form of the "irrational" can be useful and positive in certain contexts. Of course, this sounds strange and incompatible with Enlightenment values. However, Meinecke can be called anti-Enlightenment only on the condition that Enlightenment signifies the blind use of reason without any critical capacity; and it has been explained in Chapter 6 that this is not what Enlightenment is supposed to be. Sternhell's rejection of Meinecke might not be totally unfounded since a revolutionary syndicalist thinker like Georges Sorel, who inspired fascists as much as Marxists, was anti-rationalist in a way very similar to that of Meinecke. For Sternhell, Sorel "stigmatized all forms of rationalist optimism, whether Greek philosophy or the natural rights of man" and identified such "rationalist" values with those of the bourgeois class of his day (Sternhell 1996: 78). This is the kind of anti-Socratic anti-rationalism that we also find in Nietzsche. What speaks against Sternhell's interpretation of Meinecke is that the latter experiments with the concept of the "irrational" in a book intended to be a smashing critique of fascism. This shows the complexity of the topic and the impossibility of classifying any of those "irrational" lines of thought (Nietzsche's, Sorel's, Meinecke's) as simple anti-Enlightenment thinking or even as fascist.

What does Meinecke mean by the "equilibrium between the rational and the irrational" and by the disturbed equilibrium that brought down communities? Is it not the *lack* of reasonable structures that entails the breakdown of communities? For Meinecke the contrary is the case. Overrationalization and technologization of society cancel communitarian structures. When people are submitted to rational structures that are purely utilitarian but lack feeling, spirituality, and intrinsic cultural values, they will overturn them by referring to irrational sources. This creates the reverse effect of what strategists of rationality initially intended: it leads to the reinforcement of community structures in terms of race and exaggerated nationalism. Still the root of the problem had been the use of formal, technocratic, and "reasonable" patterns in politics. This is Meinecke's argument in a nutshell.

Meinecke's ideas, developed in his book *The German Catastrophe*, offer alternatives to the "rational" culture spread all over the globe. Similar to the arguments of contemporary critics of algorithmic civilization that will be dealt with in the next chapter, Meinecke points to the negative sides of *both* "the calculating and planning intellect" of a new era that attempts to cancel or circumvent more cultural ways of thinking such as "spiritual understanding" and phantasy. Meinecke's main argument is that in Germany before the First World War "the balance between rational and irrational motives was disturbed in part by an overemphasis on the technical-rational" (42). Culture tips over into irrationality when an empty and meaningless concept of "reason" based on technocratic considerations is applied in a totalitarian fashion. Then spiritual forces and phantasy dormant in every society and in all individuals "run wild" and declare war on reason and intellect at large. Fascism is for Meinecke a typical manifestation of this mechanism. Fascists fought against a culture that they deemed too rational and, as a result, they became irrational. Fascism attempted to conquer a world beyond reason through "concentrated will-power" (37).

Meinecke's interpretation of fascism differs from that of Friedrich Hayek, who insists in *The Road to Serfdom* (1943) that Nazis were socialists and that Nazism was the result of the German attachment to socialism. "Socialist policies prepared the way for the forces which stand for everything they detest" (Hayek 2003: 39). Like Meinecke, Hayek sees that "the Germans, long before the Nazis, were attacking liberalism and democracy, capitalism, and individualism" (43). Socialism prepared them for Nazism. As a matter of fact, this does not entirely contradict Meinecke's argument. Hayek writes that "fascism, [which] is the stage reached after communism, has proved an illusion, and it has proved as much an illusion in Russia as in pre-Hitler Germany" (48). Fascism is a reaction against communist rationalism. This is compatible with Meinecke. The only difference is that Hayek does not recognize the same kind of naive rationalism present in liberalism. Hayek believes that a further liberalization in the form of industrial freedom fosters the free use of knowledge and science. This prerogative, which is the essence of neoliberal thinking, has led to today's culture of excellence relying on measuring and control.

Before pondering how Meinecke's theory can be read as a premature critique of contemporary "rational" neoliberal algorithm culture (to be further examined in the next chapter), it needs to be established what could have been meant by "reasonable" in Germany around 1910. For the liberal Meinecke, "reasonable" signifies the culture of degenerated liberalism. Meinecke argues in the tradition of Nietzsche, who had characterized a certain kind of liberalism as flat and shallow. In Section 38 of *Twilight of the Idols* (1997: 74), Nietzsche explains that liberalism's "herd-animalization" has undermined the peoples' will to power. The will to power is always "anti-liberal to the point of malice." In spite of this, Nietzsche concedes that liberalism can be positive while it is still being fought for, because then liberal institutions "really promote freedom in a powerful way." However, once liberalism is achieved, it is no longer fighting for freedom but becomes the "type of well-being dreamed of by shopkeepers, Christians, cows, females, Englishmen, and other democrats."

Like Nietzsche's, Meinecke's thought is complex enough to be easily misunderstood. Though the purpose of *The German Catastrophe* is to reveal the evils of fascism, Meinecke also has surprisingly harsh words for the "liberal" culture preceding fascism, a criticism that is spread through the entire book. Meinecke takes fault with a "bad" kind of liberalism that brought about the irrational counterreaction of the Nazis. He understands fascism as a counterreaction to superficial, rational-liberal culture. The liberalist "superficial rationalization" (36) began by "stamping a mechanistic character on life, in normalizing the aims of life, and in lessening the spontaneity of spirit" (35). Meinecke vividly describes "the elaboration of the system of training and examination for professional positions in the public service" where "the rational calculation of what is helpful . . . supersedes the free inclinations which are nourished by the spirit" (35).

The malaise Meinecke describes is similar to the malaise we encounter in our contemporary postmodern centralized culture of algorithms. Meinecke focuses on the last phases of the German Empire and on Prussia. The three decades preceding the Second World War were characterized by a sort of decultured rationalization comparable with our present algorithm culture. For Meinecke, a deficient form of liberalism has created a "one-sided, exaggerated peak-production of one force at the expense of the other" (38). Meinecke quotes the prefascist ideologue Max Hildebert Boehm who wrote in 1917: "The new era that is now really approaching will be characterized by techniques, rationalism, bread-rationing, socialism, by a pitiless ethos guided not by the heart but by the head" (25). Meinecke explains that in Germany around 1910

technology's expansion into all walks of practical life has . . . created a new social class whose psychological structure is markedly different from that of previous social classes, both those of the old agrarian state and those of the new bourgeoisie which has blossomed out of the agrarian state. An intellect sharply concentrated upon whatever was utilitarian and immediately serviceable took possession of mental life. Through it great things could be achieved, resulting in an astonishing progress in civilization. (37)

The country's engineers were proud of the technological progress; however, human capacities, represented by drives, the spiritual, and emotions, were neglected. Meinecke calls those capacities "irrational" as opposed to rational and observes in "the crazy madness of many of the upper class members after Bismarck's time, the despiritualization and materialization" (95). The new technological reason so enthusiastically advanced by technocrats represents an "enormous exaggeration of purely strategic considerations" (42). For the Prussian officer, to be "reasonable" was reduced to a technique. The deficiencies of the purely rational methods became particularly obvious in the draft of the Schlieffen Plan.[1] Those technicians were unable to fully understand "the totality of historical existence": everything that resided "beyond the grasp of technical-military comprehension" would not exist for them. According to Meinecke, those deficiencies led to the "fatal blunders" of the First World War (42).

Unfortunately, the worst was yet to come. At some point those predicators of a very limited form of rationalism became unsatisfied with their own "rational" existence and longed for "the spiritual." Nazi ideology takes shape here. Now the inarticulate desire for the "beyond" produces the wildest forms of irrationalism. This is not Meinecke's cultural irrationality mentioned above, which aims to integrate a "spiritual understanding," phantasy and feeling into thinking. Now irrationalism has a clearly negative meaning.

A better liberalism

Today the disturbed state of "the psychological equilibrium between the rational and the irrational" (51) as described by Meinecke has its most radical manifestation in terrorism. It perfectly coincides with Olivier Roy's explanation of Islamic fundamentalism as the result of secularization. Roy's thesis is that the separation of religion from culture does not secularize religion but isolates religion from culture enabling its pursuit in the form of anti-cultural purification. This sounds just as counterintuitive as Meinecke's idea that the rationalization of Prussian society led to the irrationality of the Nazis. However, both arguments are plausible. Like Meinecke, Roy believes that liberalism contributed to the malaise of present Islamic culture. Liberalism and secular societies helped producing religious fundamentalism through "deculturation."

However, another kind of liberalism *does* exist in religious culture and Roy does not fail to mention it. In religion, it is represented by the Protestants Friedrich Schleiermacher, Dietrich Bonhoeffer, and Harvey Cox (Roy 2013: 143). In this liberal theology of secularization, religion is supposed to merge with secular elements. Roy's theory perfectly coincides with Meinecke's idea that the irrational should merge with the rational. And the later Protestants' desire to separate state and religion is just another kind of "bad" liberalism. Religion becomes "decultured" through secularization, exactly like Prussian military culture becomes "decultured" through the technocratic spirit of "rational" strategists. Evangelism and Salafism are modern forms of religious life, too. Religion begins living outside its proper cultural reality and will "run wild," to use Meinecke's expression.

When Meinecke analyzes this phenomenon with regard to the emergence of Nazism, we are reminded of fundamentalism. Deep down, young German engineers built up a "suppressed metaphysical desire" (Meinecke 1963: 36). Formerly rational people were attracted by irrational ideologies and began searching for a reality beyond reason.[2] Meinecke calls Goetheian or humanist culture what liberal theologians like Schleiermacher and Bonhoeffer saw as a secular, cultural religion. The problem is that this culture remained inaccessible to the technocrats. The "higher reason of Goethe" did not fare well in the advancing technological age (38). Instead of looking for answers in culture or traditional religion as transmitted through a liberal theology and humanism, those new fanatics chose one-sidedly irrational ideas. Most commonly they would perceive them in the form of revelations. Since those protagonists are unacquainted with the "free, humane culture which came down from the days of Goethe" (21), they go for the other extreme, which is irrationality. Now "the technician changes into a prophet, into an enthusiast, perhaps into a fanatic and monomaniac. Thus arises the type of man who wants to reform the world" (36). Meinecke points to cases of prominent Nazis who were affected by this syndrome: Rosenberg suddenly shifted from a technocrat to a preacher of a "wild historical-philosophical complex of ideas" (37). The result of this process is the disappearance of both reason *and* culture. Though fascism wanted to bring back culture, it becomes a perfect example of deculturation: "Man's other spiritual forces, so far as they were not suppressed, avenged themselves either by those wild reactions just mentioned or fell into a general decay and debility. Feeling and phantasy, as it were, had the choice between running wild or withering" (37).

It has been shown above that fundamentalism and the neoliberal ideology of deculturation have the same roots. Following Roy and Meinecke, it can be concluded that the root of fundamentalism is concentrated in this pattern: a "definitely rational concept acquired absolute dominion over all irrational elements in men" (Meinecke: 39). Meinecke's "irrational" has thus two meanings that are entirely opposed to each other. First there is the useful irrational input provided by culture in its Goetheian or humanistic sense. No culture worth its name is purely reasonable, but in any culture, we observe the interplay of rational and irrational elements: "A sound, natural, and harmonious relationship between the rational and the irrational forces of life is all important for men of modern culture and civilization. For it is precisely modern culture and civilization which by its peculiar character threatens its equilibrium" (34). When culture is reduced to a totalitarianism of reason, that is, to a rationalism seeing itself as autonomous without considering "other" cultural elements such as feeling, spirituality, and phantasy, then the resulting imbalance produces a malevolent form of irrationalism. This phenomenon can quickly become uncontrollable and it happened when Hitler took power. The Hitler movement represents according to Meinecke a "special complete break" separated from all movements of the past (96).

Meinecke offers a critique not just of fascism but of modernity at large. In any one-sidedly technologized world the balance between the rational and the irrational is necessarily disturbed. The hermeneutic concept of balance contradicts the idea of straightforward, technical appropriations of reason. The concept of balance suggests a dialectic in which reason manifests itself as a self-reflexive and self-critical equilibrium able to reflect itself against cultural elements that are *not* reasonable: "To reach its highest and best, [reason] must also nourish itself upon irrational forces. Feeling must guide the way to the good, to the curbing of selfishness, to all moral and religious purposes; phantasy must guide the way to beauty and to the freeing of the mind from egoistically inclined desires" (34).

Community and culture

What is Meinecke's opinion about communitarianism? Liberalism "allowed old ethical ties such as family, custom, and social stratification to relax while no energetic consideration was given to the creation of new ties. Society was in danger of becoming amorphous. Already young people were growing up more or less neglected" (72–73). Again, Meinecke puts forward his concept of balance. Most important for the subsistence of healthy communities is the balance of rational and irrational structures. Going against an entire Platonic tradition of ethics, Meinecke holds that the curbing of selfishness and the suppression of egoistic desires are not purely reasonable projects. On the contrary, reason might even tell us that it is *good* to be selfish. What is needed are cultures or religions to implement such "irrational" impulses. The Prussian degenerated form of liberalism, which concentrated on the functionally reasonable and imposed itself upon German culture before the Nazis, took the contrary approach. Originally, the aim of liberalism had been to defend the individuality of humans and their actions, which the liberal Meinecke sees as positive. But by doing so it also loosened communitarian links. The resulting problems could probably have been dealt with, had German culture continued to foster the communication between the rational science and the irrational spheres of culture. However, the "shallow" and degenerated form of liberalism that had invaded the country no longer permitted this communication. As a result, a superficial rationalism destroyed communitarian life.

Julius Evola

Another critic of rationalized liberalism is the esoteric philosopher and painter Julius Evola who was initially close to the Italian futurists, but later decided to walk along the more mystical, techno-critical paths for which he became famous. After the Second World War, Evola became a major source of the Italian Neo-Nazis. Evola's itinerary is complex and contradictory. In spite of his mystical and fascist tendencies, he emerged between 1920 and 1923 as "Italy's foremost exponent on Dadaism" (Griffin 2007: 39). Similar to Meinecke, Evola criticizes that reality had ceased being a matter of touching, feeling, and sense perception and had been reduced to a quantitative evaluation of probabilities: "All scientific certainties have an essentially statistical character" (Evola: 131). Evola talks about the time immediately preceding the Second World War. For Evola science had taken the wrong path at the moment it "had freed itself from immediate data of sense experience" (137) because this kind of "'objectivity' consists solely of being ready at any moment to abandon existing theories or hypotheses, as soon as the chance appears for the better control of reality" (132). The main problem is relativism. Einstein's ideas on relativity, originally destined to solve the positivist crisis of science, made reality disappear behind abstractions. Absolute certainties adopted a purely formal character because the new scientific perception of reality was absolute only "through the flexibility granted to it by its exclusively mathematical and algebraic nature" (133). The world had been reduced to "gross physical perceptions and an abstract, mathematical intellect" and ceased "to project feelings and subjective, emotional, and imaginary contents" (143). Knowledge was no longer qualitative but quantitative. Therefore, Evola suggests the creation of an "integrated man," able to perceive the world in its multidimensionality and not only from the mathematical and cerebral point of view of the latest physics. The contrary of the integrated man, the "one-dimensional" man, reverts to

> the realm of pure mathematical thought, of number, of undifferentiated quantity, as opposed to the realm of quality, of meaningful forms and living forces: a spectral and cabalistic world, an extreme intensification of the abstract intellect, where it is no longer a matter of things or phenomena, but almost of their shadows reduced to their common denominator, gray and indistinguishable. (136)

Evola is not alone with this criticism of science and quantification. It was also expressed by the German poet Gottfried Benn who fought "the progressive 'cerebralization of the world' which was allegedly draining it of primordial energy, [which] led to his enthusiastic conversion to the 'vitalism' of National Socialism" (Griffin 2007: 17). Italian futurists attempted to reveal the world's essence by avoiding the "comfortable" formalisms dictated by authoritative forms of reason. The target of all those currents was liberalism. Liberalism produced the scientific worldview that "concerns itself solely with hypotheses and formulae." For Evola, "the apogee of the myth of physical science" coincides with that of the bourgeois era and he fights this culture. Evola's alternatives are certainly debatable because, in the end, he sides with the irrationalism of fascists and even exalts their confusion and mysticism. But his diagnosis of the situation remains clear and interesting. There is a similarity with critiques of our contemporary algorithm culture that will be the topic of the last chapter.

The most striking fact is that, just like in the interwar period, in 2018, the "rational" culture of technology-driven excellence is a liberal project and not due to totalitarian political ambitions.

Jakob Burckhardt

Meinecke begins *The German Catastrophe* with an analysis of this pessimistic Swiss historian Jakob Burckhardt (1818–1897). This is no coincidence because we find a similar—slightly tortuous—bent of reflections in both historians. It is tortuous to assume that modern rationalism led to the catastrophe of irrationalism and that, above that, this irrationalism manifested itself in phenomena that were modern. Burckhardt is another representative of an alternative form of liberalism. Prussian "rationalism" destroyed the foundations of Western culture and the community of states. This is also the opinion of Burckhardt. The policies of later Prussia represent bad liberalism because they acknowledge only a limited, technological form of reason through which the national spirit became purely rational. Those policies parallel contemporary religious fundamentalism, which very similarly interprets noncultural (religious) ideologies as highly rational.

According to both Meinecke and Burckhardt, the synthesis of power and spirit, which real liberalism should practice, as well as the "blending of rational and irrational forces" (Meinecke: 35), was not on Prussian liberalism's agenda. Meinecke and Burckhardt were looking for a liberalism establishing the free human culture of Goethe in which communities can find a hermeneutic balance of the rational and the irrational, of the universal and the individual, of politics and culture. Hitler abandoned this balance by suggesting a new folk community based on natural groupings of society. This was anti-rational and also conservative: it emphasized traditions and the values of the existing bourgeois culture. And it was also irrational because it can be contrasted with the "rational" ideologies of bolshevism.

For Meinecke, modern rationalism—combined with the irrational opposition to it—led to fascism, which is a purely modern phenomenon. The provocative idea to associate the French Revolution with a sort of "terror of reason" comes from Burckhardt. Burckhardt was critical of Enlightenment to the point that he saw the "germ of a great disease" in the "optimistic illusions of the Age of Enlightenment and the French Revolution" (Meinecke: 1). Like Meinecke, Burckhardt believed that contemporary German society was modeling itself on the military, that its forms, symbols and concepts were penetrating and reshaping German society and culture in its image. This development was not, as Hayek seems to think, socialist but liberal. At his time, Burckhardt argued that the only solution, if Germany was to avoid the specter of totalitarianism, lay in a return to the spiritual. Burckhardt believed that "Germany has now made politics its guiding principle, and now it must bear that burden. O how the eyes of those wise men who are now celebrating Prussiandom, how they will open wide when they are forced to see that the desolation of Germany's spirit is dated from 1870" (quoted in Hinde 2000: 126). Political and military power grows at the expense of cultural power. This is a perhaps pessimistic but not an anti-modern position.

Burckhardt, colleague of another major nineteenth-century maverick, Friedrich Nietzsche, whom he befriended at the University of Basel, certainly did have a pessimistic view of modernity. From Burckhardt's Swiss point of view, modernity was concentrated in Berlin and Prussia. He preferred small units to states because he believed that individual liberty cannot be guaranteed in large states. The vast increase in the power of the state would destroy the creative spirit of the individual. In that sense he was a liberal. However, Burckhardt also looked nostalgically back to the ancien régime. He was skeptical of technological optimism, nationalism, centralization, mass culture, and power politics. An obsession with the French Revolution as the origin of all modern diseases brought him in opposition not only to socialism, classical (laissez-faire) liberalism but also to Prussia's militarism.

In Burckhardt's logic, the optimistic assumption that humans are reasonable, an assumption leading to the reduction of culture to purely reasonable structures, denotes irrationalism. This idea is certainly out of tune with any enlightened agenda as we know it, but it is not merely anti-Enlightenment propaganda. For Burckhardt, the state posed a direct threat to cultural production and freedom. Burckhardt chastises Prussian militarism, which is usually seen as conservative or as a trailblazer of "conservative" fascism. He claims that the naive belief in the rationality of all humans and the realization of a "liberty for all" leads to laissez-faire liberalism. The latter would today be seen as conservative. He was worried about the rise of mass democracy and socialism; then again, his conservatism remains very different from that of real anti-Enlightenment protagonists like fascists. Burckhardt fought for another kind of conservatism represented by a neohumanist agenda of *Bildung*, historicism, and historical criticism, which is a typically German intellectual model based on the work of Giambattista Vico and Johann Gottfried Herder. The entire agenda can be opposed to Rousseau's optimistic assumptions about the goodness of human nature. Burckhardt characterized those assumptions as a naive dream. He criticized a too optimistic form of liberalism producing the technocratic spirit of Prussia.

Terribles simplificateurs

Meinecke traced fascism to Prussian rationalism, or, better, to the fascist irrational opposition to Prussian rationalism. Fascism emerged from these irrational, non-balanced currents. Burckhardt goes further when suggesting that the origin of this development can be found in the French Revolution. For Burckhardt, European history is shot through with an optimistic strain of thought obsessed with the happiness of the masses that led to the modern world implemented by the Industrial Revolution and, later, technology. It also led to socialism. The "reason" issued by these movements is more like an uncritical belief in reason; and this belief has led to deculturation. The main problem with revolutionary reasonableness was that it attempted to simplify all social and cultural structures. This simplification is for Burckhardt the origin of terrorism. The *terribles simplificateurs* of the revolution sparked a radical tradition of anarchism because they believed in the unlimited "reasonable" progress of humanity. Subsequently this spirit took over European culture. The inheritors of the revolution would work in the name of progress and modern liberalism, but Burckhardt predicted a reverse effect. In a letter from 1889 to his German friend Friedrich von Preen, Burckhardt writes the following famous passage: "My mental picture of those *terribles simplificateurs* who will one day descend upon our old Europe is not a pleasant one. In my imagination I can visualize these ruffians in the flesh before my eyes and will describe them to you when we are having our pint together in September" (Burckhardt 1946: 455, my trans.). Burckhardt predicts a catastrophe. Will this catastrophe come in the form of modernity or in the form of a revolt against modernity? Of course, for the conservative Burckhardt, it was the modern undoings of mass suffrage, modern public education, and women in scholarship that was simplifying culture by imposing its rational, liberal structures on a traditional culture.

Burckhardt's anti-French-Revolution conservatism puts everything upside down. It would be comfortable to put Burckhardt into a far-right conservative niche (like Edmund Burke, another famous critic of the Revolution) and simply leave him there. However, Burckhardt's writings can also be read as a discourse on Enlightenment (which coincides with criticism of prefascist culture as developed by Meinecke) highly useful for a critique of the contemporary liberal situation whose "reasonableness" is traceable to an uncritical Enlightenment culture beginning with the French Revolution. Burckhardt is not merely old-fashioned. He shares something not only with counter-Enlightenment thinkers like Herder who see Kant's dogmatic definitions of freedom as unbearable simplifications because the organization of human life is too complex. He also shares something with representatives of modernity like the futurists. Futurism does not continue—it actually contradicts—the developmental line of European civilization beginning with the French Revolution. True, there is technological optimism, but the optimism of fascists and futurists is different from the optimism of the French revolutionaries. If we read Burckhardt and Meinecke we will find that those conservatives want another kind of modernity with more complex social and cultural structures. It is true that (as Meinecke also holds) Burckhardt predicted fascism. However, he did not predict fascism directly. Rather what he predicted was a rational, simplistic, and "progressive" civilization in which the complexity of culture is reduced to algorithms; this came true and fascists emerged as a counterreaction to this culture. The reduction of culture to "progressive" structures was thus the work of the simplifiers of the French Revolution and not that of fascists. This is not to say that fascists do not simplify things (just like fundamentalists do) but the simplification is not their primary misdeed. Their mistake is the adoption of irrational positions *when facing the simplifying rationalism of modernity.*

The pattern that I am trying to describe can be retrieved with the help of Meinecke's system, which divides reason into two types: (1) the *homo sapiens* and (2) the *homo faber. Homo sapiens*, the representative of a Goetheian "higher reason," could thrive, according to Meinecke, in classical liberalism. *Homo sapiens* is not appreciated by the *homo faber*, who prefers statistics and algorithms. In the "advancing technological age, *homo sapiens* was therefore supplanted by *homo faber.* No longer was there a striving for a harmony of the various mental and spiritual forces" (38). Fascism's and Futurism's conservative—though never anti-technological—inputs contradicted the development that had begun with the "terrible simplifiers" of the French Revolution. Noah Toly, in a post on the Christian website *Books and Culture*, could not have made this clearer when writing that Burckhardt

> dreaded a future in which increasingly complex technical capabilities would enable the pursuit and possession of unimaginable material welfare but would, at the same time, flatten social relations. He predicted that élites employing logics of generalization and abstraction would not merely enhance our capabilities but

also attenuate relationships, sharpen the division between classes, and decrease our sense of individual agency. (Toly 2015)

The revolt *against* simplification was enacted by those whom Arendt describes as people left behind by modernization and for whom "terrorism had become a kind of philosophy through which to express frustration, resentment and blind hatred, a kind of political expressionism" (Arendt: 330, 332). They were not simplifiers, but they were tired of simplifications. This needs to be pointed out clearly because it has often been assumed that Burckhardt predicted the Nazi regime because the latter represents a direct enactment of simplification. Niall Ferguson stated this recently in an opinion piece called "Simplifiers versus Complicators." Ferguson holds that Burckhardt predicted "a new generation of ruffian leaders" who would one day "make short work with voting rights, sovereignty of the people, material well-being, industry, etc." (Ferguson 2016). Ferguson refers to the Nazis but also indirectly to American president Donald Trump who is, in his opinion, the most recent manifestation of the simplifier tradition. However, the contrary is true. The voting rights and industrialization (Burckhardt mentions these) were introduced not by the complicators but by simplifiers. Burckhardt was against industrialization. He was skeptical of mass politics, the growth of democracy, and egalitarianism, and he saw the collapse of the authority of the Church as another step toward the modern age of simplifications.

How is it possible that the argument was turned around in that way? Even Meinecke's account of Burckhardt can be understood as if Burckhardt had predicted the Nazi catastrophe *directly*. However, Burckhardt did not predict the Nazi regime in such a straightforward manner. For Burckhardt there was a straight line leading from the simplifiers of the French Revolution to the rationalist simplifiers of modernity who do everything to represent the world in the form of reasonable, technological structures. Socialism continued the simplifier tradition. The Nazis were complicators while Stalin and Mao were simplifiers. Hitler spoke for those who were left behind in the rational, simplified world of a degenerated liberalism. This is the scope of Burckhardt sentences when he speaks out against "terribles simplificateurs" and ruthless demagogues who induce mass politics and mass culture to set up the functional world of industrial capitalism, progress, science, and technology, and who release culture and everything that is complicated into a whirlpool of unity and conformity. What could make us think that Burckhardt meant the Nazis? He meant a degenerated form of liberalism, and Nazis as well as futurists were against this.

For Burckhardt this unreal world of rationalism was initiated by the French Revolution and theorized by Rousseau. Burckhardt rejects some core ideas of Enlightenment as "unreal"—first of all the assumption that human nature is good. For him this is one of those simplifying Enlightenment dreams incompatible with a more complex, palpable, experienced reality. Burckhardt criticizes Rousseau for making "no use of the real, concrete life and sorrows of the French common man" and finds that the Swiss philosopher remained all his life a "theorist [and] a Utopian" (Burckhardt 1958: 243). Rousseau's *Confessions* are characterized by an "unnerving dreaminess, and virtuous feelings rather than virtue" (Burckhardt 1943: 243). Burckhardt's own work, on the other hand, was supposed to be based "on the study of the harsh reality of the human condition" (Hinde: 116). The naive belief in progress and utopias offered by liberal philosophy "was nothing less than self-deception and delusion" (Hinde: 116). It leads to spiritual bankruptcy and materialism because it gives no real account of good and evil, of fortune and misfortune.

The philosophies of Burckhardt and Meinecke are supposed to lead to more precise and more diversified perceptions of reality. Reality as it is perceived by German historicism is linked to individual values. Burckhardt writes that every age must be viewed in terms of its own immediate values. "There is no progress or decline in history, but only value filled diversity." The latter sentence was written by Georg Iggers in his *The German Conception of History* (Iggers 2012: 30). Historical reality is concrete and not abstract. It is the contrary of the globalized, standardized, and virtual reality produced today by algorithm culture. Such thoughts used to be considered in discussions of irrational fascism, and they should be reconsidered today in discussions of modern algorithm culture as well as of irrational Islamic terrorism.

Notes

1   The Schlieffen Plan was a strategic plan projecting the German invasion of
France and Belgium in 1914. Retrospectively it has been seen by some critics as a
miscalculation, which condemned the belligerents to four years of attrition warfare
(see Ritter 1956).
2   I have explained this development in more detail in Botz-Bornstein (2019).

9

The Narcissistic Culture of Quantification

Liberalism favors quantification, which contributed to its internal crisis. That's why Meinecke's and Burckhardt's criticism is of utmost actuality. Not much has changed since 1900, and contemporary techno-criticism can build on what those thinkers have begun. Nietzsche would find today that algorithm culture has entirely erased the tragic. The algorithmic engineer of excellence emerges from the Socratic culture of reason. Since 1900, technologies have become more sophisticated, but the essence of technology has remained the same. Techno-culture developed toward positivism, objectification, and quantification. The rational, simplistic, functional, and "progressive" world of industrial capitalism is the work of a new generation of "terribles simplificateurs" who release, through algorithms and personalized news on Facebook, culture and everything else that is complicated into a whirlpool of conformity. That's what Burckhardt had predicted. Neoliberalism accomplished the liberal project of quantification of around 1900 by promoting a political culture dominated by "experts." Finally, by replacing human choices, algorithms transform the consumer world into an echo chamber of the self. This is the latest simplification of the human cultural sphere and it is promoted as the highest accomplishment of liberalism because it is said to provide individual freedom.

In the 1970s, Macpherson predicted, in his *The Life and Times of Liberal Democracy*, that the so-called "will of the people" will one day be "manufactured in ways analogous to commercial advertising" (1977: 87). Neoliberalism has made this possible by implementing an algorithm culture working in the spirit of positivism. This culture is enforced by the economic surrealism of experts. Neoliberalism has established a non-tangible world that we are supposed to accept as real. The main problem is that algorithmic reason is no real reason. It is not a reason in the sense of, for example, Kant's pure reason or Aristotle's practical reason. The pseudo-reasonableness of liberalism was already the red cloth of anti-positivism around 1900. Algorithms are efficient *not* because they have acquired a particular understanding of a segment of reality (for example, a webpage), but because they measure the social force of the webpage inside the structure of the internet. This kind of functional reason overlaps precisely with the positivist (or "paleopositivist") reason that the "vitalist" philosophies of Nietzsche, Bergson, and Sorel as well as voluntarist subjectivists and neo-idealists revolted against hundred years ago. The algorithmic reason is a reason separated from the real world and hyperbolizes segments of reality. It is a self-referential kitsch reason. The kitsch metaphor imposes itself because one of the components of kitsch is that it is inappropriate or exaggerated because trivial incidents are blown up out of all proportion. Algorithm culture is kitsch. Numerical reality has become incompatible with the lived and felt reality of our everyday existences, and deculturation and dereferentialization are the supreme principles of this techno-narcissism. This emerges particularly well from the work of the aforementioned Nicolas Bouleau. Nietzsche would require that algorithms be replaced with instincts.

Liberalism and quantification

It has been said in Chapter 6 that Pope Benedict's concept of the "amputated reason" (vaguely derived from Kant's pure reason) represents an abstract form of reason or a quantified reason no longer able to handle concrete cultural and social values. Benedict indirectly addresses the concept of *quantified* reason, which is the product of liberalism's paradoxical "universal individualism." Liberalism aims to foster *individual* freedoms, though at the same time it adheres to a ratio-based form of *universalism*. In the twenty-first century, anti-liberal communitarians rally, once again, against liberalist universalism.

For Meinecke, all those who adhere to a purely technical concept of reason (a concept that he saw as being limited to the "technical-military comprehension," Meinecke: 42) believe to make universal statements. However, in reality they are unable to understand "the totality of historical existence." Those misconceptions led to the "fatal blunders" of the First World War (42) when liberal deculturation deprived the country of its intrinsic cultural values and plunged German civilization into irrationalism. Today's situation is not very different. Again, the enemy is the liberal who attempts to generalize a technicized, decultured reality by using a very limited concept of rationality.

Algorithms are the last manifestations of a movement of pseudo-rationalization. An algorithm is a self-contained mathematical operation used in data processing and automated reasoning. For techno-critics, the algorithm symbolizes a centralized "reason" through which a totalitarian system attempts to construct a new reality. Far from being merely technical tools, algorithms bring with them an emergent political project. The "reasoning" of algorithms does not merely concern the right calculation of relevant data but the calculated data create a simplified reality of their own. In the end, entire societies will live in the brave new world of numerical affinities in which reality is increasingly fabricated through "rational" calculations. The term "numerical affinities" comes from French sociologist Dominique Cardon (2015) who has plausibly shown that statistics do not merely calculate but reinvent everyday reality.

Quantification began around 1250 when European science moved away from Platonic idealism and aimed to interpret reality via uniform units such as miles, minutes, and musical notes (see Crosby 1998). Civilization took its course, probably always believing, in a liberal fashion, that it can only move toward the better. The liberal credo is to change the world and the ideal of liberalism turns out to be a numerical society. Silicon Valley is the realization of this liberal utopia. Sometimes the techno-utopia is mixed with an exalted New Age ethics, which makes it kitsch. Silicon Valley does much more than technical experiments: it attempts to create a better world. The credo becomes neoliberal when the realization of this dream is linked to spectacular economic benefits.

At present, few gestures in our lives are not influenced by calculating infrastructures: shopping, traveling, sex, personal and professional decisions, and so on. While we might not take those calculations entirely seriously, at the same time, we make no serious attempt to escape them. The driving force behind this algorithmization of everything is the assumption that our lives, our bodies, conversations, food, and sleep, are measurable and that the right calculation of their data will make our lives more efficient. One problem is that this measuring activity, to which in the past only specialists (mostly employed by governments) had access, can now be practiced by everybody. Another problem is that the logic of personalization creates a new category of the social, which is the "behavior society" in which relationships between a central authority and the (increasingly) autonomous individuals are about to be completely redefined. Our everyday reality is reinvented in terms of statistics. Humans begin to adapt to this reality, which means that algorithms do not merely calculate but *transform* reality. A bigger problem is that most of the time the calculations themselves remain mysterious. It is very easy to manipulate audience measurements, for example, through "clickbait" or through the selling of "third-party cookies" to ad-networks like Weborama, Double-Click, or Right Media, whose task is to link online commercials to browsers. The artificial fabrication of authority has become the elephant in the room that nobody dares to talk about. Fake sites are created to accommodate links and there are site farms (Cardon: 27); and Facebook and Twitter do nothing to chase away false accounts and cheaters.

Though the preachers of algorithms affirm to have overcome the traditional system of authorities (supported by journalists, editors, marketing specialists, etc.) in the name of decentralization, in reality they have created a new authority that will sooner or later exclude those who are not already in the center. Just 1 percent of internet users occupy 90 percent of the overall visibility (Cardon: 95). Attention attracts more attention, which is a narcissistic principle produced by a new generation of *terribles simplificateurs*. In the world of authority, attention is a matter of merit while in the world of "numerical affinities" it is fabricated. Cardon explains this through Gabriel Tarde's theory of "gloriometers," published in 1895 in *Lois de l'imitation*, which has recently attracted the attention of sociologists like Bruno Latour. Social networks are immense "expressive signs factories." Those signs are quantified and classified along the guidelines of an abstract form of excellence. You have to be "the best" in terms of clicks and links. The inevitable consequence is that the reality of excellence invented by algorithms becomes more and more incompatible with the reality of our everyday existences.

Excellence versus existence

A free individual has the right to make a hypothesis based on a limited number of data and to hope that this hypothesis is right. Of course, this does not sound very scientific. The quantifying positivist wants to be more "scientific" and not waste time with hypothesis. She tends to be against all theory (see Anderson 2014). The model of the persistently optimistic data scientists is provided by the exact sciences, and since computers are able to calculate an enormous amount of data instantly, hypotheses are almost unnecessary. Data provide us with knowledge about everything; all we need to do is to compare different data among each other. The only hypothesis permitted is the one suggesting that a regular and predictable character of behaviors does exist. When you have a GPS, you do not need to make hypotheses about what would be the best way to get to the destination. Knowledge is automatized. All this is efficient, but it does not submit us to the existential act of choosing. It is difficult to defend this lack of choice in terms of liberalism because it does not make us free. Instead of providing liberty it deprives us of liberty. Risk taking, one of the activities that make hypotheses interesting and "cool," is no longer possible. Universal liberty makes unfree, which was already the paradox of liberalism hundred years ago (see Chapter 6). A really free individual should have the right to reflect and to contemplate from a distance as long as he deems it necessary. A really free individual must be able to scrap his own internet profile at any moment. Only then can we govern ourselves without being essentialized in terms of our behavior and separate ourselves from the simplified and automatized and existences suggested by algorithms. So where is the freedom in this liberal society of quantification? Neoliberal freedom forces us to revel in our own narcissism. Cultural activities like choosing and creating are replaced with anticipation, prediction, and regulation. This is not merely a technical but a political revolution. Humanity becomes transparent, immaterial, and decultured.

The paradox of liberalism has crystallized more than ever before. In reality, the algorithmization of life goes against the grain of what the free citizen values most highly. People continue being suspicious of centralized powers, be it the power of politicians, journalists, or unions. People abhor being classified, believing that their individuality fits into no "box." However, the same individuals allow themselves to become locked into the bubble of algorithms because this authoritarianism is camouflaged as non-authoritarianism. On top of this, people are impressed by the "exact science" claim as well as by the speed and the effects of viral coordination. This techno-kitsch is part of the principle of excellence culture.

Existences, just like experiences, should be cultural. And as cultures they cannot be quantified. What can be quantified are clicks, purchases, performances, or interactions. Since their mere quantification is not interesting either, the data need to be calculated through algorithms to be compared with other clicks, purchases, performances, and interactions. This creates a narcissistic agitation of excellence, which reads in Cardon's text like this:

> A unified theory of behaviors is replaced by calculators with a constantly revisable mosaic of contingent micro theories formulating local pseudo-explications of probable behaviors. Those calculations are supposed to lead us towards the most probable objects. They do not need to be understood and often they cannot be understood. This inverted way of fabricating social life denotes the reversal of

the causality underlying statistic calculations. The purpose is to take into account the individualization of our societies and the increasing indetermination of the forces that determine our actions. (53, my translation)

Social indeterminism has led to a new determinism or a behaviorism of new calculation techniques. The freedom that has been acquired in postmodern societies has led to new constraints, this time imposed upon us not by dictators or by capitalism but by a neoliberal form of technology. Algorithms measure the social force of the webpage inside the structure of the internet—that is, they measure the number of times the page has been linked to. This was the revolutionary idea of Sergey Brin and Larry Page, the founders of Google. The positivism of algorithm culture claims to have overcome ideologies and traditional authorities because the latter are said to make individuals unfree. By following algorithms, the individual is merely following himself. This "self" is truly individual as it is not even linked to a larger group. The internet user who follows algorithms does not have to adhere to the "essential" tendencies of his ethnicity, nationality, religion, and not even of his/her gender. What could be freer than that? A CD is not suggested because the user is a Muslim or an American woman. No, it is suggested because the algorithm has *evaluated* the person's previous behavior. It has simply been measured. However, the freedom stops when algorithms lock us into their own dream of a quantified person. By basing all knowledge on the quantitative analysis of interests, the algorithmic approach refabricates individuals and entire societies in a narcissistic fashion. It reduces individuals to their own behaviors from which they will have difficulties in escaping. In the end, the user will be captured in a bubble that will be explained to him as the result of maximized freedom. Existential freedom has been stifled by the calculators' ambition to construct the image of statistical regularity that we take for granted and accept as the result of our free choice. The famous "nudges" that Carl Sunstein analyzed in *Why Nudge?* can very well be construed as the kind of "voluntary paternalism" used in cults and religions to make people believe that the forced "choice" was actually voluntary.

A classic existentialist theme comes to mind when Cardon says that people submit their destiny to the "funnel of the probable" (16) because the size of the sample of personal information used for the creation of an algorithm is disproportionate. The probable has here become an essence to which we are supposed to submit our existence, instead of, as Sartre urged, to impose our own existence upon the surrounding world and to only determine potential essences *afterward*. Through algorithms the probable is no longer "interesting" (in Schlegel's sense) but becomes an essence. We accept our own essentialization through quantification and seriously explain this as an act of freedom because what has been quantified are *our own* choices. However, "can the profile that has been derived from my traces not lead to aberrant and discriminatory decisions?" asks Cardon (80). The regularity is even produced automatically, which should make us suspicious with regard to any freedom-related argument. Are automatically created choices compatible with (a more existentially determined idea of) freedom? Certainly not. People can have "interesting" existences that do not necessarily fit into schemes of regularity. To be free also means to have the right to make mistakes from which one can learn. Mistakes can make lives interesting. Being lost in a city, losing time and money, taking risks, marveling at something one doesn't really understand, assuming the responsibility for mistakes that have been made, and so on—all these are existential experiences to which an individual is entitled in the name of freedom. In the world of algorithms, we no longer have this freedom. Being lost, losing time, and so on are incompatible with any of the standards of excellence.

Big data promoters are not impressed by what educated persons might point out as "probably good" or "plausibly good" about a website as derived from cultural contexts. Quantification fundamentalists disqualify human-made judgment and believe in truths that have been revealed by machines. The positivism of the algorithm culture of the internet refuses ideologies or traditional authorities because the latter are believed to make individuals unfree. The algorithmic approach bases its knowledge on the quantitative analysis of "the peoples'" interests. However, by doing so, it refabricates societies and reduces individuals to their quantified behaviors from which they will have difficulties in escaping. Quantification culture creates a new reality in the name of excellence. Only the best and most valuable ones should be valorized. But valuable in terms of what? In ancient Greek philosophy, values were ethical and could make sense only inside a cultural context. Neoliberal values are monetary and utilitarian or perhaps not even that they are narcissistic as they refer merely to themselves. In algorithm culture, this means that individualized data will be compared with other individualized data and knowledge will be derived from this comparison alone and not from the cultural content of the item in question. The world is no longer described in terms of cultures but in terms of a fundamental truth representing a strange and fallacious combination of religion and scientific thought. Liberal truth is abstract and quantifiable, which means that there is no truth. The absolutism of quantification culture has killed subjective experience. As a result, humans are lost in relativism. The paradoxical shift from absolutism to relativism needs to be explained one last time.

Hundred years ago, the obsession with mathematical calculation sparked the anger of vitalist philosophers, as has been shown in the preceding chapter. We can observe similar reactions today. Pope Benedict reflects about the "fake reality" problem in Aldous Huxley's *Brave New World*. In a conversation with Benedict, Peter Seewald summarizes Huxley's novel, pointing out that here the world is objectified to a degree that truth or reality have been eradicated. The objectifications bring about the loss of subjective reality:

> In his futuristic novel *Brave New World*, the British author Aldous Huxley had predicted in 1932 that falsification would be the decisive element of modernity. In a false reality with its false truth—or the absence of truth altogether—nothing, in the final analysis, is important anymore. There is no truth, there is no standpoint. Today, in fact, truth is regarded as far too subjective a concept for us to find therein a universally valid standard. The distinction between genuine and fake seems to have been abolished. Everything is to some extent negotiable. Is that the relativism against which you were warning so urgently? (Ratzinger 2010: 50–51)

The pope agrees, which means that he accepts a paradoxical definition of relativism. Relativism is not produced through subjectivity or through an exaggerated reliance on subjectivity. Relativism is rather the consequence of the liberal insistence on quantifiable, universally valid standards. When truth is universal, truth disappears. What needs to be brought back is subjective experience. The pope requires the reinstallation of religious experience as a subjective ground. Objective, quantified, standpoint-less truths should be challenged by religion. We do not have to agree with the pope that the alternative to the "loss of truth" is religious truth. What matters is the call for subjectivity that can come in forms other than religion. Suggestions how the loss of reality can be fixed have been offered by thinkers like Bloom, Meinecke, and Burckhardt. Their suggestions have been discussed above. Like Huxley, who was writing his novel in the 1920s, those thinkers of the twentieth century see a particular kind of relativism as the core problem. It is a relativism produced by an absolutizing form of rationalism.

Unfortunately, many anti-liberal philosophies are more vulgar and simplistic than those formulated by the above authors. Once deculturation has created a cultural wasteland, the counterreactions to techno-kitsch will be just as unsophisticated and violent. Fascism is one example. At the time of the First World War, when, according to Arendt, "all traditional values had evaporated (after the nineteenth-century ideologies had refuted each other and exhausted their vital appeal)" vulgarity with its cynical dismissal of respected standards and accepted theories "was more acceptable than reasonable theories and old traditions" (Arendt: 334). Meinecke describes how "the technician changes into a prophet, into an enthusiast, perhaps into a fanatic and monomaniac" (Meinecke: 36). When cultural truth has been buried under a fake reality, there is very little cultural ground on which absurd propositions could be refused. In the conclusion I will suggest more alternatives.

Conclusion: The Hermeneutic Solution

Neoliberal culture and fundamentalism produce alternative realities by following the principles of kitsch and alternative truths. Truth is manipulated. The most commonsensical reaction would be to call for scientific verification of all truths. However, science itself has become part of an alternative truth game. Reason and even the most rational methods inherited from Enlightenment produce kitsch (as well as its ethical version called "bullshit"). Once they have become self-referential and narcissistic they are looking merely for excellence.

Who can lead us out of this world of scientification where even science, assisted by a corporate culture of quantification, is unable to check reality and where science creates an alternative reality on its own? Only the traditional human sciences or what I call the "hermeneutic humanities" can consistently check the kitsch production of post-capitalist societies. "Humanists" have always been most critical of scientific kitsch culture. In education, quality monitoring, quality reporting, and quality measuring meet with particularly strong skepticism by the faculty of the humanities.[1] It's the humanists who find the quantifying and evaluating hyperactivism of administrations most disturbing and ridicule the obsession with control, standardization, and questionable ideals of competition and excellence. Bill Readings, the author of *The University in Ruins*, was a professor of comparative literature. Humanists, not natural scientists, criticize the arbitrary quality of the weighting of factors and sense the dubiousness of quantitative indicators of quality. Humanists see that the standardization methods are often derived from or even directly provided by quality management agencies based in the industry. Being confronted with the new apparatus of measuring and evaluation tools, colleagues from the humanities often believe that the purpose of the entire quantification project is to control how they think. Or, even worse, that one wants them to stop thinking all together and simply adapt to signals sent out by computers.

Reculturation can only happen via the humanities. Humanists are fighting against a powerful enemy because neoliberal corporatization and the scientization of academic life work in parallel. Both business and science tend to absolutize the methods they are working with. The humanities are facing two enemies: the corporate world with its business model *and* the pseudo-scientific approaches adopted by corporate universities. This is not to say that any "for-profit" is bad. Richard Ruch has shown that this economic system provides many advantages and one should be liberal enough to admit this. Though, as Ruch affirms, the "intellectual passion, disciplinary specialty, and deep engagement with material are not particularly well understood by the business side" (Ruch: 118), and though research is less emphasized in those universities' mission statements, it would be unfair to attribute all shortcomings of the new university culture to the desire to earn money. What needs to be criticized is the combination of corporation with science, which cannot be traced to mere commercialism. The main problem with the corporate university is not that it makes money, but that it implements a bureaucratic form of reason that is incompatible with the values of education.

Contrary to what many people might think, scientification is a much older problem than corporatization. One of the founders of "value philosophy" or axiology, German philosopher of science Hermann Lotze (1817–1881), experienced the university's move toward bureaucratic centralization within an encompassing national state and criticized a materialist conception of science, which "pulverized the good and the beautiful into atomic dust" (Kraushaar: 517). In a more contemporary context, hermeneutic philosophers have put the problem of the scientification of education and of the humanities on their agenda since the 1960s. Hans-Georg Gadamer's *Truth and Method*, published in 1960, describes the conflict between truth and method-oriented sciences as typical of the post-Enlightenment situation in which the humanities and the natural sciences are trying to secure their own territories. Does the strict adherence to scientific methods provide more truth or does it not rather prevent us from finding truth? Gadamer's answer is not simple. He sketches the profile of modern hermeneutics as a hybrid of method and non-method. Hermeneutics refuses to blindly rely of formal methods but is also not naive enough to believe that "understanding" can come about spontaneously and without any theory. Truth, meaning, and knowledge are always matters of cultural interpretation, which is why the description of the humanities in terms of hard sciences is reductive. This is not relativism because the interpretation *does* have methods; however, those methods are not purely technical.

Four years after Gadamer published his *Truth and Method*, Jacques Ellul announced that "technique" now represents the "totality of methods" for the simple reason that "technique has taken over the whole of civilization" (Ellul: xxv). Still four years later, Jürgen Habermas describes what happens when "the reified models of the sciences migrate into the socio-cultural life-world," pointing out that the technocratic-positivist way of thinking distorts the ordinary frame of reference of interaction (often maintained through ordinary language) (Habermas 1971: 112). By doing so it destroys valuable ethical categories. When scientific methods are applied to cultural phenomena, the reality begins to evaporate through the process of formalization.

Fifty-four years later the anonymous author in the *Guardian* describes "the increasing impact of technology on any sort of investigation" in disastrous terms (see Introduction). We cannot be surprised because there had enough warnings. Like Ellul, the author regrets that a certain kind of "rationalism" willfully limits its own spectrum to some non-founded and uncritically accepted form of "efficiency" that will be accepted with quasi-religious fervor as an absolute value. Psychoanalysts define this "rationalism" as a "functional desire," meaning a desire of simplification that wants things simply to "function," regardless of what the functioning item actually is.

In the humanities departments, aggressive rejections of this "rationalism" become more and more frequent. "Everything that moves needs to be evaluated" writes the author in the *Guardian*. Offices produce large files of information on simply everything that exists, no matter whether it's useful or not. If this tendency continues, curriculum development, accurate teaching outcome forecasts, and new "programs" will be more important than innovative research.

By rejecting this kind of "rationalism," the humanities do not ask for a shift toward the irrational. Rationality is not bad, nor are transparency, efficiency, productivity, accountability, competition, and ranking.[2] But they *become* bad when they trace their right of existence in a circular fashion back to themselves. Qualities like transparency and efficiency must be constantly evaluated in the light of the reality of education and the aims it wants to achieve *beyond* transparency, efficiency, productivity, accountability, competition. The anonymous author in *The Guardian* thinks that the Office of Quality is not doing that. One of the problems is that the Office of Quality understands rationality mainly as an economic rationality or as what Max Weber had called a "formal rationality," which the German sociologist attributes to bureaucratic domination prominent in capitalist economies (Weber: 975). Readings developed this confrontation at some length in *The University in Ruins*. Today things are much worse: by becoming formal and instrumental, reason has become a "bureaucratic reason" tending toward the irrational.

Meinecke opposed a "Goetheian or humanist culture" to the quantifying reason of a perverted form of liberalism and an advancing technological age (Meinecke: 38). Truth needs to be established in the context of the "free, humane culture which came down from the days of Goethe" (21). It needs to be established in the context of cultures or traditional religions as transmitted by philosophically minded theologies. Truth cannot be produced instantaneously in the form of excellence or religious revelation. Meinecke was looking for a hermeneutic concept of balance or a dialectics in which reason manifests itself as a self-reflexive and self-critical equilibrium able to reflect itself against cultural elements. Any other procedure makes reason irrational. For example, rational ideas about universalized economic freedom fostering individual wealth and well-being become irrational when they are not rethought within the concrete realm of cultures. The most ethically valuable theories become irrational and unethical if they neglect the practical reality of persons and cultures to which they are applied.

Liberalism, which is a rational political movement initiated during the age of Enlightenment, has always suffered from those contradictions between the individual and the universal. The rationalism on which liberalism is based is universal and, as a result, it was not permitted *not* to think universally in liberalism. *Therefore, hermeneutics is the alternative to liberalism.* It is the philosophy specializing in the communication between the individual and the general, and solutions are most likely to be offered by this tradition. Charles Taylor presents the concept of the dialogue during which individual and universal sides are brought together (Taylor 1999). In current liberal cultures, this "organic" approach is rarely seen as valuable. Instead, one prefers to universalize pseudo-rational principles by using science for neoliberal economic purposes.

Humanists against pseudo-science

Humanists know that disciplines relying on quantification and formalization can be efficient in very limited scientific domains but are likely to distort reality once they are applied without criticism. Science must be reflected against value criteria dependent on categories like "good life" or "good education" that need to be established beforehand *and not through the hard sciences.* They should not be established by bureaucratic reason but by a philosophical reason attempting to involve a historical consciousness. The "cultural university" (in Readings's sense) that preceded the corporate one could still appeal to virtues and values anchored in the local culture by which it was surrounded. In nineteenth-century Germany, links between the Greeks and what was believed to be

"German culture" could be emphasized in a context of national revival, which would justify the existence of the classics departments. The initial idea of the university is anchored here. To be in a location meant to share local values. This does not mean that there was no external engagement. The university was rather a paradoxical phenomenon because it was place-bound, though striving at the same time for universal knowledge.

The hermeneutic perspective presented in this conclusion is supposed to summarize the point of view of the humanities in general. Hermeneutic derives from the tradition of virtue ethics the belief that philosophical problems should always be viewed within concrete contexts.[3] And education, which is supposed to produce *a certain kind* of person, is always dependent on virtue-based ethical theories. Edmund Husserl wrote in *The Crisis of the European Sciences* (1934) that the scientific objectivity characteristic of natural sciences is bound to neglect the subjective, historical, and dynamic part of human life (Husserl: 37). In the corporate academy this has led, among other things, to the overevaluation of short-term output and forced specialization. What is lost in the numbing process of "numberization" is the subject's imaginative and reflective capacity, her aesthetic responsiveness and her introspection, as well as her ethical reasoning when engaging with the sociohistorical context of the phenomena she is examining. Quantitative methods leading to "excellence" are most often dependent on a category of efficiency whose value-status has been narcissistically established by the method itself. Gadamer calls such approaches "inductive procedures" (Gadamer 1986: 4/2004: 10). There is nothing wrong with induction. In both science and philosophy inductive reasoning moves from specific instances to general statements and it does so in a logical way. Problems arise only when induction is applied in situations where the logically inducted conclusion does not bring about a real understanding of the situation. Gadamer says that "the experience of the sociohistorical world cannot be raised to a science by the inductive procedure of the natural science" (2004: 104/1986: 10). As an alternative, he refers to the notion of *sensus communis* as applied by Giambattista Vico (1668–1744), who uses this Roman term to criticize theoretical speculation in the modern science of his time (20/28). Vico worked in the humanist tradition of the Renaissance, which revived (after Scholasticism) the classical idea of a liberal arts education centered on the humanities. Renaissance humanism approached disciplines like history and philosophy not primarily as sources of information, but as living traditions able to provide examples and models to be used as guidelines for the solutions of contemporary problems.

"Common sense" is for Vico not the result of a repudiation of "ultimates" that would much later be propagated in America in the name of a "philosophy of common sense." Nor is it related to eighteenth-century Scottish commonsense realism putting forward the human innate ability to perceive common ideas. It has even less to do with the tenacious mass of inflexible and inherited beliefs that surfaces as "common sense arguments" in today's anti-intellectualist discourses. What is in question in Gadamer's and Vico's arguments is a shift from the abstract to the concrete, though this is not an appeal to empiricism. The criticism of theoretical speculation remains based on the Platonic-Aristotelian tradition of "practical knowledge" (*phronesis*) that has been maintained by European thought through centuries, mainly through the discipline of rhetoric.

What is practical knowledge? Practical knowledge looks at the concrete situation to grasp all *possible* circumstances. Thus, common sense thinking in Vico's understanding does not reject quantification and formalization to refer merely to brute facts about which we cannot speculate. On the contrary, common sense *does speculate* in its own way as it thinks about possibilities and attempts to establish what is most "likely." Gadamer finds that this kind of speculative reason, which remains closely linked to practical reason and common sense, is "the most important thing in education": "The training in the *sensus communis*, which is not nourished on the true but on the probable, the verisimilar" (2004: 18/1986: 26), is what makes a person truly educated. The educated person is not satisfied with truth in the form of numbers and empirically established facts but will find such empiricism or positivism dogmatic. Instead, the educated person wants arguments to be "plausible" (*einleuchtend*), which is "*verisimile*" in Latin where it also means "likely." More important than mastering methods dealing with quantified bits of information is to evoke concrete (historical) examples. We understand perfectly well what Vico means when we examine the logic of our contemporary financial capitalism where norms and symbolical forms have lost any link with the reality they pretend to represent. Though the calculation is right, the "truth" is detached from the problem whose solution it was supposed to represent. Norms have been established and complex protocols have been followed, but there is no practical experience in the sense of the *sensus communis*. As a result, the conclusions are not plausible.

The commonsensical (in Vico's understanding) reflection on what is most plausible is not random; there are methods about how interpretation should proceed. The important point is that the single event should not merely be split up in its abstract components, but that "the unity of experience as determined by its intentional content stands in an immediate relationship to the whole, to the totality of life," according to Gadamer (2004: 59/1986: 64). Habermas renders the same idea in his own words by writing that the "matter-of-factness of understanding" should not be effectuated "through abstraction from pre-opinions (Vormeinungen) but through a reflection of the effective historical (wirkungsgeschichtlichen) context, with which the knowing subjects are always already linked."[4]

While professors, particularly in the humanities, complain that teaching results cannot be quantified, the methods of corporate evaluation refuse to recognize anything that is not measurable. One problem is that in education, we evaluate not mere facts but possibilities. Some students are more capable of reaching certain aims within certain circumstances than others. Some things are more plausible than others. Therefore, evaluation criteria need to be dynamic. Education is not merely concerned with facts but also with emotions, choices, values, desires, perceptions, attitudes, interests, expectations, and sensibilities.

For the hermeneutic humanities, "understanding" is not based on quantification, but instead its meaning is exemplified in the phrase "we do understand each other." It would be ridiculous to suppose that people who "understand each other" have quantified and evaluated each other beforehand. On the contrary, this kind of understanding implies that quantification and evaluation has not been necessary. What does "to understand each other" mean more precisely? It means to have similar life projects. Again, this does not mean that every detail in one person's life corresponds to certain details in the other person's life. Nor do the quantities of details overlap, but the ways in which the two persons tend to see the world overlap (to some extent) with regard to their history and with regard to projects they have for the future. The projects contain not only facts but also emotions, choices, values, desires, perceptions, attitudes, interests, expectations, and sensibilities. In hermeneutics this has been called a "life world" (*Lebenswelt*).[5] Another hermeneutic philosopher, Paul Ricœur, has written that in hermeneutic understanding "the world is not represented as a totality of objects to be manipulated, but as a horizon and as a project" (1986: 54). It is precisely this world as a "life world" or as a project that is getting lost in a world of quantification, fundamentalism, and kitsch.

The criticism of scientific methods present in anti-corporate discourses is not directed against science but finds that the "naive objectivism" (Gadamer 1986b: 254) as well as pseudo-exact methods of this "science" are simply *not scientific enough* because they are not adapted to the context within which they are used. We should not forget that the initial purpose of the natural sciences has been (and still is) the submission of nature. When this science is applied in an unaltered fashion to cultural and social phenomena, it *can* only proceed by objectifying those phenomena beforehand. The human sciences, on the other hand, are sciences of interpretation and historical mediation. The human sciences do not establish facts (through quantification) but integrate memory (transmission) and expectation into the process of understanding. In other words, they do not merely look for things but for the significance of things. And as strange as this might sound to number-crunching natural scientists, they find this more scientific because it is more adequate for the purpose.

The purpose of science should be to create a unity of life and knowledge. The natural sciences have big difficulties doing this. So why should the human sciences imitate them? A realistic vision of the world cannot be established by putting together atomized and objectified bits of experience. This does not mean that human scientists cannot learn the one or the other thing from their colleagues in the natural sciences. They have actually learned a lot for more than a hundred years by developing new disciplines and merging older ones, exactly as it happened in the natural sciences. Dialogues like that between philosophy of mind and neurosciences are exciting because they transfer large amounts of knowledge and methodology from one side to the other. Many philosophers earn supplementary degrees in computer science, theoretical linguistics, mathematics, or evolutionary biology. Still it remains true that an atomized and objectified vision of the world that is typical for the natural sciences is only adequate for the analysis of limited phenomena. We cannot quantify everything and everybody. This means that the universities have become the battleground of two approaches toward reality. In the corporate university political, ethical, and spiritual dimensions of knowledge are getting lost and with them the unity of life and knowledge. As a result, reality is getting lost, too. It is replaced by a numerical reality composed of fundamentalist truths and kitsch. What is needed is the historical kind of speculation current in hermeneutic philosophy if we want to remain able to spell out what is plausible.

Bill Readings defined excellence as a concept emptied of all cultural contents because in a globalized world nation states are unable to provide concrete cultural input. We hear the echo of Vico in Readings's statement that the excellence established through surveys "allows the a priori exclusion of all referential issues, that is, any questions about what excellence in the University might *be*, what the term might *mean*" (Readings: 27). Once truth has been emptied of all cultural value and replaced with excellence, everything is possible. The parallel with kitsch is clear: once art has been emptied of all cultural value and replaced with kitsch, everything is possible. The Singapore-based QS accreditation firm visits universities to bestow "stars" for excellent learning outcomes (generally defined as the perfect coincidence of the final outcome with the "prospective outcome" announced in the syllabus) as well as "stars" for excellent campus gyms. On the one hand, this is in keeping with the principles of the commercial university. Once education is without content, new teaching topics with popular contents (or even excellent gyms) can be introduced to pander to students' popular tastes, which will attract more students. However, as has been explained above, it is equally naive to describe the corporate university as an institution merely looking for profit. The corporate university—like capitalism in general—evolved beyond that concept. The university culture of excellence with its frenzy of evaluations and measuring no longer serves an economical purpose in the first place but appears much more as an end in itself. Similar observations can be made in other domains. The ontological patterns of the corporate university, like those of financial capitalism, corresponds much more to the production of an autonomous reality based on an idea of "excellence" that constantly refers to itself and loses sight of the social and historical reality that all sciences are actually supposed to serve and analyze. Those institutions do not serve a "cultural function," that is, a "mission" defined in terms of concrete values linked to a concrete culture. Like the creation of a "virtual reality" for computer scientists, the excellent reality is an end in itself.

Teachers who still attempt to convey concrete values feel like missionaries in a land without mission. The pattern is also reinforced because many societies prefer to relegate any talk about values to religion. As a result, the humanities have no authority about "good" and "bad" but are simply supposed to be excellent. Occasionally they might be consulted for matters of deontology (right or wrong), but a virtue ethics approach addressing questions of individual happiness will most probably be found inadequate.

In the "real world" (as opposed to the virtual world of the corporate university or to the virtual world of finance capitalism), transparency, efficiency, productivity, accountability, and competition should never represent virtues but should be *means to achieve* certain virtues. The virtues themselves cannot be extracted from education with the help of objective quantitative methods but need to be understood and established historically and hermeneutically. Or, as James Simpson states in "Crisis in the Humanities," "understanding is inseparable from narrative and process." Also, Simpson believes that the problem with formal methods is that they "bypass historical interpretation."

He points out that the humanities are the only discipline refusing to offer formalized "X-ray visions" of the world because they do not describe the world in terms of numbers and some basic abstract principles (for example, human rights), but "transmit a certain humility before the complexity of narrative experience. . . . We offer situated understanding" (Simpson 2007).

In the end, through their integration into the corporate university, the humanities become really inefficient and useless (which is perhaps what corporatization wanted them to become in the first place). Think of the clash between religion and science when it comes to evolution. Only the humanities are able to negotiate here between the two camps. But how can they do this if they have nothing to offer other than excellence? Only a discussion of values and a potential elaboration of *common values* is worthy of the name of "communication" between different communities. We need examples, history, concrete virtues, and culture. Then certain points can be made plausible. Scientism, this most mutilated form of science to which technocrats appeal, kills any commonsense as well as any real debate because the idea of finding the "plausible" has been abandoned. In the same vein, corporate capitalism pretends that no debate is necessary because, contrary to other social models (like socialism, pragmatism or virtue ethics), capitalism pretends to have no ideological grounding. Capitalism is said to be simply the natural thing humans tend to do anyway. No debate is necessary, only (bent) statistics that prove the point. This book has shown that this is a wrong assumption. Corporate capitalism submerges us with an ideology that can be called the "ideology of the non-ideology," which is the worst ideology of all because it evades debate on principle. It pretends to work "merely" in the name of excellence (or of the natural inclination toward capitalism), which means that it *must* be right, no matter what you are saying. To make the fallacies of this strategy obvious, humanities scholars should refuse to be excellent or simply refuse bullshit.

Notes

1 See: Wolin (2011); Strickland (2002); Paschal (2012); Marshall (2003); Greenwald (2010); Hahendahl (2005).

2 "Transparency, efficiency, productivity, accountability, competition" are elements that Thorstein Veblen declared to be foreign to the humanities. See Donoghue, 95.

3 It shares this conviction with the branch of Anglo-American philosophy that has reevaluated virtue ethics since the 1950.

4 "Die Sachlichkeit des Verstehens ist nicht gewährleistet durch Abstraktion von
   Vormeinungen sondern durch eine Reflexion des wirkungsgeschichtlichen
   Zusammenhangs, der die erkennenden Subjekte mit ihrem Gegenstand immer
   schon verbindet" (Habermas1971b: 122).

5 The term "*Lebenswelt*" is a central term in Husserl's mentioned *Crisis of the European
   Sciences* and it signifies the self-evident "primordia sphere" of everyday actions from
   which science should not cut itself entirely off. The crisis of science consists in the
   fact that science is no longer grounded in a *Lebenswelt*.

Bibliography

Abbas, Ackbar. 1996. "Hyphenation: The Spatial Dimensions of Hong Kong Culture," in M. Steinberg (ed.), *Walter Benjamin and the Demands of History*. Ithaca and London: Cornell University Press, 214–32.

Abdel-Samad, Hamed. 2016. *Islamic Fascism*. Amherst: Prometheus Books.

Adorno, Theodor. 1997. *Aesthetic Theory*. London: Continuum.

Adorno, Theodor and Max Horkheimer. 1972 [1944]. *Dialectic of Enlightenment*. New York: Continuum.

Agamben, Giorgio. 2000. "Beyond Human Rights," in Agamben, *Means without Ends: Notes on Politics*. Minneapolis: Minnesota University Press, 15–28.

Ahmed, Akbar S. 2003 [1992]. *Postmodernism and Islam: Predicament and Promise*. New York: Routledge.

Alraouf, Ali. 2005. "Dubaization vs. Glocalization: Arab Cities Transformed," paper presented at the Gulf First Urban Planning and Development Conference, Kuwait, December 12–14.

American University of the Emirates website http://www.onlinedubai.ru/education/higher/detail-american-university-emirates/

Anderson, Chris. 2014. "The End of Theory: The Data Deluge Makes the Scientific Method Obsolete," *Wired* June 23.

Arendt, Hannah. 1970. *On Violence*. New York: Harcourt Brace Jovanovich.

Arendt, Hannah. 1973 [1951]. *The Origins of Totalitarianism*. Cleveland and New York: The World Publishing Company.

Arndt, David. 2006. "The Two Cultures and the Crisis in the Humanities," *Forum on Public Policy*, http://forumonpublicpolicy.com/archive07/arndt.pdf 3. Last accessed December 18, 2018.

Arnold, Matthew. 1869. *Culture and Anarchy: An Essay in Political and Social Criticism*. : Smith, Elder & Co.

Baudrillard, Jean. 1970. *La Société de consommation: ses mythes ses structures*. Paris: Denoël.

Baudrillard, Jean. 1990. *Seduction* (trans. B. Singer). Montreal: New World Perspectives.

Baudrillard, Jean. 2012. *The Spirit of Terrorism*. London: Verso.

Berardi, Franco. 2013. *Dopo il futuro: Dal Futurism al Cyberpunk. L'esaurimento della Modernità*. Rome: DeriveApprodi.

Berman, Paul. 2010. *The Flight of the Intellectuals*. New York: Scribe.

Bernstein, Richard. 1994. *Dictatorship of Virtue*. New York: Knopf.

Black, Max. 1983. "The Prevalence of Humbug," in *The Prevalence of Humbug and Other Essays*. Cornell University Press, 115–46.

Bloom, Allan. 1987. *The Closing of the American Mind*. New York: Simon and Schuster.

Botz-Bornstein, Thorsten. 2012a. "A Tale of Two Cities: Hong Kong and Dubai Celebration of Disappearance and the Pretension of Becoming," *Transcience: A Journal of Global Studies* 3:2, 1–16.

Botz-Bornstein, Thorsten. 2012b. "From the Stigmatized Tattoo to the Graffitied Body: Femininity in the Tattoo Renaissance," *Gender, Place and Culture: A Journal of Feminist Geography* 2012, 1–17.

Botz-Bornstein, Thorsten. 2016. "A Hermeneutic Answer to the Crisis of the Universities: Reflections on Bureaucracy, Business Culture and the Global University," in K. Gray, S. Keck and H. Bachir (eds.), *Eastward Bound: The Politics, Economics and Pedagogy of Western Higher Education in Asia and the Middle East*. Lanham: Lexington, 243–63.

Botz-Bornstein, Thorsten. 2019. *The Political Aesthetics of ISIS and Italian Futurism*. Lanham: Lexington.

Botz-Bornstein. Thorsten. 2011. *The Cool-Kawaii: Afro-Japanese Aesthetics and New World Modernity*. Lanham: Lexington-Rowman & Littlefield.

Bouleau, Nicolas. 2018. *Le Mensonge de la finance. Les mathématiques, le signal-prix et la planète*. Paris: Editions de l'Atelier.

Bourdieu, Pierre. 1958. *Sociologie de l'Algérie*. Paris: Presses Universitaires de France.

Bourdieu, Pierre. 1984 [1979]. *Distinction: A Social Critique of the Refinement of Taste*. Cambridge, MA: Harvard University Press.

Boyers, Robert and Peg Boyers. 1990. "Kitsch: An Introduction," *Salmagundi*, 85/86, 197–200.

Broch, Hermann. 1975 [1933]. "Notes on the Problem of Kitsch," in G. Dorfles (ed.), *Kitsch: The World of Bad Taste*. New York: Bell, 49–76.

Burckhardt, Jacob. 1946. *Briefe* (ed. Max Burckhardt). Leipzig: Insel.

Burckhardt, Jacob. 1958 [1929]. *Judgements on History and Historians* (trans. H. Zohn). Boston: Beacon Press.

Burke, Edmund. 1998. *A Philosophical Enquiry into the Origin of Our Ideas of the Sublime and Beautiful*. Oxford: Oxford University Press.

Busarello, Renato. 2016. "Diversity management, pinkwashing aziendale e omo-neoliberalismo," in F. Zappino (ed.), *Il Genere tra neoliberalismo et neofondamentalismo*. Verona: Ombre Corte, 74–84.

Calinescu, Matei. 1987. *Five Faces of Modernity*. Durham: Duke University Press.

Cardon, Dominique. 2015. *A Quoi Rêvent les Algorithmes: Nos Vies à l'heure des big data*. Paris: Seuil.

Cilliers, Johan. 2010. "The Unveiling of Life: Liturgy and the Lure of Kitsch," *HTS Theological Studies* 66:2, npn.

Crick, Philip. 1983. "Kitsch," *The British Journal of Aesthetics* 23:1, 49–52.

Crosby, Alfred W. 1998. *The Measure of Reality Quantification and Western Society 1250–1600*. Cambridge: Cambridge University Press.

Cross, Gary. 2004. *The Cute and the Cool. Wondrous Innocence and Modern American Children's Culture*. Oxford: Oxford University Press.

Crowther, Paul. 1989. *The Kantian Sublime: From Morality to Art*. Oxford: Clarendon Press.

Davidson, Christopher. 2011. "Higher Education in the Gulf State: From Traditional to Modern," in N. Sultan, D. Weir and Z. Karake-Shalhoub (eds.), *The New Post-Oil Arab Gulf*. London: Al Saqi, 97–116.

de Waal, Cornelis. 2006. "The Importance of Being Earnest: A Pragmatic Approach to Bullshitting," in G. Hardcastle and G. Reisch, *Bullshit and Philosophy: Guaranteed to Get Perfect Results Every Time*. Chicago: Open Court, 99–113.

Deleuze, Gilles and Felix Guattari. 1994. *What Is Philosophy?* New York: Columbia University Press.

Derrida, Jacques. 1987. *The Truth in Painting*. Chicago: University of Chicago Press.

Devecchio, Alexandre. 2016. *Les Nouveaux enfants du siècle*. Paris: Cerf.

Donoghue, Frank. 2008. *The Last Professors: The Corporate University and the Fate of the Humanities*. New York: Fordham University Press (also printed as *The Last Professors: The Twilight of the Humanities in the Corporate University*).

Dorfles, Gillo. 1975. *Kitsch: The World of Bad Taste*. New York: Bell.

Dutton, Denis. 1992. "Delusions of Postmodernism," *Literature and Aesthetics* 2, 23–35.

Eco, Umberto. 1989. "The Structure of Bad Taste," in U. Eco (ed.), *The Open Book*. Cambridge, MA: Harvard University Press, 180–216.

Eco, Umberto. 1998. *Faith in Fakes: Travels in Hyperreality*. London: Vintage. Italian: *Il costume di casa*. Milano: Bompiani, 1973.

Eisner, Lotte H. 1975. "Kitsch in the Cinema," in G. Dorfles (ed.), *Kitsch: The World of Bad Taste*. New York: Bell, 197–218.

Ellul, Jacques. 1964. *The Technological Society*. New York: Vintage Books.

Elsheshtawy, Yasser. 2004. "Redrawing Boundaries: Dubai, an Emerging Global City," in Y. Elsheshtawy (ed.), *Planning Middle Eastern Cities: An Urban Kaleidoscope in a Globalizing World*. New York and London: Routledge, 169–99.

Elsheshtawy, Yasser. 2010. *Dubai: Behind an Urban Spectacle*. New York: Routledge, 2010.

Epstein, Mikhail. 2009. "The Interesting," *Qui Parle: Critical Humanities and Social Sciences* 18:1, 75–88.

Evola, Julius. 2003 [1961]. *Ride the Tiger: Survival Manual for the Aristocrats of the Soul*. New York: Inner Traditions.

Faye, Guillaume. 1998. *Archéofuturisme*. Paris: L'Æncre.

Ferguson, Niall. 2016. "Simplifiers vs. Complicators," *Boston Globe* October 3, https://www.bostonglobe.com/opinion/2016/10/03/how-terrible-simplicity-leads-terrible-complexity/TPOZ8LyTNXBtyW9GenT8yK/story.html. Last accessed April 29, 2017.

Frankfurt. Harry G. 2005. *On Bullshit*. Princeton: Princeton University Press. First published as "On Bullshit" in *Raritan Quarterly Review* 6:2 (1986).

Freud, Sigmund. 2006 [1920]. *A General Introduction to Psychoanalysis*. Ashland, OH: Library of Alexandria.

Friedman, Milton. 1951. "Neo-Liberalism and Its Prospects," in R. Leeson and C.G Palm (eds.), *The Collected Works of Milton Friedman*. Stanford: Hoover Institution on War, Revolution, and Peace, 89–93.

Friedman, Milton. 1982. *Capitalism and Freedom*. Chicago: University of Chicago Press.

Friedman, Milton and Thomas S. Szasz. 1992. *Friedman and Szasz on Liberty and Drugs*. Washington: Drug Policy Foundation.

Gadamer, Hans-Georg. 1986a. *Wahrheit und Methode*. Tübingen: Mohr.

Gadamer, Hans-Georg. 1986b. *Wahrheit und Methode, Ergänzungsband* [supplement volume]. Tübingen: Mohr.

Gadamer, Hans-Georg. 2004. *Truth and Method* (trans. J. Weinsheimer and D. G. Marshall). London: Continuum.

Giesz, Ludwig. 1975 [1969]. "Kitsch-Man as Tourist," in G. Dorfles (ed.), *Kitsch: The World of Bad Taste*. New York: Bell, 156–74.

Godart, Elsa. 2016. *Je Selfie donc je suis*. Paris: Albin Michel.

Gori, Roland. 2013. *La Fabrique des Imposteurs*. Paris: *Les liens qui libèrent*.

Green, David G. 2006. *We're (Nearly) All Victims Now! How Political Correctness Is Undermining Our Liberal Culture*. London: Civitas.

Greenberg, Clement. 1961. "Avantgarde and Kitsch," in C. Greenberg (ed.), *Art and Culture: Critical Essays*. Boston: Beacon Press, 3–21.

Greenwald, Richard A. 2010. "Graduate Education in the Humanities Faces a Crisis. Let's Not Waste It," *The Chronicle Review* April 4.

Gregotti, Vittorio. 1975. "Urban Kitsch," in G. Dorfles, *Kitsch: The World of Bad Taste*. New York: Bell, 254–64.

Griffin, Roger. 2007. *Modernism and Fascism: The Sense of a Beginning under Mussolini and Hitler*. London: Palgrave.

Griffiths, Paul. 2014. *Decreation: The Last Things of All Creatures*. Waco, TX: Baylor University Press.

The Guardian. 2014. "Universities Focus Too Much on Measuring Activity, not Quality." Article by An anonymous Professor. August 15. http://www.theguardian.com/ higher-education-network/blog/2014/aug/15/academics-anonymous-universities-measure-activity-not-quality?CMP=twt_gu. Last accessed December 18, 2018.

Habermas, Jürgen. 1970. *Toward a Rational Society: Student Protest, Society and Politics*. Boston: Beacon Press.

Habermas, Jürgen. 1971a. *Knowledge and Human Interests*. Boston: Beacon Press.

Habermas, Jürgen. 1971b. "Der Universalanspruch der Hermeneutik," in J. Habermas, H.-G. Gadamer, K.-O. Apel (eds.), *Hermeneutik und Ideologiekritik: Zu Gadamers Wahrheit und Methode*. Frankfurt: Suhrkamp.120–59.

Hahendahl, Peter Uwe. 2005. "The Future of the Research University and the Fate of the Humanities," *Cultural Critique* 61, 1–21.

Hardcastle, Gary. 2006. "The Unity of Bullshit," in G. Hardcastle and G. Reisch (eds.), *Bullshit and Philosophy: Guaranteed to Get Perfect Results Every Time*. Chicago: Open Court, 137–50.

Hardcastle, Gary and George Reisch (eds.). 2006. *Bullshit and Philosophy: Guaranteed to Get Perfect Results Every Time*. Chicago: Open Court.

Hari, Johann. 2009. "The Dark Side of Dubai," *Huffington Post* April 7 http://www.huffingtonpost.com/johann-hari/the-dark-side-of-dubai_b_183851.html. Last accessed July 7, 2011.

Harper, Christopher. 1997. "The Daily Me," *American Journalism Review* April. http://ajrarchive.org/article.asp?id=268. Last accessed September 7, 2017.

Harries, Karsten. 1979. *The Meaning of Modern Art*. Chicago: Northwestern University Press.

Hayek, Friedrich. 2003 [1943]. *The Road to Serfdom* [condensed version]. London: Institute of Economic Affairs.

Hegel, Georg Wilhelm Friedrich. 1986. *Vorlesungen über Ästhetik I* (Werkausgabe Bd. 13). Frankfurt: Suhrkamp.

Hepburn, Ronald W. 1993. "Trivial and Serious in Aesthetic Appreciation of Nature," in S. Gaskell and I. Kemal (eds.), *Landscape, Natural Beauty, and the Arts*. Cambridge: Cambridge University Press, 65–80.

Hinde, John R. 2000. *Jakob Burckhardt and the Crisis of Modernity*. Montreal: McGill-Queen's University Press.

Holliday, Ruth and Tracey Potts. 2012. *Kitsch: Cultural Politics and Taste*. Manchester: Manchester University Press.

Horkheimer, Max and Theodor Adorno. 1992. *Dialectic of Enlightenment: Philosophical Fragments*. Stanford: Stanford University Press.

Hume, David. 1918. "Of the Standard of Taste," in D. Hume (ed.), *Of the Standard of Taste and Other Essays*. London: Allyn and Bacon, 3–24.

Husserl, Edmund. 1985. *Die Krisis der Europäischen Wissenschaften und die Transzendentale Phänomenologie*. Hamburg: Meiner. Engl.: *The Crisis of European Sciences and Transcendental Phenomenology; An Introduction to Phenomenological Philosophy* (trans. David Carr). Evanston: Northwestern University Press, 1970.

Iggers, Georg G. 2012. *The German Conception of History: The National Tradition of Historical Thought from Herder to the Present*. Middletown, CT: Wesleyan University Press.

Indiana University Newsroom. 2015. "Not-so-Guilty Pleasure: Viewing Cat Videos Boosts Energy and Positive Emotions, IU Study Finds," http://archive.news.indiana.edu/releases/iu/2015/06/internet-cat-video-research.shtml. Last accessed March 8, 2017.

Junemo, Mattias. 2004. "Let's Build a Palm Island: Playfulness in Complex Times," in Mimi Sheller and John Urry (eds.), *Tourism Mobilities*. New York: Routledge, 183.

Jung, C. G. 1967. *Two Essays on Analytical Psychology* in *Collected Works* 7. Princeton: Princeton University Press.

Kalisch, Volker. 1992. "Mozart und Kitsch: 'Ein musikalischer Spaß'?" *International Review of the Aesthetics and Sociology of Music*, 23:1, 43–60.

Kant, Immanuel. 1764. *Beobachtungen über das Gefühl des Schönen und Erhabenen*. Königsberg: Kanter. Documentation Center, Das Bonner Kant-Korpus

(AA [Akademieausgabe] II, 205)] https://korpora.zim.uni-duisburg-essen.de/kant/
aa20/001.html. Last accessed November 6, 2017.

Kant, Immanuel. 1838. "Der Streit der Fakultäten," in *Immanuel Kants Werke: Sorgfältig revidirte Gesammtausgabe in zehn Bänden*, Vol. 1. Leipzig: Modes und Baumann.

Kant, Immanuel. 1911. *Critique of Aesthetic Judgement* (trans. J. Creed Meredith). Oxford: The Clarendon Press.

Kant, Immanuel. 1965. *Observations on the Feeling of the Beautiful and the Sublime*. Cambridge: Cambridge University Press.

Kant, Immanuel. 1977 [1793]. *Kritik der Urteilskraft* (second edition). Stuttgart: Reclam.

Kimbrough, Scott. 2006. "On Letting It Slide," in Hardcastle and Reisch, 3–18.

Koons, Jeff. 1992. *The Jeff Koons Handbook*. New York: Rizzoli.

Kraushaar, Otto F. 1938. "What James's Philosophical Orientation Owed to Lotze," *The Philosophical Review*, 4:5, 517–26.

Kulka, Tomáš. 1996. *Kitsch and Art*. University Park: Pennsylvania State University Press.

Kundera, Milan. 1999. *The Unbearable Lightness of Being*. New York: Harper & Collins.

Lasch, Christopher. 1979. *The Culture of Narcissism: American Life in an Age of Diminishing Expectations*. New York and London: Norton.

Lea, John. 2008. *Political Correctness and Higher Education: British and American Perspectives*. New York: Routledge.

Lebensztejn, Jean-Claude and Kate Cooper. 1981. "Photorealism, Kitsch and Venturi," *SubStance* 10:2, 75–104.

Legutko, Ryszard. 2016. *The Demon in Democracy: Totalitarian Temptations in Free Societies*. New York: Encounter Books.

Levet, Bérénice. 2017. *Le Crépuscule des idoles progressistes*. Paris: Stock.

Lévi-Strauss, Claude. 1962. *La Pensée sauvage*. Paris: Agora.

Lipovetsky, Gilles. 1983. *L'Ere du vide: Essais sur l'individualisme contemporain*. Paris: Gallimard.

Lipovetsky, Gilles and Sébastien Charles. 2004. *Les Temps hypermodernes*. Paris: Le Livre de poche.

Lugg, Catherine A. 1999. *Kitsch: From Education to Public Policy*. New York and London: Falmer Press.

Lurton, Douglas Elsworth. 1956. *The Power of Positive Thinking*. New York and London: McGraw Hill.

Lyotard, Jean-François. 1991a. *Lessons on the Analytic of the Sublime*. Stanford: Stanford University Press.

Lyotard, Jean-François. 1991b. *The Inhuman*. Stanford: Stanford University Press.

MacIntyre, Alasdair. 1981. *After Virtue*. Notre Dame: University of Notre Dame Press.

Macpherson, C. B. 1977. *The Life and Times of Liberal Democracy*. Oxford: Oxford University Press.

Maes, Hans and Katrien Schaubroek. 2006. "Different Kinds and Aspects of Bullshit," in Hardcastle and Reisch, 171–81.

Makiya, Kanan Mohamed. 2011. "What Is Totalitarian Art? Cultural Kitsch from Stalin to Saddam," *Foreign Affairs* 90:3, 142–48.

Mann, Michael. 2004. *Fascists*. Cambridge: Cambridge University Press.

Marginson, Simon. 2001. "Intro to Part I," in R. King, S. Marginson and R. Naidoo (eds.). *Handbook on Globalisation and Higher Education*. Cheltenham: Edward Elgar Publishing, 3–9.

Marshall, Gregory. 2003. "A Liberal Education Is Not a Luxury," *The Chronicle of Higher Education* December 12, 50:3, B.16.

Marshall, Tim. 2011. "Muammar Gaddafi: The Kitsch Dictator," *Foreign Affairs* September 5. https://uk.news.yahoo.com/muammar-gaddafi-kitsch-dictator-162327388.html. Last accessed December 18, 2018.

Martin, Clancy W. 2006. "Review of Harry Frankfurt, On Bullshit," *Ethics* 116:2, 416–21.

Martinot, Steve. 2016. "The 'Fundamentalism' in Police Operations," *Black Agenda Report* July 20. https://www.blackagendareport.com/fundamentalism_in_police_operations. Last accessed December 18, 2018.

Mayer, Hans. 1967. "Rhetorik und Propaganda," in H. Mayer (ed.), *Zur deutschen Literatur der Zeit*. Hamburg: Rowolt, 119–31.

McIntyre, Elisha. 2014. "Rescuing God from Bad Taste: Religious Kitsch in Theory and Practice," *Literature & Aesthetics* 24:2, 83–108.

McLuhan, Marshall. 1964. *Understanding Media: The Extensions of Man*. New York and Scarborough, Ontario: Prentice Hall.

Meinecke, Friedrich. 1963 [1946]. *The German Catastrophe*. Boston: Beacon Press.

Michéa, Jean-Claude. 1999. *L'Enseignement de l'ignorance et ses conditions modernes*. Paris: Climats.

Michéa, Jean-Claude. 2007. *L'Empire du moindre mal : Essai sur la civilisation libérale*. Paris: Climats.

Montesquieu. 1748. *L'Esprit des lois*. Geneva: Chatelain.

Morreall, John and Jessica Loy. 1989. "Kitsch and Aesthetic Education," *Journal of Aesthetic Education* 23:4, 63–73.

Motz, Marilyn Ferris Motz. 1983. "'I Want to Be a Barbie Doll When I Grow Up:' The Cultural Significance of the Barbie Doll," in C. Geist and J. Nachbar (eds.), *Pop Cultural Reader*, Bowling Green: Bowling Green University Popular Press, 122–36.

Ngai, Sianne. 2012. *Our Aesthetic Categories: Zany, Cute, Interesting*. Cambridge, MA: Harvard University Press.

Nietzsche, Friedrich. 1997 [1889]. *Twilight of the Idols or how to Philosophize with the Hammer* (trans. R. Polt). Indianapolis: Hackett.

Nye, David E. 1994. *American Technological Sublime*. Cambridge, MA: MIT Press.

O'Grady, Sean. 2009. "Is Dubai the 'New Lehmans'?" *The Independent* November 26. http://www.independent.co.uk/news/world/middle-east/sean-ogrady-is-dubai-the-new-lehmans-1828328.html. Last accessed July 7, 2011.

Olalquiaga, Celeste. 1998. *The Artificial Kingdom: A Treasury of the Kitsch Experience*. New York: Pantheon.

Paschal, Mark. 2012. "Against Humanities: The Self-Consciousness of the Corporate University," *Viewpoint Magazine* September 10.

Patterson, Orlando. 1998. *The Ordeal of Integration: Progress and Resentment in America's "Racial" Crisis*. New York: Civitas.

Pawek, Karl. 1975. "Christian Kitsch," in G. Dorfles (ed.), *Kitsch: The World of Bad Taste*. New York: Bell, 143–50.

Popper, Karl. 1966 [1945]. *The Open Society and Its Enemies* Vol. 1. Princeton: Princeton University Press.

Popper, Karl. 1999. *All Life Is Problem Solving*. London: Routledge.

Preston, Alex. 2015. "The War Against Humanities at Britain's Universities," *The Guardian* March 29. https://www.theguardian.com/education/2015/mar/29/war-against-humanities-at-britains-universities. Last accessed December 18, 2018.

Prezzolini, Giuseppe. 1903. *Vita intima*. Firenze: Lunachi.

Prezzolini, Giuseppe. 1991 [1907]. *L'arte di persuadere*. Firenze: Lunachi.

Ratzinger, Joseph. 2003. *Truth and Tolerance: Christian Belief and World Religions*. San Francisco: Ignatius Press.

Ratzinger, Joseph. 2005. "Apostolic Journey to Cologne: Vigil With Youth at Marienfeld Area," August 20. http://w2.vatican.va/content/benedict-xvi/en/speeches/2005/august/documents/hf_ben-xvi_spe_20050820_vigil-wyd.html. Last accessed January 20, 2017.

Ratzinger, Joseph. 2005b. "Mass 'Pro Eligendo Romano Pontifice,'" http://www.vatican.va/gpII/documents/homily-pro-eligendo-pontifice_20050418_en.html. Last accessed January 20, 2017.

Ratzinger, Joseph. 2010. *Light of the World: The Pope, the Church and the Signs Of The Times. A Conversation with Peter Seewald*. San Francisco: Ignatius Press.

Rawls, John. 1971. *A Theory of Justice*. Cambridge, MA: Harvard University Press.

Rawls, John. 1993. *Political Liberalism* (expanded edition from 2011). New York: Columbia University Press.

Readings, Bill. 1996. *The University in Ruins*. Cambridge, MA: Harvard University Press.

Reiber, Bettina. 2009. "The Sublime and the Possibility of Meaning," in L. Pajaczkowska and C. White (eds.), *The Sublime Now*. Newcastle: Cambridge Scholars, 77–91.

Reisch, George. 2006. "The Pragmatics of Bullshit, Intelligently Designed," in G. Hardcastle and G. Reisch (eds.), *Bullshit and Philosophy: Guaranteed to Get Perfect Results Every Time*. Chicago: Open Court, 33–48 (44).

Ricœur, Paul. 1986. *Du texte à l'action. Essais d'herméneutique II*. Paris: Seuil.

Ritter, Gerhard. 1956. *Der Schlieffenplan: Kritik eines Mythos*. Munich: Oldenbourg.

Rosenberg, Harold. 1959. *The Tradition of the New*. New York: Horizon Press.

Roy, Olivier. 1994. *The Failure of Political Islam*. Cambridge, MA: Harvard University Press.

Roy, Olivier. 2013. *Holy Ignorance: When Religion and Culture Part Ways*. Oxford: Oxford University Press.

Ruch, Richard S. 2001. *Higher Ed, Inc.: The Rise of the For-Profit University*. Baltimore: Johns Hopkins University Press.

Saisselin, Rémy G. 1992. *The Enlightenment against the Baroque: Economics and Aesthetics in the Eighteenth Century*. Berkeley: University of California Press.

Schlegel, Friedrich. 1797. "Über das Studium der griechischen Poesie," in *Ästhetische und politische Schriften*. Neustrelitz: Michaelis.

Schlegel, Friedrich. 1986. *Athenäums-Fragmente und andere Schriften*. Stuttgart: Reclam.

Schlegel, Friedrich. 1991. *Philosophical Fragments*. Minneapolis: University of Minnesota Press.

Schlegel, Friedrich. 2001. *On the Study of Greek Poetry*. New York: SUNY Press.

Schneider, Michel. 2002. *Big Mother: Psychopathologie de la vie politique*: Paris: Odile Jacob.

Scruton, Roger. 1999. "Kitsch and the Modern Predicament," *City Journal* https://www.city-journal.org/html/kitsch-and-modern-predicament-11726.html. Last accessed December 18, 2018.

Seelow, Soren. 2014. "Jeunes, de gauche et fans de Dieudonné," *Le Monde* January 8.

Selle, Gert and Peter Nelles. 1984. "There Is No Kitsch, There Is Only Design!" *Design Issues* 1:1, 41–52.

Simpson, James. 2007. "Crisis in the Humanities? What Crisis?" *Harvard Press Author Forum*. http://harvardpress.typepad.com/off_the_page/james_simpson/. Last accessed December 18, 2018.

Snow, C. P. 1959. *The Two Cultures and the Scientific Revolution*. Cambridge University Press.

Soboczynski, Adam. 2016. "Sie hassen die Moral der Eliten," *Die Zeit* 10, February 22, 39.

Solomon, Robert C. 2004. *In Defense of Sentimentality*. Oxford: Oxford University Press.

Sorel, Georges. 2003 [1908]. *Réflexions sur la violence*. Geneva: Entremonde. Engl.: *Reflections on Violence* (trans. J. Jennings), Cambridge: Cambridge University Press, 2004.

Soros, George. 1998. *The Crisis of Global Capitalism: Open Society Endangered*. New York: Public Affairs.

Sowell, Thomas. 1993. *Inside American Education: The Decline, the Deception, the Dogmas*. New York: Free Press.

Spengler, Oswald. 1938 [German: 1917]. *The Decline of the West*. New York: Knopf.

Steinvorth, Ulrich. 2016. *Pride and Authenticity*. New York: Palgrave.

Sternhell, Zeev. 1996. *Neither Right nor Left: Fascist Ideology in France*. Princeton: Princeton University Press.

Sternhell, Zeev. 2010. *The Anti-Enlightenment Tradition*. New Heaven: Yale University Press.

Strickland, Ronald. 2002. "Gender, Class and the Humanities in the Corporate University," in *Genders: Presenting Innovative Work in the Arts, Humanities and Social Sciences* 35.

http://www.colorado.edu/gendersarchive1998-2013/2002/01/10/gender-class-and-humanities-corporate-university. Last accessed December 18, 2018.

Sykes, Charles J. 1995. *Dumbing Down Our Kids*. New York: St Martin's Griffin.

Tapp, Robert B. 2010. "Review of *The Last Professors: The Corporate University and the Fate of the Humanities*," *On the Horizon* 18:2, 147–53.

Taylor, Charles. 1985. *Philosophy and the Human Sciences: Philosophical Papers 2*. Cambridge: Cambridge University Press.

Taylor, Charles. 1999. "Conditions of an Unforced Consensus on Human Rights," in J. R. Bauer and D. Bell (eds.), *The East Asian Challenge for Human Rights*. New York: Cambridge University Press.

Tétreault, Mary Ann. 2012. "Soft Power Goes Abroad," in Kathryn L. Kleypas and James I. McDougall (eds.), *The American-Style University at Large*, Lanham: Lexington Books, 53–76.

Tibi, Bassam. 2007. "Europeanisation, Not Islamisation," *Sign and Sight* March 23.

Tietge, David J. 2006. "Rhetoric is not Bullshit," in G. Hardcastle and G. Reisch (eds.), *Bullshit and Philosophy: Guaranteed to Get Perfect Results Every Time*. Chicago: Open Court, 229–40.

Toly, Noah. 2015. "Terrible Simplifiers: Failing to Account for the Agency of the Marginalized," *Books & Culture: A Christian Review* May/June. http://www.booksandculture.com/articles/2015/mayjun/terrible-simplifiers.html. Last accessed May 21, 2016.

Tomlinson, John. 1991. *Cultural Imperialism: A Critical Introduction*. Baltimore: The John Hopkins University Press.

Trilling, Lionel. 1993 [1943]. *Beyond Culture: Essays on Literature and Learning*. New York: Viking Press.

Turner, Bryan S. 1998. "Universities, Elites and the Nation-State: A Reply to Delanty," *Social Epistemology* 12:1, 73–77.

Vattimo, Gianni. 1997. *Beyond Interpretation: The Meaning of Hermeneutics for Philosophy*. Oxford: Blackwell.

Volli, Ugo. 1975. "Pornography and Pornokitsch," in G. Dorfles (ed.), *Kitsch: The World of Bad Taste*. New York: Bell, 224–50.

Vora, Neha. 2013. *Impossible Citizens: Dubai's Indian Diaspora*. Durham: Duke University Press.

Weber, Max. 1968 [1921]. *Economy and Society*. New York: Bedminister.

Wheeler, Kathleen. 1988. "Friedrich Schlegel," in D. Simpson (ed.). *The Origins of Modern Critical Thought: German Aesthetics and Literary Criticism from Lessing to Hegel*. Cambridge: Cambridge University Press, 177–178.

Wiseman, A., N. Alromi and S. Alshumrani. 2014. "Challenges to Creating an Arabian Gulf Knowledge Economy," in Alexander W. Wiseman, Naif H. Alromi and Saleh Alshumrani (eds.), *Education for a Knowledge Society in Arabian Gulf Countries (International Perspectives on Education and Society, Volume 24)*. Bingley: Emerald Group Publishing Limited, 1–35.

Wolin, Richard. 2011. "Reflections on the Crisis in the Humanities," *The Hedgehog Review* 13:2, 8–20.

Würzburg University. 2017. "Narcissism and Social Networking," *Science News from Research Organizations* April 18. https://www.sciencedaily.com/releases/2017/04/170418094255.htm. Last accessed October 1, 2017.

Zemmour, Eric. 2014. *Le Suicide français.* Paris: Albin Michel.

Žižek, Slavoj. 2007. *The Universal Exception.* London: Continuum.

Index

www.ingramcontent.com/pod-product-compliance
Lightning Source LLC
Chambersburg PA
CBHW050423280326
41932CB00013BA/1966